creating theatre

creating theatre
The Art of Theatrical Directing

AUGUST W. STAUB

Louisiana State University, New Orleans

Harper & Row, Publishers

New York, Evanston, San Francisco, London

contents

preface

This book is written for the student who has had some experience with theatre, for directing should not be attempted without prior experience in all areas of theatre art. Directing is the most extensive and demanding of the theatrical arts, and those, no matter how talented, who have not informed themselves about acting, costuming, designing, and playwriting are not likely to be wholly satisfactory directors.

There are no rules in the art of directing, but there are principles. These principles, however, are so hedged in by the contingencies of the play script, the acting talent, the set, the costumes, and the technical facilities of the production organizations that the overriding touchstone of all directing is total flexibility of approach. To demonstrate how specific cases change the application of directing principles, this book has drawn its examples from highly divergent plays: *Oedipus, Hamlet, The Imaginary Invalid, From Morn to Midnight, The Waltz of the Toreadors,* and *Death of a Salesman.* The limitation of the number of sample plays has the advantage of providing an easily read and remembered body of dramatic literature common both to the teacher and to the student of directing.

Wherever possible, traditional theatrical terminology has been used, but new terminology has been introduced, sometimes for the sake of clarity, sometimes because no present terms exist. The latter is especially true for the problems and issues of kinetic composition.

A textbook on theatrical directing owes much to the great artists of the theatre, past and present; in this case a particular debt is due the writings of Adolphe Appia, Ted Shawn, Gordon Craig, and Alexander Dean. A greater debt is owed to the actors, designers, playwrights, and directors with whom the author has worked throughout his career in the theatre, and especially to Don F. Blakely.

But the greatest debt is owed to those closest to the final construction of this book: the author's students, co-workers, and family, especially the author's wife, Patricia Gebhardt Staub, who designed the diagrams and illustrations.

August W. Staub

a note on
the model plays

The play scripts used as principal examples in this work are available in single volumes as well as in anthologies. Most may be purchased in inexpensive paperbound editions. *Oedipus, Hamlet,* and *Death of a Salesman* are all to be found in *A Treasury of the Theatre,* edited by John Gassner, 3rd college edition, New York, Simon & Schuster, 1953. *Hamlet* and *Oedipus* are listed in the very modestly priced Crofts Classics Series published by Appleton-Century-Crofts, New York. *Oedipus* is translated by Peter Arnott in this series and *Hamlet* is edited by R. C. Bald. *Death of a Salesman* may be ordered in a paperbound acting edition from Dramatists Play Service, 440 Park Avenue South, New York.

The Crofts Classics Series is also an excellent source for a translation of *The Imaginary Invalid.* As translated by Morris Bishop, the Molière work is titled *The Would-Be Invalid.* Under the title of *The Hypochondriack,* the play may be found in *Molière's Comedies,* Volume II, Everyman's Library Series, London, J. M. Dent & Sons, Ltd., 1956. An acting edition of *The Imaginary Invalid* may also be purchased from Samuel French, Inc., 25 West 45th Street, New

York. Samuel French also has acting editions of *Hamlet* and of *Waltz of the Toreadors*.

In addition to the Samuel French edition, *Waltz of the Toreadors*, as translated by Lucienne Hill, is published in a single volume by Coward McCann Geoghegan, New York, 1953. *From Morn to Midnight* may also be obtained in a single-volume translation by Ashley Dukes, New York, Brentano's, 1922. *From Morn to Midnight* is also found in Dickinson's *Chief Contemporary Dramatists: Third Series*, Boston, Houghton Mifflin, 1933. However, the most available source for the Kaiser play is *Masters of Modern Drama*, an anthology edited by Haskell M. Block and Robert G. Shedd, New York, Random House, 1962.

creating theatre

CHAPTER 1

the nature of theatre

THE BASES OF THEATRE

If you have recently read a review of a local theatrical production, you might have come across a statement such as "the production had life and energy, but it suffered from lack of consistent style." Or you might have been told that the production lacked pace, that the characterization lacked depth, or that the director missed the author's point. It is all so clear that we wonder why the defects were not corrected before opening night, or why, having been pointed out, they were not immediately remedied before the second performance.

As we know, although theatre as an art product may appear simple, the creation of that art is actually complex, so complex that theatre

1

artists of long years' experience are often hesitant to comment on any particular aspect of any given production. Before venturing an assessment they want to know which of the contributing artists—the playwright, the actor, the director, the various designers—was responsible for what, when, where, and to what degree.

The reason an actor's characterization lacked depth may be simply that the actor lacked the necessary talent and skills. However, many other possibilities exist. The director may have desired, for stylistic reasons, a certain shallowness of character. The scene designer or the costumer may have detracted from the actor's characterization by an inappropriate setting or costume. Perhaps the lights were too warm, too cool, too bright, or too dim. In short, it is not impossible that in attempting to remedy a problem in characterization we may find ourselves in the light booth, reworking the patch plot. Theatre is indeed complex.

Because of its complicated nature, theatre can be understood and discussed intelligently only by beginning with an analysis and definition of its basic components. To start with root words, when we attend a play we go to a *theatre,* a word taken from the Greek term for "a place for seeing." We seat ourselves in an *auditorium,* a word meaning a place for hearing; and we watch one or more human beings *act,* a word that means "the doing of a deed." In the words *theatre, auditorium,* and *actor* we have named the three basic components of theatrical art: the theatre-visual, the theatre-auditory, and the theatre-kinetic.

THE THEATRE-VISUAL

The theatre-visual is all that part of theatre which appeals directly to the eye. It begins with light, since light is essential to vision. Lighting may be simple illumination coming directly from the sun, or it may be as elaborate and carefully controlled as the involved and constantly shifting light patterns of many contemporary theatrical productions. In its latter form, light calls for the services of one of the theatre's contributing artists. The artist may be a specialist, or he may combine his duties as lighting designer with those of scene designer, costumer, or director.

In addition to light, the theatre-visual requires space. This space might be the highly conventionalized, finite area behind the proscenium arch of many modern theatres, or it might be no more than a simple clearing in a crowd of spectators. Space has the potential of being reshaped and decorated for each new scene, performance, or production. When space is shaped and articulated, it calls forth the services of several theatrical artists: the theatre architect, the scene designer, the director, the actor, and the costumer.

Although the architect who designs a given theatre is too often but dimly aware of his responsibilities, he sets the essential limits upon what the other visual artists can do with space. For instance, an architect who designs a traditional proscenium theatre prevents productions given in such a theatre from ever escaping the picture-frame metaphor.

Once the architect has delivered the theatre building to the remaining theatre artists, he is replaced by the scene designer, whose task is to manipulate the received space so that it provides both a visual comment on the play as a whole and an acceptable environment for the work of the actors and director. The scene designer is followed by the director and the actors, who further design the space with their bodies so that additional visual comment is made. With the appearance of the actor in space, a final significant aspect of the theatre-visual is introduced—the decoration of the actors, that which they wear and carry. Here again the services of one or more contributing artists—the costumer, the makeup specialist, or the creator of properties—may be demanded.

In sum, the theatre-visual is that part of the theatre which deals directly with visible space, space essentially separated from time and motion. It is the spectacle that gives a name to the entire art form: *theatre*—a place for seeing.

THE THEATRE-AUDITORY

The theatre-auditory is that component which makes its chief appeal to the ear. In its simplest form it may be any noise, perhaps merely the pounding of feet upon a board. Normally it is the spoken word. Sometimes it is poetry; sometimes poetry that is accompanied by music. As language, whether sung or spoken, the theatre-auditory demands two separate artistic functions—the creation of words and a structure for such words, and the oral presentation of those words and structures. These services may be performed by a single artist, but more often they are assigned to at least three: the writer as deviser of vocal patterns, the actor as vocal instrument, and the director as arranger of suitable and meaningful auditory relationships between actor and audience. The writer might create merely a speech, a poem, or a song. Usually he creates a story involving speaking or singing characters. The director and actors then add their vocal contribution both through interpreting the vocal base contributed by the writer and by creatively enlarging on that base. When the theatre-auditory involves music, the artistic services of musicians and music director may also be needed.

Just as the theatre-visual is an essentially spatial art, so the theatre-auditory, which makes its statements to the ear, is an essentially temporal art. It is this temporal aspect of the art—the theatre as sound in time—that gives us the words for auditorium and audience.

THE THEATRE-KINETIC

The final component of theatre is the theatre-kinetic, the theatre as movement. One component of theatre appeals to the eye, another to the ear, while the theatre-kinetic appeals to our kinesthetic sense, our perception of motion. The theatre-kinetic is the most familiar and the least understood of the theatre components. Too often it is confused with the theatre-visual through the assumption that movement is a perceptual function of the eye alone. All senses are, of course, interdependent. We hear a speaker more easily when we can see him; we see noisy things more rapidly than silent ones. Undoubtedly, kinetic perception depends heavily on vision, but equally certain is the fact that there are separate and specialized sense perceivers for movement and balance. Moreover, these perceptors can indeed operate independently of vision. All of us have had the experience of sensing a movement we have not yet seen, or of having our muscles tighten in response to the emotional (and consequently hidden) muscular strains of another individual. However, without belaboring the point we may say that there is a clear distinction between that which moves and that which does not move.

4

The theatre-kinetic, then, makes its appeal to our sense of motion, which means that it is an art of space-time. The artists whose primary function is kinetic work directly with the problem of visible space transversed by a body in actual time. Essentially the immediate concern of the actor and the director, the theatre-kinetic is that part of theatre which weds space to time and in doing so creates motion. Other theatre artists, such as the scene designer with a moving set or changing lights, may be said to have secondary kinetic functions, as does the playwright with a developing story. The theatre-kinetic gives us the terms *act, actor,* and *action.* In the art of filmed drama, we obtain the terms *motion picture, movies,* and *cinema* (i.e., *kinema*).

THE RELATIVE VALUE OF THE BASIC COMPONENTS

Having identified the three aesthetic constituents of theatre, the question arises immediately: Which of the three is most vital? The answer is that in the art as we understand it today all three components are indispensable; to remove one would be but to weaken the remaining pair. The total theatrical metaphor is the judicious blending of all three constituents.

However, a judicious blending requires an understanding of relative values. Critical literature in the theatre often refers to so-called "actor's theatres," "playwright's theatres," and "designer's theatres" or "spectacles." Each of these terms indicates a need for realizing that choices exist, and that in certain places or periods of history one component has been stressed above the other two. When such imbalance takes place, the art is certainly endangered. To avoid imbalance, we must make certain value judgments, acquire principles that can later be adjusted to meet a given situation.

Most theatre historians will agree that theatre begins in dance. What is essential is a body, usually a human body, in visible space. A body and space are the sole preconditions of the art. The art itself begins when that body begins to move. It need not speak; it need not be decorated in any way. The body will make a better total artistic statement if it is accompanied by sound, voice, even music, and if it is meaningfully and beautifully decorated in a meaningful and striking stage setting. But the latter additions can be absent. After all, sound can retreat into the arts from whence it came—music and literature. The theatre-visual can return to sculpture, painting, and architecture. If a moving body, the actor, still remains, we are still in the presence of theatrical art. Moreover, if the visual and auditory arts are to be joined, a synthesizing agent must be present. That agent is the theatre-kinetic, an element which combines both space and time through motion.

The significance of the theatre-kinetic in the total art form is so obvious that any discussion of the point may seem redundant. However, we have for so long been bred on a literary tradition that the concept of the playwright as the essential creative artist of the theatre is regarded as a truism. All our formal education tends to emphasize the word as supreme in value and dignity. And, indeed, literature is a mighty and noble art. But in the threefold nature of the theatre, the dramatist is one of a number of contributing creative artists. What is more to the point, his contribution can, if necessary, be absent without totally destroying the art form. One need only to have had the experience of observing any highly skilled pantomimist hold an audience enthralled for two hours to realize that while the theatre sincerely desires the playwright, it can exist without him. In short, the theatre's essential ingredient is the actor, not as a speaker or reciter of lines, but as a deed-maker. It is not by sheer accident that our word *drama* comes from the Greek term for "a doing." Moreover, our words *play* and *player* connote physical activity rather than speaking or thinking.

But to realize that the theatre-kinetic is the irreducible element of the art is not to see it as the element that must be emphasized above the other two. Rather we must understand it as a base and touchstone for a proper balance of all parts. It is the synthesizer that creates the proper interplay of the three components of the theatre.

THE INTERPLAY OF THE THREE COMPONENTS

The viewpoint that the play script is the sole purpose of the theatrical metaphor is an easy one to assume but a difficult one to maintain. Often the script does little more than raise problems; specific solutions are left to the visual and kinetic theatres. Consider *Oedipus Rex.* Is

A Streetcar Named Desire by Tennessee Williams. The Ohio University School of Theatre.

Director: Dennis Dalen   Production Assistant: Robin Lacy

Note the romantic style produced by using transparencies to expand the normal densities of some forms, while the deliberate softening of the normal lines of other forms adds to the air of mild nostalgia and decay.

Oedipus wearing a short skirt or a long gown? Does he or does he not walk with a pronounced limp? Choice of costume or walk will say much about the character, as much perhaps as all the words he speaks—yet on these two points the playwright gives no instructions. Again, exactly what does the skeleton in the tree look like in *From Morn to Midnight*? Kaiser tells us little, and yet the visual impact of the skeleton is a central feature of Kaiser's argument. These two examples point out the fact that subordination of the visual and kinetic theatres to the auditory theatre is not the manner in which the art achieves its best results. Coordination, not subordination, is the process through which theatre is created. To understand the manner in which the three constituents coordinate, it is necessary to attempt an understanding of the Aristotelian concept of *action*.

In his *Poetics*, Aristotle claimed that action was the end of tragedy (and by extention, all drama). So important was action in Aristotle's mind that he argued that a play could exist without characters but not without action. Character, he said, is merely present on account of action. Just exactly what *action* meant to Aristotle would be impossible to say, but clearly he saw it as something different from plot or story line, for he used the word *mythos* for plot. If action is not plot, then it is not merely an intrigue invented by a playwright and passed on to actors. What then might action be?

In its broadest sense, we understand action to be any sort of change. It is a major aspect of life and the human experience. On its most immediately preceptible level, action is physical, tangible movement from one position in space and time to another. On intellectual and emotional levels, action is the change from one idea or emotional condition to another idea or condition. In all probability physical, emotional, and intellectual action must ultimately take the form of something physical, such as writing, kissing, laughing, or building a bridge. Action, then, is an aspect of life itself; it is the change inherent in all life.

However, art is not life. Therefore action in art cannot be the same as action in life. Aristotle was very careful to make this point. Drama, he said, is not the creation of an action; it is an "imitation of an action. As a natural phenomenon action can be imitated by a number of arts, each with their special imitative advantages and limitations.

Music can imitate particularly well the temporal and auditory aspects of action, as can literature. Literature's forte is the imitation of intellectual and emotional actions. Painting, through color and form, can imitate certain spatial features of action. Dance and pantomime can imitate outward physical attributes of action. No art is wholly adequate to imitate action in all its manifestations and implications. By calling forth the cooperation of a number of contributing arts with the art of motion as their base, the theatre can move far in the direction of totally encompassing the imitation of an action; but it often gives up in depth what it gains in breadth.

The advantage theatre has in all-encompassing breadth is, however, the reason Aristotle singled it out as the form most directly concerned with imitating action. Indeed, because of its kinetic base, the theatre has no other choice or goal. Other arts may elect not to imitate action, but the theatre has no other true function. The theatre's imitation of action proceeds through the cooperation of its contributing arts, each contribution imitating action in its own special fashion, but with each art subordinating some of the advantages of its form in order to secure the cooperation of the other forms. The process might begin at any point. Traditionally it begins with the play script, but it could as easily begin with a scene design or an improvisation in an acting studio.

The playwright, then, contributes an imitation of an action. The imitation is not the reality action, but a verbal analogue, containing dialogue, plot, and dramatic agents, of natural action. Since the basis of the play script's imitation is language, the imitation is essentially temporal; that is, the imitation is presented in terms of characters and events succeeding each other in a time rhythm. Moreover, since the playwright is seeking the cooperative assistance of various spatial and kinetic artists, he deliberately avoids introducing actual spatial reality into his play. Because dramatic literature is a time art, the playwright has no real spatial restrictions. A novelist, for example, may have his characters climb mountains in an introductory adverbial clause, or leap tall buildings in a single bound. The playwright, by deliberate choice, assumes spatial discipline. Miller does not have Willy Loman take his suicide drive on stage, for this would present impossible problems to the spatial artists of the theatre.

It can be said that the writer becomes a playwright not so much by

9

what he does as by what he does not do. A dramatic story becomes a playable script when sufficient allowance is made by the playwright for the creative functions and spatial requirements of the kinetic and visual theatres. A play script is as valuable in what it allows the actors to be and do as in what it gives them to say.

Just as an action can be imitated in words, so it can be imitated in space. The artists of the theatre-visual, having recognized the particular action imitated in the script, then proceed to imitate the same action in terms of space. They are not, if they are worthy of the name artist, merely providing a visual aid for the dramatist. Their major task is twofold: to comment directly on the action through the media of the plastic arts, and to provide an environment, both tangible and atmospheric, which will aid and promote the work of the theatre-kinetic. By imitating the underlying action through line, color, and shape, the theatre-visual contributes to the breadth of statement and strongly reinforces the comment made by the theatre-auditory. Here again the theatre-visual is also asked to exercise discipline. Scene, costume, and light design are purely spatial statements. As such, they are not restricted by the demands of time nor the needs of movement. The scene designer could, if he so wished, state the whole action of the play in a huge narrative mural. The costumer could so build his costumes that the actors become merely display models, incapable of free movement.

The theatre-visual normally does not exploit the full potential of its arts, only because to do so would mean the shutting-out of the effects of the other theatrical components.

Finally the theatre-kinetic, for whose sake the other arts have sacrificed so much, is required in turn to exercise its share of self-denial. Kinetic art lies closest to the physical action to be imitated, and it provides an immediate and vivid analogue for intellectual and emotional action. Kinetic art, however, often lacks subtlety, and for this it needs the aid and support of the spatial and auditory arts.

Since the art of motion is neither a purely temporal nor a purely spatial art but rather an art of space-time, it does not have the severe limitations of literature on the one hand nor the space restrictions of painting, sculpture, and architecture on the other. A mime actor could, for example, state the entire temporal action of *Oedipus Rex* in a few quick movements. Moreover, the same mime actor could ignore the limits of scenic architecture and make his statement without regard or reference to any place or locale.

The theatre-kinetic, however, should not step beyond the time sequence of the play script nor transgress the spatial environment created by the scene and costume designers. The actors and the director, the two artistic forces most active in the theatre-kinetic, must be willing to forego many of the freedoms and advantages of the space-time form in order to obtain the breadth of imitation possible only with the cooperation of the auditory and visual theatres.

THE BASES OF THEATRE: A SUMMARY OF AN AESTHETIC

Action exists. It may be defined as any sort of change in life. Literal action is not capable of being created in an art, but it may be imitated. To imitate action merely to give it record is of little artistic value, but as action is imitated in an art it is also given a distinct and individual form. This form reveals the artist's attitude toward the action under imitation, and thus action obtains meaning and human value. A number of forms are capable of imitating and informing action. Among these arts is theatre, whose whole function is solely the imitation of action.

Theatre begins as a physical thing, a human moving in space. In its kinetic form, theatre imitates through physical motion. In order to broaden its imitative ability, theatre seeks the cooperation of the visual arts. Through the modulation and decoration of space and actor, these arts both imitate the action in their own media and enhance the imitative power of the physical theatre. For its statement to be as encompassing as possible, theatre also seeks the aid of the time arts, principally literature, but often music as well. The arts of sound imitate action in terms of temporal sequences; in so doing they greatly expand and deepen the temporal dimensions of the theatre as well as provide exciting reinforcement for the kinetic and visual theatres.

Of the three components of theatre, that of the theatre as physical movement is most vital, but it is dangerous to talk of any separation. Remove any of the points of the triangle, and the whole structure rapidly disintegrates. The actor and the director may go it alone, as they did in the *commedia dell'arte,* but they are unhappy and are constantly seeking the aid of the scenic artist and the playwright. As for equating the theatre with dramatic literature, history has repeatedly demonstrated the sad result of attempts to make the theatre merely a "hearing place." In Rome we are reduced ultimately to the outrages of Senecan melodrama. In the Italian Renaissance, we have the endless volumes of gray closet dramas on the one hand, and on the other, a stage filled with meaningless spectacle and vacuous landscapes. Our own time has given us the radio soap opera.

The contemporary emphasis on theatre as visual spectacle has created the sorry phenomena of the Hollywood extravaganza and the television special, both of which have reduced the actor to a prancing clothes horse and the playwright to a composer of quips and doggerel.

Subordination is not only dangerous but impossible in true theatre. The theatre is an art of cooperation, not one of subordination. As it advances toward its goal of public performance, first one and then another of its basic triad is the one which at any specific moment gives the art its informing vision. But when the form is complete, when it is in its ideal state before an audience, the essential values of each component should be present with equal effect. Each constituent—kinetic, visual, and auditory—must make its demands and its sacrifices. The demands are the price the other two must pay for value received; the sacrifices are the purchase of cooperation and enhancement.

CHAPTER 2

the function of
the director

In Chapter 1 an approach was made to an understanding of the nature of the theatre, but only in general terms. Since this is a book about directing, our discussion will proceed henceforth from the viewpoint of the play director. The first need is to understand the function of the director in the art of theatre. Usually the function of any artist can be obtained from a study of the literature devoted to that artist. Unfortunately, the literature devoted to the art of play direction is comparatively slight. Moreover, much of it comes from so late a date that one sometimes meets the assertion that the director is a phenomenon of the modern theatre only. This assertion is far from correct, and a brief glance at the director as a historical entity might help lay the ground for an understanding of his modern function.

THE DIRECTOR IN THE HISTORY
OF THE THEATRE

The director, under one title or another, undoubtedly has always existed in the theatre, for his function is essential and can be performed by no other artist. He may conceal his art under the title of another, as did the Greek playwrights who were both poet and director, but he is usually present. In fact the combination of playwright and director might, in some cases, prove the ideal one, but we must remember that although one man performs both functions, he operates at different times as different artists. When the Greek author wrote his play, he was a playwright; when he directed that play, he became a director. Interestingly enough, the Greek word for poet can be used for both functions, for the term means "a maker" and can be compared to the modern theatrical term *producer*. Moreover, the Greek playwrights had the knowledge and artistic skill to combine the arts of writer and director, for they were educated in dance and rhetoric as well as in literature. Modern playwrights are usually not so well equipped. Then, too, even the Greeks did not always direct their own works. We know, for instance, that Aristophanes allowed Kallistrates and Philonides to produce *Lysistrata, The Babylonians,* and *The Birds.* Nor did the director disappear from the Roman theatre. In the mime troupes, the mimeograph contributed the play script, but if he were a nobleman as was Decimus Laberius, his position prevented him from exercising any other function. Consequently, the task of directing was assumed by the archmime, who was also the leading actor. The evidence from the prologues of Terence's plays is unmistakable; his producer and director was Ambivius Turpio. In the Roman art of pantomime, a single mime was director, actor, and playwright, a combination which leads to highly cohesive theatre, but, without doubt, a painfully circumscribed art.

From the massive pageantry of the French medieval theatre comes the title "master of the play," and so highly respected and desired were these professional directors that one, Jean Bouchet, was actually bribed to stage a particular village's production. The Italian Renaissance provides us with a long list of commedia directors, who sometimes also doubled as actors and sometimes as composers of scenarios. A fascinating document from sixteenth century Italy, the *Dialogues of Di Somi*, a professional director, provides additional proof of the continuing existence of the theatrical director. The *Dialogues* are in themselves as valuable in terms of theatrical theory as they are in terms of history, and the insights they offer are important enough to make them required reading for any student of dramatic production.

Shakespeare leaves us two excellent insights into his work as a theatre director. The first is the renowned "speak the speech," which contains the so-often-unheeded advice not only to "suit the action to the word," but also to "suit the word to the action." The other reference is the charming spoof found in the Pyramus and Thisbe subplot of *A Midsummer Night's Dream*. Molière has also left a record of himself as a director in his short work, *The Impromptu at Versailles*. Both of these men were trained in all the arts of the theatre and could therefore more successfully unite the duties of playwright and director.

From the eighteenth century on, the existence of the director as a separate theatre artist is too clearly marked to need further comment. For instance, we are coming to realize that David Garrick's major contribution may not have been his acting (as it was certainly not his playwriting), but it could well have been his directing. After all, it is not his ability as a dramatist, nor his genius as an actor, which Kitty Clive makes so much ado about, but his achievement in taking an average company and making them "actors without genius . . . having made them pass for such."

The theatrical records of the nineteenth and twentieth centuries leave little doubt that the director is a vital functionary of the modern theatre, but as our brief history demonstrates, he has always been so.

That the director emerges as a somewhat shadowy figure historically is the direct result of the nature of the art, for the director's task is to use his art advantageously to promote the other artists of the theatre. His greatest achievement is not to have undue recognition, but rather to have the praise that might accrue to him be lavished on the actors, scenery, and the dramatic script itself. Only theatre intimates might know the precise work of the director on a given production, and even professional directors cannot mark the exact point where a fellow director's art stopped and the art of others began.

THE DIRECTOR AS INTEGRATOR

When we say that the director's task is to promote the various arts of theatre, we do not mean that he is merely the willing servant of the actor, the playwright, or the scene designer. Indeed, the situation is quite the reverse. The director is the master of all the arts of theatre. He is the core artist. Without his will the kinetic, visual, and auditory components of the theatre are incapable of proper union, and will for the most part remain juxtaposed rather than coalesced. It is the director's task to integrate the three constituents of theatre. To accomplish this, he must create a metaphor which can contain and incorporate all three. This metaphor is what the audience receives, and, consequently, it is the director's vision that makes the ultimate statement of the play.

We must realize that though the director is the master, not the servant, of the other theatre artists, he also is not the unreasoning tyrant. He is responsible to the other artists, and if he refuses to acknowledge his responsibility he is punished by loss of willing cooperation, a loss which means the disappearance of his tools and thus of his art. The director can design his own set, or hire a scene designer. If he works with a visual artist, he may accept or reject the solutions provided by the designer, but he should refrain from dictating those solutions. Again, the director may write his own play, but if he is using the literary work of another, he should respect that work. He does not have to accept a given script, but once having accepted it he should not willfully make major rearrangements in the literary form. Finally, who does or does not act for him is usually the director's prerogative, but once having cast an actor he should respect that actor's right to his own art. In turn, the director properly requests allegiance and willing devotion to his conception of the theatrical performance. He expects the playwright to provide a script which can be reasonably combined with the arts of vision and motion. He expects the actors to go where he tells them and to respond to the patterns established. He looks to the scene

16

Biedermann and the Fire Bugs *by Max Frisch. Louisiana State University, New Orleans.*
Director: August W. Staub   Designer: Gerald B. Forbes   Costumer: James M. Ragland

A purely constructivistic set and deliberately outlandish costumes contribute to the unreal effect of Frisch's neo-Expressionistic play. Note the emphasis gained by counterfocus.

designer to reinforce the play script and to provide both a spatial vision for the production and an acceptable environment for the statement that he and the actors are seeking to make.

With an overview of the integrative functions of the director in mind, let us examine more particularly the tasks that face him in each of the three components of theatre.

THE DIRECTOR AND THE THEATRE-AUDITORY

The director's first problem in the auditory theatre is to select the play script. Since a director has the accumulation of over two thousand years of dramatic literature from which to choose, just why might he select one play and reject thousands more? Of course a number of extra-artistic reasons might dictate his choice. But let us assume the conditions under which the average noncommercial theatre director operates. Assuming that the play is in English or in a good translation, the director probably uses three additional guidelines: (1) the play is good literature, (2) the play can be mounted in terms of his production situation, and (3) the playwright's view of the human experience agrees in main with the views of the director. The first criterion implies that the director has a sturdy background in literature and literary criticism; the second implies that the director has a good grasp of the capabilities of his audience, production plant, and personnel. Regarding the third criterion, one hopes that the director is intelligent and sensitive enough to find agreeable to his tastes play scripts that make reasonably profound and compassionate statements, be they comedy or tragedy.

Once the script has been selected, the basic time sequence of the final theatrical production is generally fixed. Some alteration is always possible, but it is usually minor because major changes in temporal sequence generally do violence to the form and meaning of the script. Also, the number of characters and hence the number of actors is generally set, though this too can be altered within limits. The selection of the play script also means that the mood, quality, and a good measure of the style of the future production is given a base. Lastly, the script provides general rhythmic patterns and a basic idea of theme. None of these seminal constructs, however, is absolute. The play script provides a score, a framework upon which much of the ultimate

18

theatrical event is built. But the dramatic script is infinitely more ambiguous than the musical score. It is not uncommon to hear the director referred to as an interpretive artist, a sort of practical dramatic critic. Certainly this is one of the functions of directing, but it is impossible for a director to discover all his answers in the play script. *Hamlet,* for example, has almost as many interpretations as there are practicing Shakespearean critics. *Oedipus Rex* has been variously interpreted as a fate-tragedy, a free-will tragedy, and as a story of man's search for identity. The point is not to question the validity of these various interpretations, but to let them remind us that the director must bring his own meanings to the script. The playwright may set a ceiling on possible meanings, but in such cases as *Oedipus* or *Waltz of the Toreadors* this ceiling may be quite high.

What the director obtains from the dramatic script is a temporal narrative containing suggestions for additional visual and kinetic statements. The temporal narrative puts at the director's disposal a story of intrigue, language and verbal rhythms, and a number of dramatic characters. Armed with these elements of his craft, the director is now prepared to begin his integrating process in the visual, auditory, and kinetic theatres.

THE DIRECTOR AND THE THEATRE-VISUAL

From the auditory theatre the director obtained a temporal sequence; from the visual theatre he must derive a space in which that sequence can occur. The play script will form the suggestive base for the space selected, but the selection will be made by the director in conjunction with the scene designer. The two artists may decide upon space existing for itself alone, having no references to locale or culture. *From Morn to Midnight* could be staged in such a space, or it could be staged in a number of units highly suggestive of such locales as the bicycle race track or the Salvation Army Hall. Whatever the choice, whether simple space or highly modulated space, director and scene designer have now sharply curtailed the manner in which the play can comment on the human situation. *Oedipus Rex* staged upon open platforms, suggestive of no place and no time, is not the same play as *Oedipus Rex* staged upon and before a formal Greek façade. Not only does space treated as space make statements and set limits, but as it is presented so it also provides the basic patterns for the movement of the actors. In other words, the whole framework, the determining base, of the theatre-kinetic is settled upon by the decisions made in the theatre-visual. The original Broadway setting for *Death of a Salesman* retained the feeling of a house within a city. It also attempted to suggest that the house had more than just an external reference in time. However, by retaining the basic floor plan of a two-story house, the scene designer threw a heavy burden on lighting to inform the audience of when the story was leaving the external reality of the house and entering the subjective world of Willy's mind. The director and scene designer had good reasons and justifications for retaining the metaphor of an actual house, but in doing so they eliminated certain movement patterns that could have been highly provocative and telling when the place of action happened to be in Willy's mind.

From the theatre-visual the director, then, obtains the element of space, formed and unformed, decorated and undecorated, colored and uncolored; and the basic movement pattern for the theatre-kinetic. In addition the director brings to the theatre-visual his own kind of visual statement, the costumed actor. The human body of the actor contains all the elements of visual composition: form, line, mass, color, and texture (the latter two mainly through costume). Thus the director has at his disposal the ability to create static visual compositions which are both aesthetically pleasing and intellectually meaningful. These actor-compositions he blends with both the setting and the theatre-auditory to produce a single comment. Therefore, without moving the actors the director can make statements simultaneously in auditory and visual media through what the actors say and through how they look in relation to one another on the space assigned to them. Obviously, since the director not only cooperates with the scene designer in the design of the stage set but also operates himself as a visual artist, his education should include work in the theory and practice of fine arts.

THE DIRECTOR AND THE THEATRE-KINETIC

When the director has a story, a space, and actors, he has the tools to solve the problem of theatre as movement. Here his freedom to create is as great as or greater than in the visual theatre. Whatever decisions he

An Angel Comes to Babylon *by Friedrich Durenmatt. Department of Drama and Communications, Louisiana State University, New Orleans.*

Director: James M. Ragland   Designer: David H. Brune   Costumer: Pamela J. Mason

Note that the effect of the large upstage mass is reduced in dominance because of its low color value. The single figure on stage right is clearly dominant. His dominance is gained from high color value and from being surrounded by a significant amount of negative space. Note also that the focus of the entire composition is on an off-stage presence. The effect of an "old movie" is obtained in the surpressed energy of the arrested mass.

has previously made concerning the script, the costumes, the setting, the lights, and the actors, he has been guided by what he wishes to accomplish in the theatre-kinetic, just as when he works in the kinetic theatre he continually takes into account the needs of the auditory and visual theatres.

The designer and costumer have set limits to the amount and quality of movement in space; the playwright has set limits to movement in time. Within these limitations the director must invent a pleasing and meaningful kinetic analogue to the story being presented. For example, after Oedipus learns the awful truth about himself, he must exit from the stage. How he moves during that exit will say as much about the character as how he looks and what he says.

Directing, then, requires a knowledge of the design and composition of motion. The director must understand the factors of kinetic design—such as rate, direction, and energy—and the principles of motion design.

The actor is the director's chief kinetic tool. In terms of the actor as a moving body, the director must understand the restrictions placed on that body by the setting, the costume, the playwright's character, and the actor's own skill and talent. More important than the single actor, the director must control the kinetic relationships of all the actors. This is a task only the director can perform. He alone has sufficient overview and objectivity.

In its basic form, movement by more than one actor involves the technical problem of traffic control. But motion design goes beyond mere traffic. Take for example the scene between Willy and Howard in *Salesman*. Willy is being fired. Willy's reaction to this shock can be stated in what he says, how he looks, and what he does. Since only two actors are involved, and since two actors rarely have traffic problems or visual compositional problems, the scene rests on what the two say and what they are doing as they talk. When does Howard advance? When does Willy retreat? When is Willy moving? In what directions? With what rate and energy? The answers to these questions will give added depth and dimension to the words of the two actors.

Thus in the kinetic theatre the director works with his major tool, the moving body of the human being. Since he attempts to blend the statements made by a moving body with those made in the visual and auditory theatres, he must constantly seek areas of compromise and cooperation between all three components of theatre.

SEEKING COOPERATION: THE REHEARSALS

In the rehearsals is where the directorial compromise is achieved and where the theatrical metaphor for a finished production is created. In terms of mechanics, the director's function in rehearsals is that of clerk-of-the-works. He arranges the total schedule, supervises each individual rehearsal, maintains discipline, even acts as prompter if none is available. More importantly, he casts the actors, teaches them how to use the set and lights, sets the limits of each characterization, creates movement patterns, aids in character analysis, gives the actors individual line readings, creates the overall vocal patterns of the play, and gives shape and rhythm to the story being told. In order to do these things, the director must be conversant with the art of acting and of oral interpretation. He should know what can be done with the spoken line in terms of phrasing, pausing, emphasis, pitch, rate, and volume. He should also know what can be done with the human body in terms of walking, running, standing, sitting, kneeling, falling, and jumping. In short, especially in the noncommercial theatre, the director should be prepared not only to give directions but also to teach and coach.

In the technical and dress rehearsals the director completes the final blending. All the resources of the visual, kinetic, and literary theatres are joined in the immediately visible, speaking, moving presence of the actor. It is during technical and dress rehearsals, when each artist is making his greatest contribution, and when many have conflicting demands, that the director must act as arbiter and diplomat.

Performance is the test of how well the director has accomplished his complex function.

THE FUNCTION OF THE DIRECTOR: A SUMMARY

The three components of the theatre are by their nature self-contained. Without a single central control, a satisfactory union is less likely. To achieve a satisfactory union is the function of the director. Thus the director as unifying artist has always been present in the theatre, although not always identified by title. Theatre is a cooperating art, and the director is responsible for that cooperation. Consequently, he might be viewed as the master artist of the theatre, but his art is greatest when it is least recognized. His function is to blend the efforts of all contributing artists and to focus those efforts on the actor in performance. In this way, his contribution is disguised beneath the contributions of others.

CHAPTER 3

selecting the script

The art of theatre might begin in any of its three components. It might begin with a dance step or with a special type of stage set, but the most frequent initial point is the selection of a script by a director. In theory the director has complete freedom of choice in this matter, but in practice a number of technical and aesthetic restrictions might be placed upon him. In the noncommercial theatre, for example, the director must consider the instructional and cultural needs of his students and the community. He is usually asked to work for a balanced season and frequently must consider financial matters.

In general, however, the theatre director has the opportunity to select his own play script. Not only does he have the opportunity, but he has the duty to do so, and his willingness to meet this duty is the first test of his arrival as a mature artist. His second test as an artist is his adroitness in making good selections. A good selection can usually be measured in terms of positive audience response; in many theatres which must earn some or all of their financial support at the box office, a good selection also pays its way. Finally, a good selection satisfies the ends of theatre: a cultural and artistic experience for both theatre personnel and audience.

How does a director make a good play selection? Putting aside for the moment any extra-artistic factors, the director usually bases his choice upon the three guidelines outlined in Chapter 2. He chooses a play because it is good dramatic literature, because it appears to be able to be mounted in terms of his particular theatre, and because the statements made in the play are those with which the director agrees and can build upon.

THE PLAY SCRIPT AS DRAMATIC LITERATURE

All good drama is also good literature. Therefore, in order to judge the artistic value of a script, the director should be reasonably expert in literary history and criticism. If this knowledge is not gained in school, it should be acquired privately as quickly as possible. Moreover, such expertise must be kept up to date. The director should know the works and opinions of past and present literary critics, and he should have a general knowledge of the literature of the past and the innovations of the present. Every potential and practicing director should be a reader of literature. If possible, directors should attempt to write, because the best way to understand the potentials and difficulties of writing is by practice and trials. Two of America's outstanding directors, Harold Clurman and Elia Kazan, are also authors of considerable skill.

A strong literary background will not guarantee that plays the director selects will be good literature, but it will provide him with some skills in sampling literature and some scope in making his judgment. He certainly will gain immeasurably from knowing which writers have been recognized by reputable critics as outstanding authors. Moreover, these same authors will give him a basis of comparison. If he is aware, for instance, of Sheridan and Goldsmith, he can use the writings of these two as a means of evaluating other plays of the eighteenth century or even works from other periods. The director must also be a reader of poetry as well as prose, for much dramatic literature is in poetry. He must develop an ear for verse patterns and an eye for literary imagery.

A general knowledge of literature is indispensable, but dramatic literature is literature with a difference, and the director should educate himself to that difference. He cannot read too many plays nor ponder too long on their structure. He should constantly be reading and contemplating dramatic literature. What he is searching for in his reading is discussed in detail in the following chapter. Suffice it to say that in general the director is judging each play in terms of its dramatic elements: language, character, point of view, exposition, story, and action. He wants to know how these elements are presented and how they achieve the goals of dramatic composition and design: unity, proportion, emphasis, variety, rhythm, and theme.

The use of the elements of drama to achieve the goals of dramatic composition and design is what gives each play its style. *Style* may be defined as the total effect produced by a given work of art, in this case dramatic art. Style has two aspects: an individual and a group character. Every artist belongs to some tradition. This tradition includes the artist's experience; his general education; his artistic education; and his social, economic, and historical position. Goldsmith and Sheridan, for example, have great similarities that grow out of their both being eighteenth-century English playwrights. Jonson and Shakespeare are also much alike. Here too we have contemporaries. On the other hand, Anouilh's *Waltz of the Toreadors* reminds us of Molière, though the two French playwrights are separated by three centuries. In this case, Anouilh's education and training must be taken into account.

Each artist also has an individual style, and one test of the excellence of an artist is the degree to which his personal style transcends the stylistic tradition in which he is working. A playwright's style is his peculiar use of the elements and goals of dramaturgy. Sometimes, in the case of poor artists, the personal style is very distinct, but it falls below the artistic level of the tradition in which he is working. Sometimes, with great writers, it exceeds the level. More often the style maintains a place near the center of the tradition. In order to judge

27

What Price Glory by *Maxwell Anderson and Lawrence Stallings. Louisiana State University, New Orleans.*

Director: August W. Staub   Designer: Peter Casanave   Costumer: James M. Ragland

The line of soldiers following the trailing vacuum of the leader are seen in dynamic tension created by the lone soldier moving in a slightly different direction in an upstage plane.

individual style, the director must know the traditions of past and present. He must understand the values of a tested technique and be alive to the merits of new techniques and cautious of their dangers. Originality is exciting, but it must be judged in terms of whether it is merely a break with a perfectly workable traditional technique, or whether it offers a new method which the old could not accomplish.

Good literary style means good literature; good dramaturgic style means good dramatic literature. The director will need to have a background in literature in general and dramatic literature in particular in order to select a play script of sound literary merit. His literary background and his experience in selecting and producing plays will contribute to his "dramatic instinct" for what is a valuable script and what is less worthy.

THE PLAY SCRIPT AND THE SPECIFIC PRODUCTION SITUATION

Among the play scripts of sound literary value, many will be rejected by the director because they do not meet the requirements of his specific production situation. To know the peculiarities of every production situation is impossible, but most directors will face one or more of the following issues whenever they select a play: (1) the type of theatre in which the play is to be produced; (2) the material resources of that theatre; (3) the artistic resources of the theatre, including design and acting talent; (4) the purpose for which the theatre produces plays; and (5) the potential audience.

In terms of the first issue, it is obvious that not all plays can be produced in all types of theatres. An outdoor arena will hardly do for some plays by Ibsen, while *Oedipus* would go quite well outdoors. Tiny stages are not well suited for spectacles; large stages often have to be pulled in drastically for drawing-room comedy. In this respect even the size of the auditorium may affect the choice of a play. Large, echoing auditoriums simply do not encourage a feeling of intimacy, no matter how effective the on-stage activity.

Closely tied to the type of theatre is the problem of the material resources of a given theatre. Physically the theatre plant must support the production. An arena stage with little place to store and move scenery is not a felicitous place to stage a multiset show. Lighting and lighting control must always be a consideration when selecting a play script. Dressing rooms, scene shops, sewing rooms, rehearsal space, and audience control are all problems that may greatly influence a choice of play.

The third issue, that of artistic resources, is in many ways the most crucial one. If the design and acting talent simply are not capable of producing a given script, the director may have to pass it over. This problem is a very real one in the noncommercial theatre. For instance, the director may have a good core of talent, but simply not enough to mount *Hamlet*. Certainly the literary value of the play is unquestionable, and certainly the people involved would gain greatly from the educational experience. The theatre plant and resources may be quite sufficient. But if the artistic skills of the theatre would be so overstrained that producing *Hamlet* might cause an artistic disaster, the director might be wiser in postponing that particular play to some future date. After all, a bad production might do more educational harm than good, and certainly it would offer little in the way of artistic satisfaction. Since most noncommercial theatres have professional designing talent on staff, the issue of artistic skill is often centered on the talent and skill of the actors. Most directors give considerable thought to the potential of their acting pool before they select a play.

Our fourth issue is the purpose for which the play is produced. Plays, particularly in noncommercial theatre, are produced for a variety of reasons. Most are done for their educational value, but this value will vary with specific situations. One play might be done to give the actors experience in doing farce; another because the theatre is partaking in a college-wide Spanish culture festival. A third might be produced because each year the theatre does an original play. A musical might be done both as light entertainment and as a money-maker to support the remainder of the season. All of the above examples and many more will color the director's choice of play and playwright.

The final issue is the audience for whom the play is intended. A theatrical production, like a public speech, is intended for an immediate audience. This audience has some prejudices about what it expects to see in the theatre. While the director as artist need not address himself to every wish of his audience, he must understand and make allowances for their prejudices if he is going to communicate at all. Consequently some scripts might have to be rejected because at the moment they are too shocking for a potential audience, too involved, or too far from their experience realm. Whatever might be the specific case, the director usually attempts to understand his particular audience and to consider that audience when he comes to make his choice of a play.

Thus in addition to selecting the best possible dramatic literature, the director also considers his specific production situation when he chooses a play. He takes into consideration his theatre, its material resources, its artistic resources, the purpose for which the play is produced, and the audience for whom the play is intended.

PLAY SELECTION AND THE DIRECTOR AS ARTIST

As a final guide to play selection, the director considers himself as theatre artist. Unlike the commercial director, the normal noncommercial director need not do a play which offers to him a disagreeable philosophic premise. For other reasons he may elect to do the play, but most directors select play scripts that do not conflict seriously with their own view of the human experience. The director himself is an artist, and not surprisingly he wishes also to communicate ideas and experiences through his art. He will better communicate these things if he and the playwright are philosophically compatible.

Most plays, except those that are thoroughgoing propaganda, offer sufficient philosophic breadth to the average director. More confining, however, is the artistic style of the play. Like the writer, every director has a general style and an individual style. The general style grows out of his training and contemporary directing practices; the individual style develops as the director grows in artistic maturity. Every director, consciously or unconsciously, seeks a personal style. At first this style may be merely a potpourri of the styles of others. Every beginning director goes through such a period, and the experimentation is healthy. But the mature director builds a style of his own. This style begins with the kind of play scripts he selects and continues with his handling of all the elements of the visual, kinetic, and auditory theatres. It is good and necessary that a director achieve an individual

Hamlet *by William Shakespeare. Pioneer Memorial Theatre, Theatre Department, University of Utah.*

Director: David E. Jones

Note the choice of a different costuming period for the play. The period selected gives the play a modern feeling yet it is clearly removed from the world of business suits and everyday realities. The foils are used to extend line and gain emphasis. The curve in Hamlet's body indicates weakness and complexity.

style, but that very achievement acts as a restriction on his choice of plays.

Some directors have a broad and relatively elastic style and thus have a greater freedom of choice in scripts; others have a circumscribed style which immediately eliminates many worthy scripts. Of course no artist is prevented from experimentation, but while experimentation might lead some directors to a broader style, it might lead others to a striking but more narrow range. The beginning director should constantly take inventory of the nature of his style. As early as possible he should begin determining what he directs well and what he does not. He may find that some very good plays are simply not suitable for his approach.

A director may find the general style of a play to his liking but reject it because it does not provide the artistic opportunities he desires. While the play may provide an excellent base in the auditory theatre, it may so circumscribe the opportunities in the visual and kinetic theatres that the director will forego its production. For example, a play might present excellent dialogue between interesting characters in a strong situation, but it might occur in a darkened hospital room with all characters bedridden. Certain directors, in certain periods of their careers, might feel the play would not offer enough visual and kinetic material.

Thus the final consideration in play selection is the director as artist and philosopher. While the latter concern is less of a problem, directors for the most part avoid plays that run counter to their own philosophic views. As to artistic concerns, directors might accept or reject a play because of its style in terms of their own capabilities. Finally, a director might accept or reject a play on the basis of the opportunities it affords him in his own creative efforts in the auditory, visual, or kinetic theatres.

SELECTING THE PLAY SCRIPT: MISCELLANEOUS PROBLEMS

A number of miscellaneous problems may affect script selection. Such problems vary from theatre to theatre, year to year, and director to director. For instance, many directors will not do a heavy drama or a tragedy during the summer. Some theatres have a tradition of a classic drama or a Shakespeare every year; other theatres always start their season with a big-cast show. Another type of problem might be the scheduling of rehearsal time and space.

In many theatres the problem of music is a major one. Some non-commercial theatres do an opera or a musical every year. The demands of certain operas and musicals might greatly affect their selection. During play selection time, the director must be on guard for miscellaneous problems inherent in his production situation.

SELECTING THE PLAY SCRIPT: A SUMMARY

Every director is faced with the problems of his own situation when selecting a play script. But whatever his specific needs, he will usually choose a play in light of its value as dramatic literature, its relation to his own producing situation—that is, his theatre, its physical and artistic resources, the purpose for production, and his audience—and its relation to himself as a theatre artist. He may also be concerned with various miscellaneous problems, not the least of which is music.

CHAPTER 4

initial decisions
in the theatre-auditory

*Preliminary Evaluation of
the Play Script*

A play script under serious consideration by a director should meet
certain standards of dramaturgic form before it is finally accepted for
production. This is not to say that there are rules to which every script
must conform. In fact, the whole concept of literary excellence is
merely an initial starting point. It matters little how many times a play
"breaks the rules," or how nicely it conforms to accepted patterns. In
the end, the only sure way to judge a play is by its effectiveness in the

theatre. But before a play is actually produced, the director must depend upon his literary and theatrical training and experience to guide him in deciding what may or may not be effective drama.

The director's key to script evaluation is a knowledge of the means and ends of dramaturgy. In the preceding chapter, the elements of dramaturgy were listed as language, dramatic agents, exposition, story, point of view, and action. The aims were dramatic composition and dramatic design. *Dramatic composition* may be defined as the realizing of unity, proportion, emphasis, variety, and rhythm in the play script. *Dramatic design* may be defined as the use of the elements of dramatic composition to achieve meaning in the play. The overall effect of elements and goals may be called the style of the play.

THE ELEMENTS OF DRAMATURGY

The elements of dramaturgy are the tools by which the author achieves his goals. They are analogous to the tools of line, form, color, mass, texture, and space, by which the visual artist gains his goals. The elements of dramaturgy are found also in narrative fiction, but in the latter art they take a distinctively different turn. Our present concern is only with playwriting, and before we examine each element separately, we might remind ourselves that in the well-constructed play, as in any work of art, the dramaturgic elements are not mutually exclusive, but rather all work in unison to support and enrich each other and to make more effective the compositional and design goals of the playwright.

INITIAL EVALUATION OF LANGUAGE

One of the basic tasks of the playwright is providing words for actors to speak. While a play might exist without words, most plays are based upon the spoken word. Moreover, it is in the concept "spoken" that dramatic language finds its most significant test. Plays are sometimes monologues, more often dialogues; the language of a play is meant to be said aloud or sung by actors and heard by an audience. Thus we ask the playwright to give us, first of all, speakable language and then, if possible, "beautiful language."

A line is more easily spoken when it is as close as possible to the rhythms of normal speech. Hence most English verse drama is in iambic meter because the iamb is the verse foot closest in rhythm to spoken English. However, dialogue need not sound as if it could have been heard on any street corner. Dramatic language is an element in a work of art; it is not reality, nor should it be. On the other hand, some language simply cannot be spoken intelligently by an actor nor understood by an audience. In this regard the director should be wary of language that is consciously obscure; filled with adjectives and modifiers; built of long, periodic sentences; or composed of highly involved and convoluted syntax. As the director gains experience in reading plays, he normally becomes more adept at judging the oral and aural qualities of dialogue. He can be greatly helped in this problem by a background in acting and oral interpretation. Many directors read a play aloud to themselves or arrange to have parts of the play read by skilled readers.

Language should not only be speakable; it must be listened to and understood by an audience. To understand a speech or a set of dialogue, the audience must be able to remember its premises as well as follow its conclusion. In doing this the audience depends heavily on its ears. The longer and more involved a speech, the harder it is for the listener to remember its points or follow its progress. While long speeches are not a dramaturgic weakness per se, directors tend to be cautious of a play that seems "too talky."

In order for an audience to listen intelligently, they must want to listen. Audiences want to listen to language when it is interesting, which implies that dramatic dialogue should incorporate the principles of good rhetoric. That is, the language should be unique enough not to seem trite, but must at the same time appeal to the audience through reference to the familiar. Through the use of image and diction, language should arouse curiosity but not cause confusion.

Language should also be appropriate to the speaker as well as to the audience. *Hamlet* is a verse play, but not all the characters in the play speak verse of the same quality. Some, such as the Gravediggers, speak no verse at all. The lyric poet may never vary his style. The dramatic poet should always endeavor to have his lords speak as lords and his clowns as clowns. The question of beauty in dramatic language is really one of consistency with the quality of the play. Pretty or elegant language would seem at odds with the state of frenzy desired by Kaiser in *From Morn to Midnight*, while the telegraphic speech of Kaiser's work, which has its own intense beauty, would hardly do for elegant manners of Molière's people.

When he makes his initial assessment of language in a play script, the director usually asks if the language is speakable, clear, sufficiently concise, rhetorically sound, and appropriate to the speakers and the quality of the play.

INITIAL EVALUATION OF DRAMATIC AGENTS

Plays contain events and events demand agents, entities who by their presence or activity initiate or maintain events. Since dramas are designed for human consumption, the most common dramatic agents are human beings, or, more precisely, dramatic imitations of human beings usually called characters. Dramatic agents are not limited to characters, however, for the skeleton in the tree in *From Morn to Midnight* is as important a dramatic agent as are the judges at the bicycle races.

Some dramatic agents are not human but possess human characteristics, such as the Lion in Shaw's *Androcles and the Lion*. Shaw's Lion is an affectionate beast who likes to dance and practices the golden rule. However, unless an agent is human or bears human implications, audiences tend to ignore it. Hence the first test of dramatic agency is its humanness or its implication in the human experience.

Other evaluations of agents are more complex. An agent human enough to be classified as a character must also be simple enough not to present the bewildering complexity of an actual person. A play is a work of art that lasts but a brief while, and characters as elements in that art must be adjusted to its brevity. Hence characters must be relatively concise.

A dramatic character is composed of two aspects: his manners and his motives. His manners constitute those things he must do; his motives constitute those things he desires to do. For instance, as a king Oedipus must condemn and search out the murderer of his father; as that same murderer, he could hardly have the motive to expose himself. Hamlet's manners as Prince of Denmark demand that he avenge his father; his motives tend to make him shy away from the bloody deed. At times a character's manners and motives are at variance; at times they are in harmony. For instance, Argan in *The Imaginary Invalid* is in complete harmony when his manners as a hypochondriac give him the motive for wishing to marry his daughter to a physician.

In both manners and motive patterns we expect a character to perform his particular agency with economy. Polonius has a function in *Hamlet;* we expect him to fulfill that function and no more. No matter how fascinating we may find him, it would be a weakness of dramatic structure if Shakespeare stopped the progression of the play in order further to investigate the reasons that Polonius became chief advisor to the King. Thus economy of function is sometimes more significant than complexity of manners or motives. For example, Argan, the Cashier, and Oedipus are all less complex than Hamlet and St. Pé; yet all five are superb dramatic agents because each satisfies the demands of his drama with economy.

Just as dramatic agents should be more economical than real, they should also be more consistent than the average human. That is, it is less important for a character to seem as if he were a living man than it is for him to behave in a manner consistent with the audience's expectations. To do otherwise confuses an audience and interrupts communication. Consistency commences in manners patterns and extends into motives. Polonius, for instance, is less a flesh-and-blood person than he is the epitome of a conservative court advisor. The advice he gives Laertes is just what we expect from a man of his manners; indeed, imagine how bewildered an audience would be if Polonius should have finished his famous speech to Laertes by remarking, "Above all, endeavor to have a good time; soon you'll be as old and tired as I." Yet many a sound, right-thinking father has said as much.

Later in the same scene, the ultraconservative manners pattern of Polonius gives rise to a motive: he desires Ophelia never to encourage Hamlet again, because Hamlet is a prince and she is of lesser rank. A marriage between the two, even the prospect of marriage, is quite too liberal a thought. In this regard it is interesting to note that Laertes also warns Ophelia away from Hamlet. However, true to the manners of a young gallant, Laertes argues that Ophelia may stumble into an illicit love affair.

To take an example from another play, the audience watching the end of *Waltz of the Toreadors* might be saddened but not surprised that Anouilh concludes his play by having General St. Pé begin to seduce the new maid. In this case, although St. Pé is strongly motivated not to repeat his old patterns, his fixed manners are too strong, too consistent. Such consistency in this case is both sad and gratifying to an audience. Hence Anouilh describes his play as bittersweet. Motives as well as manners should have their consistency, and between the consistency of motives and that of manners there is an interplay and tension that aids in the creation of the story and action of a play. Thus Willy Loman's motive is to see Biff as a successful man. His concept of success is derived from the manners of a salesman—success to Willy is public financial success. Moreover, Willy's manners are heightened by his age, fatigue, and personal failure as a public success. When Biff fails to secure a job, Willy's manners and his motives bend on securing money at all costs, even if this means committing suicide.

In order for us to understand a character's economy and consistency, the agent must be clearly defined and differentiated from other agents. Such definition usually begins with manners patterns and follows with a revelation of motives as they occur. As pointedly and as soon as possible, the playwright should make clear the probable patterns, in both manners and motives, of each of his agents, and he should also make evident the qualities that distinguish one agency from another. This does not mean that all agents should be individualized, only that there should be enough distinction to avoid confusion. The chorus in *Oedipus* is a group functioning as a single agency. Without individualizing each member of the chorus, Sophocles has managed to distinguish the chorus, in both manners and motives, from Oedipus, Creon, or Jocasta.

The major burden of outlining various agents is the function of another element of dramaturgy: exposition, which will be discussed next. Before turning to exposition, however, we might pause to observe the relationship between character and language. The playwright attempts to make a dramatic character human, functional, consistent, and clearly outlined. Toward each of these ends language contributes heavily. First, simply by talking a character becomes more human. Second, by what he says about himself and others, a character aids in exposition, story, action, and viewpoint. Third, a character contributes to his own consistency and clarity of outline by his speech. The long-winded rhetoric of Polonius brands him a "foolish, prating knave" long before Hamlet identifies him as such. Again, St. Pé's speech is peppered with campfire metaphors, while the language of his daughters is shrill and girlish.

INITIAL EVALUATION OF EXPOSITION

The function of dramatic exposition is to provide sufficient information throughout the temporal sequence of the play so that the audience may follow the story, identify the agents, understand the point of view, and respond to the action. An audience must follow a play as it progresses; there is no going back for rereading. Exposition permits the audience to follow the play. This does not mean that *all* information is provided at once about all elements of the dramatic situation (for that would remove opportunities for suspense and surprise), but it does mean that necessary information is presented in time to prevent complete audience bewilderment. Through his exposition the dramatist outlines the manners and exposes the motives of dramatic agents; sets the situation of the story in time, place, and circumstance; encourages our expectation and knowledge of a chain of events; and lays bare the underlying action of such events. In order to accomplish exposition, the playwright has recourse to some or all of the elements of dramaturgy. Through language the playwright tells us information; through the manners and motives of characters we obtain further knowledge; through the way characters act or through the pattern in which events grow one out of the other we are further instructed. Finally, through the point of view accepted by the playwright we receive additional facts.

No matter what his method, the good playwright never bores us with his exposition. There is no right or wrong expository method. Numerous techniques are employed. Ibsen, for example, structures many of his plays around withholding an important bit of exposition from an audience, thereby constantly arousing their interest in exposition. Other playwrights, notably those in eighteenth-century England, tell almost the whole process of the play in an initial scene between two servants. In *Oedipus*, Sophocles has a priest give Oedipus information about the plague—information, by the way, which Oedipus undoubtably already knows, but of which the audience is ignorant. In a different manner, Miller gradually informs us of the problem in *Death of a Salesman* through exposition presented as a series of flashbacks. In *Hamlet* the exciting figure of the Ghost gives us much of the basic information of the play. What is not said directly by the Ghost is passed on to us through the tense conversation of the soldiers as they wait for or recover from the visits of the apparition.

Most of the basic expository information of a play takes place in the opening scenes, but exposition is a continuing process, and one test of a playwright's skill is how aptly he contrives to provide necessary exposition without causing the story undue delay. Thus exposition should be both interesting and concise.

Another test of exposition is its clarity. While an audience expects to be confused at times, it usually resents being constantly bewildered. To know the whole story beforehand is often boring, but it is just as boring not to be able to understand it at all. Hence, expository information—whether in terms of character, action, or story—should be clear, or at least unambiguous enough to prevent total confusion. The audience wants to know, and expects to know sooner or later, just why Biff is so bitter toward his father, and the flashback in the hotel room satisfies their desires and expectations clearly, concisely, and interestingly.

The hotel room sequence in *Salesman* illustrates the final task of exposition—timeliness. Expository information given too late frustrates the audience's desires and expectations; information presented too early takes the edge off their curiosity. How expertly Miller lets us see the deep rift between Biff and Willy, and how adroitly he hides its real basis until the moment when our desire for information is highest! Yet if Miller had waited much longer, our anticipation for further information might have dwindled into exasperation.

Exposition is that element which allows the audience to understand the other elements of dramaturgy. In order to obtain exposition, the playwright uses one or more of the other dramaturgic elements, and he attempts to make his exposition interesting, concise, clear, and timely.

INITIAL EVALUATION OF POINT OF VIEW

Closely tied to the problems of exposition is the issue of point of view as a dramaturgic element. The term *point of view* has various meanings in general parlance, but in a literary context point of view may be taken to mean the perspective from which the author tells his story. Several such perspectives are open to a playwright. He may first of all elect to be omniscient, or to act as a sort of literary god who sees the thoughts and deeds of all characters. Such is the viewpoint taken by Shakespeare in *Hamlet*. Not only do we see the external activities of the various characters, but we observe their inner thoughts as well. Shakespeare's technique for presenting interior thought is a language device —the interior monologue or soliloquy. Nowhere is Shakespeare's use of the omniscient point of view more dramatically effective than in the scene in the chapel when the interior thoughts of both Hamlet and the King are presented. By employing omniscience Shakespeare is able to demonstrate that Hamlet does not know what the King is thinking. Believing that the King is praying, Hamlet does not kill him.

Other playwrights elect to use a third-person objective viewpoint. A hallmark of Realistic drama, the third-person objective point of view endeavors to present only what can be seen or heard externally; interior states must be implied through exterior ones. In other words, the playwright pretends to act merely as a recording device. The Realistic plays of Ibsen are excellent examples of third-person objective point of view. Many directors may understand Sophocles' *Oedipus* as being presented in this manner; others might feel that the play is more subjectively projected.

A third form of point of view is the subjective viewpoint. There are two types: one form in which the playwright directly projects the play from his own personal subjective vision, and one form in which the subjective vision of another, generally a character within the action of the play, is used as a perspective on the story. Both of these forms of subjective viewpoint might be called first-person subjective. In fiction the technique, in its most extreme form, is often known as "stream of consciousness." Perhaps the most outstanding example of a play in which the author directly tells the story through his own subjective viewpoint is Strindberg's *The Dream Play*. Kaiser's *From Morn to Midnight* is a good example of a play told through the subjective vision of a character within the story, in this case the viewpoint of the Cashier. In fact, a distinguishing characteristic of most plays of the Expressionist style is the use of first-person subjective viewpoint, just as third-person objective is a feature of Realism.

Many playwrights use a mixture of points of view. One such mixture is found in *Death of a Salesman*, where Miller shifts constantly from the third-person objective world of Willy's family to the first-person subjective of Willy's interior life. In a more subtle manner, Anouilh makes use of the same mixture in *Waltz*. For the most part the play is presented objectively, but more and more frequently, as the play progresses, we move into the interior world of General St. Pé. While Miller uses the flashback to present Willy's interior life, Anouilh uses the time-honored devices of the aside and the soliloquy. In fact, Anouilh's use of asides and soliloquies might lead one to assume that he is actually employing an omniscient viewpoint, until one considers that only General St. Pé uses asides and soliloquies.

Just as in his use of exposition, the playwright obtains and maintains his point of view through the employment of other elements of dramaturgy. For example, the "telegraphic" language in *From Morn to Midnight* enhances the subjective quality of the play, while the very story, by constantly featuring the Cashier in every weird episode, forces the audience to understand the play through the Cashier's eyes. Exposition is both an end and a means of presenting the subjective viewpoint in *Salesman*, for it is in Willy's subjective states that the most interesting and vital expository information is presented, and the exposition is most interesting at those times because of the shift in viewpoint.

Character patterns, particularly manners patterns, aided Shakespeare greatly in achieving an acceptable omniscient viewpoint. All of his great lords are given to talking aloud in corners, perhaps because we expect great people, particularly great people in plays, to think aloud—certainly we are all aware that the great have little privacy, even for purposes of thinking.

The function of point of view is to provide the playwright with an excuse for telling a story and a means for presenting that story to an audience. One type of viewpoint is no better than another; the adroit use, not the type selected, is what makes a play strong or weak. Good use of point of view means that it allows the other dramaturgic elements to be effectively employed. For example, since Shakespeare was interested in the clash between Hamlet and his uncle, his use of omniscience allowed him to present not only the overt manners and motives of the two but the interior motives as well. On the other hand Anouilh concentrates entirely upon St. Pé's viewpoint, since the play concerns the struggle within that character, the struggle between his manners and his motives.

In order to be effective, point of view should be clear. While the audience might expect to grope about a bit especially at first, in a play that uses a subjective viewpoint they should be able to realize as quickly as possible what viewpoint is being employed. Thus by the third scene in *From Morn to Midnight* the Cashier is delivering a long interior monologue on an empty stage. By the same token, in establishing his omniscient point of view, Shakespeare has Hamlet delivering a soliloquy by the end of the second scene.

In addition to clarity, point of view should be consistent. Consistency does not mean only one type of viewpoint, though a single viewpoint will achieve consistency. It does mean, however, that shifts in viewpoint should be clearly marked and contain an interior consistency. When Willy engages in his reverie, he remembers Biff, Happy, and Linda as much younger. The characters in the reverie, particularly the boys, must therefore change in manners and motives. Moreover, language, exposition, and action should all remain consistent to the prevailing viewpoint. An interesting Japanese motion picture, *Roshomon*, provides a good study in consistency of viewpoint. The same story, an assault upon a woman traveling through wooded country, is told from the several subjective viewpoints of the participants. Each time the story is retold, the characters, the incidents, the action, the exposition, even the language alter to suit the prevailing point of view.

Thus each playwright in presenting his drama to an audience must assume some type of point of view—omniscient, objective, subjective, or mixtures thereof. The purpose of viewpoint is to allow the playwright effective use of the other elements of dramaturgy. In order to achieve this purpose, a viewpoint should be clear and consistent.

INITIAL EVALUATION OF THE STORY

The story of a play involves the location of incidents and their progression in time. For purposes of evaluation and analysis, story may be separated from both action and character. The story, of course, needs agents to locate an incident and to progress through a series of incidents, and quite naturally such progression contributes greatly to the action of a play. However, the same story can be used to incorporate many different characters and actions. Without belaboring the point, consider how often the classic Hollywood Western has used the story of a lynching to portray many different characters involved in widely varied actions.

Story is composed of time, place, and incidents. In order to achieve each of these, the playwright must use the other elements of dramaturgy. In establishing initial time and place, exposition is heavily depended upon, but language (i.e., word choice and style), character, point of view, and action are also used. After the initial incident is established, most playwrights depend more heavily on the other elements of dramaturgy and less on exposition. For instance, an expository speech by the priest and a message from Apollo set the initial time, place, and incident in *Oedipus*. Thereafter, the King's own manners and motives cause one event to progress into another quite rapidly. On the other hand, in a more leisurely style, Shakespeare takes more than two acts before moving from the initial situation, and it is only by the introduction of a new dramatic agent—the strolling players—that a progression of events takes place.

Time and place pose two types of evaluation problems—literary and theatrical. In terms of dramatic literature alone, time and place should be interesting, appropriate to the play's overall purposes, economically used, and clearly established for the needs of both audience and play. For example, *Waltz of the Toreadors*, which takes place at about the turn of the century in the study of General St. Pé and in his wife's bedroom, meets all the literary requirements. The time is far enough removed from our own to be romantically intriguing; the time is appropriate because the play deals with a continuing human problem; the place is economical in that only two locales are called for; and the time is quite clearly established through language, exposition, character, story, action, and viewpoint. A very good but different example is found in *From Morn to Midnight*. Set in a series of locales in the present century, *From Morn to Midnight* achieves part of its interest through rapid change of place, which though less economically employed is nevertheless appropriate to the play. Appropriate, too, is Kaiser's use of modern times, since the play deals with a modern problem.

As with spoken language, time and place immediately affect the physical theatre, so that these two, although used excellently in terms of literature, might make for a poor theatrical piece. Whatever the locale of a play, be it the open space suggested in *Oedipus* or the multiple locales called for in Kaiser's play, that place must be translated into actual theatrical space. When evaluating a play the director should keep in mind his own theatre and its ability to create, suggest, and support the locale called for by the dramatist. Such ability on the part of the theatre will include both the physical space and the costumes. Much in this regard of course depends on the imagination of the director, scene designer, and costumer.

Time in drama is quite complicated. In terms of the story, there is the metaphorical time of the play; in terms of the theatrical production there is also actual playing time. Metaphorical time may be progressive chronology, as in *Hamlet,* regressive chronology, or mixed chronology. The latter form is quite common in such modern plays as *Death of a Salesman.* Whatever the temporal sequence, good use of time holds the audience's interest, makes its progression clear, and does not stretch the credulity of the spectators. The latter issue is a difficult one to resolve. Kaiser, in *From Morn to Midnight,* is able to suggest a long day of feverish activity in approximately two hours; Shakespeare suggests months in his somewhat longer play. Miller ranges over a man's whole married life. All are successful. Yet other playwrights have been criticized for packing too much into too short a span of time. A sure test of a dramatist's skill is how well his metaphorical time retains credence.

A play translated into the theatre also faces the test of actual playing time. How long an audience will watch a play without becoming unduly restless depends not only on the play but on social customs of the audience. Shakespeare's audience expected over three hours in the theatre; today's audience finds three hours slightly exhausting. Many an excellent play is never produced because its playing time is too long. As a final comment on playing time, many directors have learned through unhappy experience that playing time is related not only to the length of the written script but also to the kind and number of locales. Often a script of seemingly handy size is so weighted down with necessary scene shifts that the playing time is greatly increased.

Just as time and place should be generally interesting, appropriate, and clear, so should be the incidents of a story. An interesting incident should be sufficiently unique without causing confusion, sufficiently familiar without being dull. Willy Loman's being fired is a familiar enough event, but Miller's use of the tape recorder to add to Willy's distress makes the scene both novel and touching.

An appropriate incident should state the story, contain within itself the possibilities for a new incident, and suit the general purposes of the play. Consider in this regard the scene between Hamlet and his mother. In this incident, Hamlet reveals his position and attitude to his mother, sees again his father's ghost, and kills Polonius. The killing of Polonius moves the story forward, while the confrontation between mother and son provides Shakespeare with an opportunity to comment on the complex relationship between Hamlet and Gertrude.

A clear incident is one in which the audience can follow, as much as is necessary at the moment, all the operative elements of dramaturgy. For instance, in the scene mentioned above, Shakespeare makes it clear to the audience, both in earlier scenes and just before Hamlet enters, that Polonius is to be completely hidden so that he does not detract from the scene between the mother and the son. Therefore, though the audience is clearly aware of Polonius, they also are allowed to give their attention to Hamlet and Gertrude.

Dramatic incidents do not, however, exist in isolation; they are parts of a chain. Thus not only should each specific incident be clear, but a good play also contains reasonable clarity of story line. This does not mean that the audience always knows what *will* happen, only that they can easily recall what *has* happened and can at least keep abreast of what *is* happening. Moreover, the story line of a play should not only be clear but also consistent. Events should grow out of other events. Consistency does not require a strict temporal progress nor absolutely logical probability; it does imply, however, that there is some aesthetic relationship between incidents. For instance, it is neither temporally necessary nor strictly logical that Willy should go into a restaurant washroom and remember the day his son surprised him with another woman. But, given Willy's tendency toward reverie, given Miller's use of shifting viewpoints, and given the impact of Biff's stealing a fountain pen and his own loss of a job, it is probable that Willy would withdraw into his own world—in short, the flashback has artistic consistency with what went before in the play.

Finally, the chain of story events should be artistically economical. That is, the number of events is not as important as their selection and arrangement. Out of the countless number of events available, the good playwright gives the impression that the ones he has chosen tell the story most economically, and he gives the further impression that no other arrangement would do as well. Directors who have had experience in cutting plays will usually agree that the better written a play is, the harder it is to cut and rearrange incidents.

To sum up, the story of a play, while it uses all elements of dramaturgy for its ends, is a separate element. It consists of time, place, and events. Time and place are judged both as literary and as purely theatrical problems. Time, place, and events should be interestingly, clearly, economically, and consistently selected and presented.

INITIAL EVALUATION OF ACTION

The final element of dramaturgy is action. As with all the other elements of drama, action does not stand alone but is dependent upon contributions from story, character, language, viewpoint, and exposition. In its turn action contributes conflict, crisis, and resolution. Action is change, and change is achieved in drama when time, place, incidents, or characters are caught up in a *conflict* which produces a crisis. A *crisis* is a condition in which conflicting forces are so arranged that a continuance of the status quo is no longer possible, and consequently a change takes place. The resulting change is the *resolution* of the crisis. Most resolutions are not permanent but actually give birth to new conflicts which in turn engender new crises. And so the action of a play progresses: situation, conflict, crisis, resolution, conflict, crisis, resolution—until a final resolution is reached, or until the playwright simply breaks off the action.

The number of fully completed action cycles in a play and the kind and quality of their resolution varies so widely from play to play that a quantitative evaluation of action is of little importance. What is vitally important to a good play script is that action does exist. In fact, it may be argued that the single major evaluative test of any play script is the presence of its action. Lest this sound like "double-speak," it might be clarified by saying that when a director reads a play he should always seek to discover if the playwright has, whenever possible, united every element of his play to one or more actions. The conflict-crisis-resolution cycle is what divides the dramatic from the expository; the dialogue story from the drama. By considering each element of action separately, we can gain some insight into how a dramatist may imbue his whole work with action.

The initiating aspect of action is conflict. The concept of conflict has its subtle as well as obvious manifestations. While most plays contain such marked and obvious conflicts as that between Hamlet and the King, skilled dramatists use conflict as a vitalizing force in every element of dramaturgy. Sometimes such conflict is merely the use of contrast in sentence structure. Take for instance Hamlet's famous line: "To be or not to be, that is the question." The first half of the line establishes a conflict between two equal ideas—life and death. A crisis takes place in the pause or cesura indicated by the comma. A resolution follows—"that is the question." The resolution, however, is not final; it merely relieves the crisis for the moment.

Conflict occurs in, or may be engendered by, character, story, and viewpoint, as well as language. Conflict may even take place in exposition. For example, the contrasting stories of the death of Laius are a major source of conflict in *Oedipus*. Character conflict may not necessarily be between agent and agent. As observed earlier, a major conflict in *Hamlet* is the contrast between his manners as a young prince and his motives not to kill. *Waltz of the Toreadors* has also been cited as a play in which the major conflict springs from a split between the manners and the motives of the central character. Intercharacter conflicts may be rather subtle. For example, there is a conflict between Hamlet and Young Fortinbras; the first cautious and crafty, the second militant and direct. This conflict, of which Hamlet is only too well aware and which prompts one of his famous soliloquies, is brought to resolution when Young Fortinbras reappears in the final scene of the play and receives the kingdom from the dying Prince.

Conflict is also present in point of view. Perhaps the major feature of

Miller's *Death of a Salesman* is the conflict between the objective viewpoint of the world around him and the subjective viewpoint of Willy Loman. In another technique, we have already noted how effectively Shakespeare uses the omniscient point of view in the chapel scene in *Hamlet*. Through showing the inner thoughts of each man, Shakespeare demonstrates the conflict between what the King actually thinks and what Hamlet believes he is thinking. As a final example of conflict through point of view, note the contrast between the subjective visions of the Cashier in *From Morn to Midnight* and the implied objective view of his crime by society in general. This conflict is resolved when the Cashier confesses his crime and rejoins the objective world, only to be forced into suicide.

Conflict, of course, is always found in the time, place, and incidents of the story. Locale produces strong conflict in *Hamlet*. Had the Prince faced his uncle anywhere but in the latter's own castle, Hamlet might have effected his revenge immediately. Had the message from Apollo come at any other time than during a period of national disaster, Oedipus may not have been so quick to issue his unhappy dictum. Had Biff not come home at the very time Willy was fired, the father may not have placed so much importance on the necessity for some form of instant success for his son.

In terms of incident, had Oedipus questioned the shepherd before talking to Creon, Tiresias, or Jocasta, most of the conflict of the play would not have developed. Had Hamlet not killed Polonius, the King would not have gained an ally in Laertes, and Hamlet might not have had to face the young noble in so deadly a duel.

A final source of conflict is action itself. Conflict, crises, and resolution make for new conflicts, crises, and resolutions. General St. Pé is faced with several conflicts simultaneously (an excellent thing for the health of the play). He has his own internal conflict, the conflict with his wife, and the conflict between his confused motives and manners and the desire on Ghislaine's part for him to divorce his wife and marry her. The first crisis in these multiple conflicts is his wife's attempt at suicide. When St. Pé rushes to his wife's aid, Ghislaine realizes that he will never marry her. A new conflict is now created in her character. Should she continue under the present circumstances, or should she commit suicide? She elects suicide. Her vain attempt at self-destruction introduces her to the young secretary, and new conflicts result.

Conflict leads to crisis—the joining of opposing or contrasting forces. In discussing conflict, we observed crisis occurring in as minute a place as the pause in a line of poetry. Crisis also has its moments of grandeur: our frequently cited praying scene in *Hamlet* is a major moment of crisis. A crisis in viewpoint takes place when Kaiser's Cashier rejects his personal vision and accepts the viewpoint of the crowd in the Salvation Army Hall. A crisis in character is presented when Willy Loman relives the moment when his son caught him with another woman. Small crises build toward larger crises. Some plays, such as *Oedipus*, have a single large crisis; others, such as *From Morn to Midnight*, have a series of coordinate crises. However it is used, crisis is the most exciting part of most actions, and therefore the most exciting part of most plays. A play whose crises seem flat, or a play that cannot seem to achieve a significant number of major and minor crises, should make the prospective director especially wary. On the other hand, overly frequent major crises make for a play "too exciting" to be truly interesting.

Most crises contain within themselves the elements of their own resolution. That is, the opposing forces are either neutralized or discover an outlet. When the opposing forces are neutralized, the action of a play, at least in the direction it has previously taken, is at an end. When the opposing forces find an outlet, there is usually the potential for new action. When Hamlet confronts his mother, he brings her life with the King to a crisis. Were it not for the appearance of the Ghost, and, more significantly, the murder of Polonius, Hamlet may well have neutralized her affections for the King and gained an important ally. Frequently the web of crises becomes so involved that a playwright cannot discover a probable solution. At such times he often has recourse to frankly artistic, as opposed to logical, resolutions. In *Ghosts*, Ibsen simply calls for the final curtain just in the middle of a gripping crisis. Molière frequently resorts to a messenger from the king who arbitrarily sets the conflict in balance. Anouilh in *Waltz of the Toreadors* employs a similar device when he has a priest, an early acquaintance of St. Pé, suddenly show up with some interesting information about St. Pé's amourous adventures, information which not very logically, but certainly very artistically, resolves the play's conflicts.

While an action in progress is clearly tied to the story, and while a completed action is often indistinguishable from the story, it is no more interrelated to the story than to any of the other elements of dramaturgy. Action needs to be evaluated as a separate element. The story of *Oedipus,* for example, could well contain other conflicts, crises, and resolutions than the ones Sophocles invented. The same story could, for instance, be told from the subjective viewpoint of Jocasta. Using an identical story, an interesting but clearly different action pattern could then be developed. This has been done for *Hamlet* with the play *Rosencrantz and Guildenstern Are Dead.*

As observed earlier, the initial evaluation of action is its presence. Without action a nondramatic form of literature results. As with the other dramaturgic tools, action should be interesting, clear, economical, consistent, and appropriate to the purposes of the play. It should also provide a means for allowing the playwright full use of the other aspects of dramaturgy. An interesting action utilizes conflicts that are unique enough in their complications, crises, and resolutions that they arouse curiosity and maintain interest. A clear action is familiar enough in construction to permit understanding. A king who condemns and searches out a murderer of his predecessor is a clear enough action; that that king is married to his own mother and is himself the unwitting murderer whom he seeks certainly adds interest to the action. Economical action uses the most efficient and most effective number of conflicts, crises, and resolutions in both quantity and quality. What is economical will depend upon what is appropriate to the purposes of the play. Willy Loman has a conflict within himself and with his oldest son. This is enough; if he also were in open conflict with his wife, the chances are there would be too much action for Miller's purposes.

Perhaps the surest way to evaluate action in the play script is in terms of consistency. Action should be consistent with language, exposition, viewpoint, character, story, and with itself. The last is highly significant. Without undue elaboration, consider how skillfully Miller uses his flashback technique to focus language, exposition, story, and character on Willy's own special viewpoint and on the action which he alone undergoes. While it is not objectively probable that Willy, in the washroom of a restaurant, should undergo an action that happened in the past, we have already remarked on its artistic consistency. The action actually stems out of a continuing conflict between Biff and

Willy which is brought to a crisis by Willy's loss of his job and Biff's attitude. Though the crisis occurred in the past, it grows directly out of present conflict and thus is entirely consistent.

Before summarizing our discussion of action, we might note that, especially in the theatre in the presence of the living actor, action has both an external and internal dimension. Obviously such activities as fighting, kissing, standing, or sitting are capable of being classified as actions. However, such activities may be merely expository if they do not involve conflict, crisis, or resolution. Part of the evaluation of a play's action involves distinguishing between mere expository activity and genuine action. Activity for its own sake may be interesting, but it is not dramatic, and the possibility is strong that mere activity will quickly become distracting and even boring to an audience.

Less obvious than physical activity is internal action. Every thought or emotion that creates conflict or leads to a crisis or a resolution of a crisis is also part of an action. Such action must be clearly implied or else translated into physical terms. To take an obvious example, the skilled playwright will perhaps translate an interior decision to fall in love into the physical act of a kiss. The ability to imply vividly interior action, or as frequently as possible translate an interior into an external act, is one of the marks of a good playwright. For example, Shakespeare could have had Hamlet's encounter with the Ghost and his decision to revenge his father related to us in a conversation between Horatio and Hamlet. Instead Shakespeare, being the skilled playwright that he is, managed to create an exciting physical confrontation between Hamlet and the Ghost. In short, he "dramatized" the scene.

As opposed to story, action is the series of conflicts, crises, and resolutions contained within the play. A good play must have action, and such action, be it internal or external, should be interesting, clear, consistent, economical, and appropriate to the play.

THE INITIAL EVALUATION OF THE ELEMENTS OF DRAMATURGY: A SUMMARY

The elements of dramaturgy are the tools with which the playwright achieves his compositional and design goals. There are six elements: language, exposition, character, story, point of view, and action. As observed, the elements are not mutually exclusive, and while each has its special evaluatory problems, all may be judged in terms of their interest, economy, clarity, consistency, and appropriateness to the general purposes of the play.

INITIAL EVALUATION OF THE COMPOSITIONAL GOALS OF DRAMATURGY

The compositional goals are what gives a drama the effect of being aesthetically pleasing. There are five goals of dramatic composition: unity, emphasis, proportion, variety, and rhythm. These goals are analogous to the five goals of visual composition: unity, emphasis, balance, variety, and rhythm. As with the elements of dramaturgy, the goals of dramatic composition are not mutually exclusive, and we shall have opportunity to observe the manner in which one goal contributes to and shapes all goals.

UNITY AND DRAMATIC COMPOSITION

Dramatic unity is a concept whose nature has long been disputed by theorists. During the Italian Renaissance, critics were convinced that a play should have the three unities of time, place, and action. These "unities" were interpreted to mean that a play could have no subplot, that it must take place in a single locale, and that its playing time should be identical to its narrative time. Such tight restrictions would be considered invalid today, but they are not completely destructive to all drama, for *The Imaginary Invalid* is an example of an excellent play which holds to the "unities." In any age, to be aesthetically pleasing a play script should give the impression of singleness of purpose. Any or all of the elements of dramaturgy are capable of providing this singleness of purpose or unity. Some plays, such as *Hamlet,* gain unity not only from a strong central character, but also from a singleness of time, place, viewpoint, and verse language. *Death of a Salesman* ignores unity of time and depends heavily on unity of central dramatic agent. *From Morn to Midnight,* as its title implies, has tight temporal unity but little unity of place. Perhaps the most effective unifying device in *From Morn to Midnight* is not the obvious unity of strong central character, but the subtle unity of both dramatic action and point of view. Each incident in the play is quite different in story line, yet all repeat essentially the same action: a crisis of frenzied fear and a resolution in a compulsion to flight. Moreover, throughout the play the subjective viewpoint of the Cashier dominates.

Dramatic unity also has a negative aspect. Any element in the play that does not actively contribute to unity is in some way weakening the oneness of the play. There may be good dramaturgic reasons for introducing material that does not contribute to unity, but the director should be wary of play scripts that seem to sacrifice unity in favor of developing an interesting character or pursuing a bit of lyric verse. It is a rare lyric, however beautiful; a rare character, however interesting; an extraordinary incident, however exciting, that is worth more than the effect of total dramatic unity.

Dramatic unity, then, is the impression of singleness of purpose which flows from a play script. Unity may be achieved through one, two, or all of the elements of dramaturgy. Any aspect of a play that does not contribute to the total unity actually acts as a unity-destroying element. While an aesthetic goal in itself, unity may also be formed and supported by the other aesthetic goals of dramaturgy. In this respect, the goal of emphasis is perhaps the most important.

INITIAL EVALUATION OF EMPHASIS

A play with good emphasis permits the audience to focus its attention on what is important at any moment in the progress of the play. Through emphasis the significant item of exposition, the apt linguistic image, the evolution of a new motive, the nature of a conflict, the appearance of a crisis, the formation of a new incident, and the shifting of point of view are all made apparent and clear to an audience. Although all dramaturgic elements make their special contribution to emphasis, perhaps the most immediately striking is action, particularly action in crisis. A well-constructed crisis grips the audience so completely that an almost automatic emphasis is achieved. Many playwrights take advantage of this situation to present to the audience such otherwise hard to emphasize elements as exposition and hidden character motives. Moments just before and just after tense crises are also used for emphatic purposes. Thus Shakespeare uses the impending appearance of the Ghost to give emphasis to dull but necessary exposition, and he adds further expository information immediately after the appearances of the Ghost.

Language, particularly shifts in a fixed language pattern, is another means of gaining or maintaining emphasis. Unusual manners patterns, unsuspected motives, sudden or surprising shifts in time, place, or incident, interesting uses of point of view, and even the revelation of new expository material are all used by the skillful playwright to secure or perpetuate emphasis.

Emphasis need not be singular. True, when Hamlet delivers his soliloquies, he needs almost exclusive attention. At other times, however, emphasis may be divided. For example, in the second scene in *Hamlet*, even while the King receives primary emphasis, secondary emphasis might be placed on Hamlet. Thus emphasis can be divided, as when two characters share a scene. A more complicated form of emphasis is diversified emphasis, in which one element may receive primary emphasis, another secondary emphasis, a third and fourth tertiary emphasis. Such emphatic distribution is possibly implied in the final scene in *Hamlet*, where the dead and dying are strewn about the stage, each demanding a share of attention, while Hamlet dominates all.

Diversified emphasis involves the third compositional goal—proportion. Before discussing this issue, one might take note of the manner in which emphasis and unity reinforce each other. By providing focus, emphasis prevents the play from seeming to have digressive elements, whereas unity, encouraging singleness of effect, makes emphasis easier to achieve by removing possible diverting influences.

INITIAL EVALUATION OF PROPORTION

Good scripts give a sense of proportion, that is, an impression of thoughtful organization which, while providing for unity and emphasis, gives each element of dramaturgy its just attention. Thus a play with good proportion does not slight language for character, nor character for action, nor action for exposition, story, or point of view. A play with good proportion is one in which its unity is not achieved at the expense of all other goals and in which its emphasis is not so pointed that it obscures all but the emphasized element. Thus in the final scene in *Hamlet,* though the Prince's death takes major emphasis, proportionate secondary emphasis and tertiary emphasis are also given through language, action, incident, and even exposition (Laertes tells Hamlet of the King's part in the poison plot) to the Queen, the King, Laertes, and lastly to Horatio and Fortinbras.

In terms of finer detail, a play with good proportion does not concentrate all its action in the beginning or the middle or the end. If it is comparing viewpoints as in *Death of a Salesman,* it does not overweigh one viewpoint at the expense of another, does not pay undo attention to the motives of a character and too little attention to his manners, build a conflict to more significance than the crisis can bear, nor finish a major crisis with an abbreviated resolution. *Hamlet* has good unity because of strong central character, but it has good proportion in that the character is not allowed to dominate every scene.

Proportion gives direction to emphasis and organization to unity; it is an aesthetic check placed by the playwright on the goals of emphasis and unity. On the positive side, it receives from emphasis the means of distributing through subordination and coordination the elements of dramaturgy, and from unity those elements germane to organization. In acting as a check on the simplifying goals of unity and emphasis, proportion promotes the vitality of the fourth compositional goal—dramatic variety.

INITIAL EVALUATION OF VARIETY

Too much of even the best of things is dull. Consequently variety is a major structural goal of dramatic composition. Any play seeks variety, and most audiences demand diversity. For instance, because *Oedipus* was so short, Sophocles could tell his story without comic relief; but in the longer *Hamlet,* Shakespeare realized the need for humor, however grim. So, too, Molière has us cry a bit with Argan and his family simply to prevent our becoming tired of laughing at them.

Most plays seek their initial variety in uniqueness of story. However, *Waltz of the Toreadors* offers us variety of time, *From Morn to Midnight* enormous variety of place and an unusual treatment of language, and *Oedipus* in its situation presents variety of incident. *Salesman,* with an ordinary enough story and language, contains variety in viewpoint and expository technique; *The Imaginary Invalid* makes use of variety in character, particularly in the outlandish manners patterns of the central character. *Hamlet* exemplifies unusual variety in its striking use of the English language.

Playwrights seek to attain variety not only in dramatic elements but also in dramaturgic composition. Thus the superior play script achieves unity and emphasis by multiple means, and the same script's proportion usually features a wide distribution of all the elements of dramaturgy. In the soundly skilled dramatist, the need for variety stimulates him to seek constantly fresh methods of creating unity, emphasis, and proportion. At the same time, the three latter goals restrain the playwright from seeking out change for its own sake. For variety, as an aesthetic goal, is always variety with a purpose, variety that complements but does not sacrifice unity, emphasis, and proportion. Such variety sustains the final, and perhaps ultimate, compositional goal—dramatic rhythm.

INITIAL EVALUATION OF RHYTHM

When a visual artist speaks of rhythm, such as the rhythm of a line, he usually has in mind the pattern which that line follows. Thus he might say of a painting with many curved lines that it has a curvilinear rhythm. Drama also has patterns, but being a temporal art, dramatic patterns progress; that is, they change, so that rhythm in drama is both pattern and change. Thus we might define dramatic rhythm as patterned change. In this respect dramatic rhythm and musical rhythm are similar. Similarly nature has a patterned change in its progression from spring to summer to fall to winter to spring. But drama differs from both music and nature in that the elements by which it achieves rhythm are peculiar and specialized.

Playwrights achieve dramatic rhythm through the patterned changes in the elements of dramaturgy. Of these elements the most fundamental to rhythm is action. With its implied change from conflict to resolution and with its pattern of conflict (or tension), crisis, and resolution (or relaxation), action gives to dramatic rhythm its most unique quality and *the* quality that draws the theatre-auditory closest to the theatre-kinetic. Of this matter more will be said in a later chapter. In passing, though, it might be interesting to wonder if this special relation between dramatic rhythm and action is not what prompted Aristotle to argue that the end of drama is action.

Because action is so closely united to story, dramatic rhythm also is based upon patterned change in time, place, and incident. And because story requires agents, rhythm also is achieved through the changes characters undergo as they participate in the story and undergo action. Finally, although rhythm relies mainly on action, story, and character, rhythm also draws a base from language, exposition, and viewpoint through their contributions to the other elements of dramaturgy.

In its major manifestations, rhythm can be seen in any worthwhile play. *Oedipus* reveals a pattern of growing conflict in the King's search for the murderer, the crisis of his discovery of that murderer, and the gory resolution of that crisis. Willy Loman, a modern Oedipus in reverse, is caught in a pattern of attempting to avoid a search for the truth, a crisis of recognizing that truth, and a resolution of the crisis in suicide.

Rhythm exists not only in major patterns but in many smaller patterns of change, and not only in action but in story and character. Take, for example, the pattern of change in Laertes from an open and amiable young man, to a bereaved son and brother, to a wily conspirator in a dark plot, to a final resolution in confession and death. Or, as an example of simple rhythm of locale, recall the swift pattern of scene shifts in *From Morn to Midnight,* or the simpler and perhaps more awesome shift of locale from St. Pé's bright study to the sick room of his wife. In that room a crisis of character, action, and locale occurs, a crisis partly resolved by a change back to St. Pé's study.

Rhythm permeates and controls the well-composed drama. Notice the pattern of change in shift of viewpoints as Willy Loman's conflict deepens and his crises become more intense. Observe the quickening of language in *Hamlet* in the tense scene between himself and his mother, or observe how the verse breaks down into the savage cry of "dead for a ducat, dead," as Hamlet kills Polonius, and then how the language returns to calm lyricism as Hamlet realizes what he has done. Dramatic rhythm is a patterned change which follows a cycle of tension, crisis, relaxation; this pattern is closest to the conflict-crisis-resolution cycle of the element of dramaturgic action. In this respect dramatic rhythm is unique. Rhythm is also achieved through all elements of dramaturgic structure, and in creating rhythm by multiple means, the playwright satisfies the need for variety. Rhythm also contributes to proportion by imposing its pattern on action, character, and story. By its variety, by its pattern, and by its potential for change, rhythm further aids the playwright in achieving unity and emphasis.

Strong dramatic rhythm not only aids the playwright in accomplishing his other goals, but his other goals in turn support rhythm—unity, by simplifying the quality of rhythm; emphasis, by calling attention to rhythm; proportion, by organizing the pattern of rhythm; and variety, by adding interest to the quantity and quality of rhythm.

INITIAL EVALUATION OF DRAMATURGIC GOALS OF COMPOSITION

Composing a drama means making the play script aesthetically pleasing. Unity, emphasis, proportion, variety, and rhythm are the goals of composition. To achieve these goals the playwright makes use of the six elements of composition. Evaluation of these goals involves judging how well each of the goals is achieved through the use of the six elements and through use of the remaining goals. In the completed play, an overall impression of the interrelation of all the goals is the effect sought by the playwright.

INITIAL EVALUATION OF DRAMATIC DESIGN

Dramatists write not only to give aesthetic pleasure but also to make a statement about life, particularly about the human experience of life. The manipulation of the elements and goals of drama in order to make such a statement may be called the theme or *design* of a play. In a soundly written play, as each of the elements of dramaturgy are organized to achieve dramatic composition, they are simultaneously structured to produce a design, for design is not an idea superimposed on the script but a theme united with and growing out of the very play itself. In fact, a theme superimposed on the play script actually injures the unity, proportion, and rhythm of the composition; and, while it might add variety by introducing new material, it certainly makes difficult the achievement of satisfactory emphasis.

Therefore in seeking a meaning for a play, most critics will look to its total form as a clue to its ultimate design. Let us take but one example; doubtless others will occur to you. Several times already the use of point of view in *Death of a Salesman* has been discussed. Let us see how this one element works in both composition and design. Two points of view are contrasted—the subjective and the objective—thus providing a base for variety. Willy Loman shares in both viewpoints, thus achieving a sense of unity. In both viewpoints Willy is dominant while Biff is subordinate, hence providing a sense of proportion. When Willy's viewpoint prevails, Biff is usually the object of contemplation, thereby securing one type of emphasis. When the objective view prevails, Willy is usually emphasized above Biff. The movement from one to the other point of view provides the rhythm for the play. Finally, after Willy's death, the viewpoints are resolved in a single objective view. An organic theme or design is present in Miller's use of point of view. Quite simply, one of the major themes of *Salesman* is the tragic disparity between the world as the individual conceives it and the world as it actually is. In fact, Miller has elsewhere said that he sees tragedy resulting from the conflict between the interior world of the individual and the exterior world of society. His composition and design of viewpoint in *Salesman* vividly expresses this attitude.

Not only the elements of dramaturgy but also the goals of composition will reveal the design of the playwright. Unity restricts theme, and the unity of central character in *Oedipus* is a clear example. Emphasis calls attention to theme. Note in this respect how Argan's morbid and foolish interest in medicine is reinforced by the stupidity of the doctor whom he intends to be his son-in-law. Proportion gives value to theme. While Biff's acceptance of life as it is is given attention, Willy's rejection of life as it must be lived receives greater stress. Variety adds interest to design. St. Pé's unfortunate predilection for seducing women and his inability to engage in real love is restated through Ghislaine, Madame St. Pé, the Dressmaker, St. Pé's dislike of his own daughters, and his return to his old habits at the close of the play.

Rhythm sustains design. Not only in the changes that rhythm brings but in the patterns of those changes is design supported and communicated. Willy Loman changes to the extent that he recognizes at least the real conflict between himself and his son; but because of the pattern of recognition, because he is old, broken, mentally tormented, and rejected as a salesman, he cannot permanently accept his new insights. His crisis of recognition merely encourages him to revert to his old habits, to seek resolution in once more being a salesman—this time selling his own life in a vain attempt to obtain insurance money.

INITIAL EVALUATION OF STYLE

As we discussed earlier, the total effect of a play may be called its style. In particular, the use of dramaturgic elements to obtain compositional goals, the use of composition to present design, gives a play its specific and its general style. Another way of looking at the same issue is to say that style is the result of the way in which a playwright solves, with his tools, the problems he creates for himself. If a director feels a play has good style it normally means that the playwright has achieved his compositional and design goals. However, not all good styles make good directing choices. Which styles appeal most to a director depend upon his tastes, but the director who most often makes good play selections has trained his tastes to suit not only his own skills and abilities but also his knowledge of sound dramaturgic structure.

INITIAL EVALUATION OF THE PLAY
SCRIPT: A SUMMARY

A play script is a work of art. To achieve success in that art form, the playwright uses the tools or elements of dramaturgy to obtain the goals of dramatic design and composition. In his initial evaluation of a play script with an eye to its production, the director should investigate as thoroughly as possible the playwright's skill in attaining his ends. He should further examine those ends in terms of his own skills and ability as a director. If his evaluations are positive, and if the conditions stated in Chapter 3 have also been met, the director should feel safe in selecting the play under consideration. With his script selection completed, the director is now ready for a thorough analysis of the play. Before this can be completely accomplished, however, he must reach certain initial decisions in the theatre-visual and theatre-kinetic.

CHAPTER 5

initial decisions in the theatre-visual

The Director and the Theatrical Designers

THE THEATRE-VISUAL

There are six primary areas of visual theatre: the theatre building or the location, the scenery, the lighting, the costumes, the makeup, and the actors. This chapter will be concerned primarily with the first five, which are commonly called the design areas. There may be a separate visual artist for each of the design areas, or one or more design responsibilities may be combined for a single individual. For ease of discussion, a separate personage will be assumed in each case, though the principles involved remain essentially the same when design areas are combined. The most fundamental problem in regard to visual design is directorial responsibility, and the most difficult problem is director-designer communication.

THE ISSUE OF DIRECTIONAL RESPONSIBILITY

Whether the director executes his own designs or whether he seeks the contributions of others, he should remember that, just as in the matter of play selection, the responsibility for failure remains with him. In all things in the theatre, the praise goes to others, while the blame starts and stops with the director. Having once asked for the cooperation of the designer, the director's responsibility is: (1) to secure what he needs from the designer, (2) to give the designer as much artistic freedom as possible, and (3) to respect the artistic integrity of the designer's work as much as he respects the playwright's work. Establishing communication between designers and director will go a long way toward helping the director successfully discharge his responsibility.

DESIGNER-DIRECTOR COMMUNICATION

During the process of play selection and evaluation, the director is dealing with a verbal art. When the director turns to the theatrical designers, he enters the realm of nonverbal or only partially verbal communication. Hence the director's background in the visual arts should be as strong as his training in literature. Only with such a background can the director hope for effective communication between himself and the contributing visual artists. Many of the concepts and terms necessary to technical communication in the visual arts are detailed in Chapter 7. At the moment we might simply observe that not too much dependence can be placed on words. In the end, the director and the designers must communicate directly in visual images.

Until such images are created, however, preliminary discussions will be mainly through language. How much discussion is needed will depend on how long the director and the designers have worked together and how successfully they have communicated in the past. With relatively new designers, and even with many old colleagues, the director must fabricate a communicative structure as soon as possible. While such a structure is tenuous at best, if all concerned have a strong background in theatre as well as in their respective arts, matters are far from hopeless. The best basis for establishing initial communication is in terms of simple technical problems. From there discussion can proceed to more abstract matters.

TECHNICAL PROBLEMS IN THEATRICAL DESIGN

The first technical matter in theatrical design is deciding upon a theatre architecture. We have touched upon this problem in terms of play selection; it now recurs in regard to play production. Some theatres have only one form, and the matter is thus settled. Other theatres have more than one producing space, or the available producing area can be converted into several forms. In consultation with the designers, the director might, if he has not already done so, select a theatrical form—proscenium, arena, thrust. This selection, of course, is not mere whimsy, although that may play a part at times. Some plays work better in one form, some in another. For the better part of the twentieth century the proscenium was considered the ideal form. In both dramaturgy and production, styles have recently been changing, and many directors produce as often in the arena and the thrust as in the proscenium. Moreover, the proscenium, in its strictest "fourth wall" form, is best suited for plays of the Realistic school. Most dramatic literature has been and is continuing to be written with non-fourth-wall theatres in mind. Today, both live theatre and movies and television productions may elect to go on "location."

For instance, *Oedipus Rex* was originally intended for a large outdoor arena, *Imaginary Invalid* for an apron-plus-proscenium stage, and *Hamlet* for a large thrust platform. *Waltz of the Toreadors*, written in the Molière tradition, might work well on an apron stage, and certainly *Death of a Salesman* strains under the restrictions of the traditional fourth wall.

Nevertheless any play can be adapted to almost any type of staging with the proper imagination. Consequently, initial design discussion

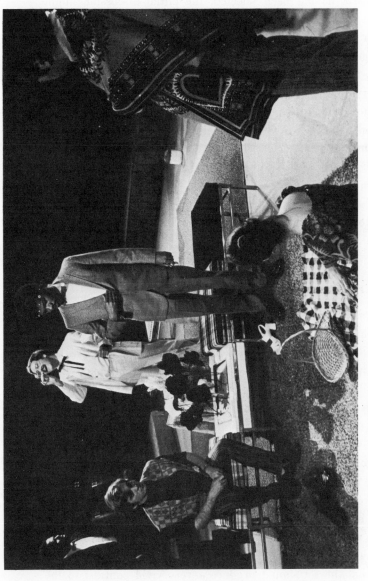

Get Together by Sybil Kein. Department of Drama and Communications, Louisiana State University, New Orleans. Written under the direction of Beverley Hamer Peery

Director and Designer: August W. Staub   Costumers: Kay deMetz and Barbara Coleman

This is a photograph of an arena production. Note that actors are not arranged to clear sightlines for a single point of view. Note also the need for miminal vertical scenery and for such items as backless chairs and couches.

will be concerned with choice of theatre architecture, or adaptation of the play script to the architecture on hand.

A theatre form having been selected, the initial discussion might fruitfully take up preliminary technical problems. For instance, the scene designer might want to know the approximate number of necessary set changes or the number of required entrances. The costumer might want to know if the costume changes called for in the script are really necessary. Matters of finances, work time, technical staff, theatrical organization, construction material on hand, and channels of communication, if not already fixed, might be discussed in an initial conference. Most directors feel it is important that they are aware of the technical facilities and material of their theatre before they make specific design requests. While they respect the fact that particular technical decisions are usually the prerogative of the individual designers, directors usually wish to avoid making requests that cannot be realized.

AESTHETIC PROBLEMS IN THEATRICAL DESIGN

Initial technical problems out of the way, the director-designer conferences turn to aesthetic matters. Since the designers have also read the play, they will have their own opinions of structure and style. The director must now attempt to communicate what the play means to him, and how he will generally accomplish that meaning. In other words, he will attempt to coordinate his own visions and desires with those of the designers. To do this, the director might place the play in terms of its general style—i.e., Elizabethan, German Expressionism, Molièresque —and then explain how the play is individually distinct from the general style. Words may not be sufficient. He may have recourse to pictures, comparisons to other productions, comparisons to music, or even to some of his general intentions in the kinetic theatre. He may refer to single visual images as metaphorical suggestions. For example, he may say he feels the costumes should be all in warm yellows and oranges and that the set should produce a very vivid contrast to the costumes.

In his initial aesthetic discussion the director should be as specific as possible without dictating precise solutions. But if the director wishes to do *Hamlet* in modern dress, then he should say so. If he wishes no specific changes of locale for *From Morn to Midnight*, desiring instead to suggest changes through props and light, then he should also make this need clear. When the initial discussion period is completed, the designers are ready for preliminary visual solutions. The work of the scene and lighting designers can begin immediately. Much of the work of the costumer must wait until the actors are cast.

THE DIRECTOR AND THE SCENE DESIGNER

The director's next important contact with the scene designer comes with the presentation of a preliminary sketch. Depending upon the theatre, this sketch will take the form of a rendering or a pencil drawing and a preliminary floor plan. The rendering states the general outline of the set in visual composition and style. If the director is satisfied with its general quality, he may ask for a model and a floor plan, or simply a floor plan. If he is dissatisfied, he at least has something concrete and visual about which he can talk. The matter of requesting major alterations in a preliminary design may require all the director's powers of persuasion and sense of tact. On the other hand, the director may be so pleasantly surprised with the design that he might ask for even more development in the direction indicated, even though that direction was not the one originally anticipated. No matter what the case, the director should be prepared to be flexible in terms of the setting. He cannot be sure what to expect until he sees the preliminary design.

With the preliminary design in hand, the director and the scene designer are able to talk concretely for the first time about the five issues of theatrical scene design: (1) the general vertical and horizontal treatment of space, (2) the lighting of space, (3) the number and location of entrances, (4) the kind and number of shifts of locale, and (5) the quantity and quality of furniture and properties. As with everything else in theatrical art, these issues are not mutually exclusive, for one leads into another; and the problems of one issue may well be the solutions of another.

The first issue, that of general vertical and horizontal treatment of space, means in technical terms the architectural, painted, or draped forms and masses the designer has devised to rise up from the stage floor and the treatment the designer has given to the stage floor in the way of platforming, steps, or raking. In aesthetic terms, the general treatment of space means the designer's use of line, form, mass, color, texture, and space to make a comment on the play and create an environment for actors. Technically the director will want to assess the preliminary design in regard to sight lines, practicality of horizontal and vertical units, and traffic patterns established by such units. The matter of sight lines involves principally the question of whether most of the audience will be able to see most of the setting and the actors on that setting. The issue of practicality of units means that the director should ascertain which units shown in the design can be touched, moved, walked on, or handled in any way by the actors. Sometimes this question is overlooked, and the director finds to his dismay that what seemed to be a perfectly usable platform materializes in the final set as merely a profile piece. Reading the preliminary floor plan along with the rendering will sometimes provide most of the answers about practicality. In reading the floor plan the director should note the height involved in each change of level and the angle or pitch of rake in each ramp. Too sharp a pitch will make a ramp impossible to walk on and therefore impractical; similarly, rises in level of over six inches or surface treads under ten inches wide make climbing up and down rather awkward for actors.

Aesthetically the designer's horizontal and vertical treatment of space should satisfy the director in terms of spatial comment on the play script. With some plays, such treatment must be obviously narrative; that is, a particular and specialized statement of time and place must be made by the horizontal and vertical forms. Other plays may use more abstract or suggestive statements. Much depends on the director's final aims; one director might want the façade of a Greek temple in his production of *Oedipus*, while another might merely wish an interesting arrangement of platforms.

Aside from narrative needs, the setting must provide a suitable environment for the actors. What constitutes a suitable environment varies from play to play, but a basic issue is whether the set seems to overpower the actors. In every play that is not created strictly as a scenic spectacular, the burden of communication falls on the actors. A setting which through horizontal or vertical treatment competes for audience attention with the actors is a setting that creates artistic disunity in the final production.

Another basic aesthetic issue is whether the director wishes the actors to make the sole vertical statement or whether he wants the set to cooperate in vertical statements. If the former condition is desired, then the setting should concentrate on horizontal treatment only, while the vertical treatment should be as negative as possible. A final matter to consider is whether the director intends the actors to be in the set or in front of the set. A set which is background only tends to be more painterly; one which is environmental is usually more architectural.

The second issue of theatrical space design—lighting—may involve a lighting specialist as well as a scene designer. But the two designers must operate as a coordinated unit. Lighting will materially affect the vertical treatment of a set in line, form, mass, color, and space. By control of specific lighting areas, the horizontal quality of the set can also be shaped or reshaped. Before accepting the preliminary design, the director, the scene designer, and the lighting designer should agree about the overall type and quality of lighting.

The third issue of scene design, the number and location of entrances, is intimately tied to the horizontal and vertical elements of setting. First, the director and designer must decide if entrances should be marked vertically; that is, should there be doors or arches? If so, should the doors or arches contain practical units? The matter of masking is also involved. Where do the actors go after an exit or before an entrance? Will the masking be done architecturally or will changes in light be used to accomplish masking? Not only the type of entrance but the exact number of entrances may be very important. Sometimes the play script demands a specialized entrance. For example, *Waltz of the Toreadors* calls for four entrances: one to the wife's bedroom, one to the outside, one to an anteroom, and finally a window large enough to jump out of. The director may wish to have all four of these entrances, or he and the designer may combine one or more. For instance, a large upstage arch with French windows in the middle might be used for three of the four entrances. The French windows could lead to the outside; a hall stage left would be the anteroom, and a hall stage right the entrance to the bedroom. Multiple entrances give the director greater freedom in traffic patterns but might make for a rather motley-looking set. Fewer entrances place a greater burden on the director's inventiveness but may simplify his traffic problems.

Along with the number of entrances is the problem of location of entrance. In a highly realistic box setting, the location of entrances should be consistent with implied architectural conformation of the set. That is, exterior and interior doors must not seem to lead to the same area. Traffic patterns of actors are greatly affected by the location of entrances. These problems will be discussed in detail in Chapter 10. For now we might observe that in the proscenium theatre, the director must decide if he wants upstage entrances, downstage entrances, or both. In the arena the location of entrances is not as important as the problem of masking the entering and exiting actor.

The fourth scenic issue is the type and number of scene shifts. With the designer the director should settle on both the number and the type of locale changes needed in a production. *Oedipus* maintains a fixed locale throughout, but *From Morn to Midnight* has many changes. The changes can be complete or partial, much depending on the technical facilities of the theatre. In general, total changes of elaborate scenery are more easily accomplished in the average proscenium theatre than in the average thrust or arena playhouse. The exact moment in the progress of the play when shifts are accomplished is also important. Scene shifts during intermission are usually no problem. Shifts during the running of the play are more or less annoying to the audience depending on their duration and the method of accomplishment. On the other hand, some shifts done before the eyes of the audience may even enhance their enjoyment of the production.

Partial scene shifts may require no more than the rearrangement of props or furniture. Often such changes can be worked into the presentation of the play so that the shifting is done by the actors themselves. Partial, or sometimes even total, scene changes can be done with lighting. In this regard, much depends on the horizontal and vertical treatment of the set. In sets in which the vertical treatment is entirely the function of the actors, changes in lighting will often suggest a scene change. Or, in lieu of light changes, a change of costumes might be used to suggest a new locale.

The final design issue, the quantity and quality of properties and furniture, is tied directly to the number and types of locale. The director and the scenic designer should agree on the kind, amount, and placement of furniture and set properties. In this regard, the director should first ascertain the placement of furniture and then divide that furniture which is practical from that which is merely decorative. The responsibility for providing properties should be fixed, and as soon as possible the designer should be given a list of set props required. Some properties will be hand properties and might become the responsibility of the costumer. If the director knows that he will need some properties not called for in the script, or that he will not use properties mentioned in the script, he should so inform the designer. For instance, although the author had suggested that the ingenue carry a bouquet of flowers, the director might prefer a fan or a handkerchief.

If the director and the designer are satisfied with the preliminary design, the next step is the preparation of a final model or rendering, and a detailed and scaled floor plan. Models are not always necessary in proscenium design; however, most arena directors ask for a model because a rendering cannot suggest the multiple viewpoints of the arena stage.

During his work on the final design and floor plan, the director should keep in touch with the designer, so that any new thoughts or problems can be solved before too much is committed. When the designer has the final plans ready, he and the director can again go into conference. The issues at this conference are identical with those in the initial conference, except that more detailed decisions are reached and more importance is attached to each decision since it will tend to be final. If someone other than the scene designer is to do costumes, it might be well to have the costumer present at the final scenic conference.

With an architect's scale in hand, the director should carefully study the floor plan or model. He should note the relative height of platforms; the direction, height, and width of entrance ways; the placement of furniture; and the width of pathways between architectural units. Use of color is important to both the director and the costumer, for the costumer must adjust his color scheme to that of the scenery. Widths may be important to both the director and the costumer. Wide skirts on Molière's characters do not pass easily through narrow doors or between closely located units of furniture. Heights of entrances may have much to do with the kind and type of headdress worn.

Area relationships should be studied by the director. Does the sofa work best with the window or with the lamp table? Does the platform for the entranceway stand alone, or does it seem to involve adjacent areas? Such decisions will affect the kinetic pattern of the play as well as the assignment of lighting areas. Before accepting the final scene design, the director should remember that he is committing the costumer, the lighting designer, the playwright, and the entire kinetic theatre to a fixed set of visual limits and spatial patterns.

If the director is satisfied with the set, the designer is free to begin his working drawings and to commence construction. Once drawings are completed and construction begins, changes are possible but costly in time, money, and artistic morale. Before he gives his final nod, the director should try to foresee all possible problems that might arise from the set he is about to accept.

THE DIRECTOR AND THE COSTUMER

Whether they are one and the same person or two separate designers, the director will follow with the costumer essentially the same process he went through with the scenic designer. The timetable, however, will vary slightly. Before the actors are cast, the director and the costumer can engage in some general preliminary discussions, especially about the historical or modern style of the costumes and the degree of realism the costumes will attempt. Color schemes might be coordinated with the scenery and the preliminary lighting plans, but until the actors are cast, specific costume decisions are better postponed. Once the acting company is cast, the assembly of an acting company being to costuming what the choice of a theatre is to scenic design, the costumer is free to begin his designing. An initial costumer-director conference is first in order. At such a conference the three issues of costume design are raised: (1) the style and quality of costumes, (2) the number and changes of costumes, and (3) the coordination of costumes with the scenery and lights.

Concerning the first issue, the style and quality of the costumes, the director and costumer must immediately settle the narrative problem.

Second Shepherds' Play. *Anonymous.*
Florida State University.

  Director: W. Harlan Shaw
  Designer: W. Harlan Shaw

Note that the director and actors have cooperated with the costumer to stress curved line and loose, organic form. The statement is warm, casual, and earthy. The basic compositional mass is the formal triangle, but the formality is relieved by slanting the triangle to one side.

Do the costumes have a narrative function in terms of the play script, and if so, what is that function? Are certain costumes necessary to suggest time, place, manners, exposition, and even action? Many directors find that time and place are frequently better suggested by costume than by scenery, and many actors discover that a costume, simply by its presence, can establish a complete manners pattern. As with the scenery, costumes provide a comment on the play and an environment for the actors, and, as with scenery, that comment and environment may be highly realistic or quite abstract. The director and costumer must decide which they prefer. This choice might depend on the acting company. For example, the director wants a slightly ridiculous Polonius. But in tryouts, the director's only choice for Polonius is a rather handsome and imposing actor. The costumer might be then asked to do an outfit which would detract from the actor's natural attractiveness. On the other hand, an amusing little actor with a tendency toward mugging and slapstick comedy might be the director's final selection for Polonius. The costumer would then be asked to counteract the overcomic tendencies of the actor cast as Polonius by giving him a costume suggesting conservative dignity.

In order to settle on the style and quality of each specific costume, the director will probably give the designer a brief analysis of each character as he understands his place and function in the play. Frequently the costumer gives the director additional insight into character patterns by his own analysis or by costume suggestions that stimulate further analysis. The director's analysis might also include specific costume solutions, for example, an observation that the Doctor in *Waltz of the Toreadors* is a "tweedy" sort of person, or that Ghislaine seems the type of woman who would dress in pastels.

The issue of the number of costumes and the changes of costumes is both a technical and aesthetic issue. Technically, the total number of costumes the director has in mind may be impossible in terms of financial resources or technical facilities. Some hoped-for costume changes may have to be eliminated. On the other hand, the director may not desire as many costumes as are implied in the script. Whichever may be the case, the director and costumer must come to some agreement.

The same technical considerations are true for the scheduled costume changes. There must be a place for changes, a way to get to that place, means for storing costumes, and time to accomplish the necessary changes. Entrances and exits that precede costume changes must be analyzed and noted. The time allowed in the script for the change must be studied with an eye to its adequacy. The path the changing actor takes to leave the stage must be coordinated with the place of change.

Concurrent with technical decisions are aesthetic ones that will affect the number and change of costume. The addition of a new costume into the visual pattern always adds interest, but will it detract from the point of the scene or play? Sometimes such decisions involve only a partial change. For instance, a crucial decision for any production of *Oedipus* is the costuming of the tragic hero after he has put out his eyes. Is his costume now covered with blood? Is he covered with a dark cloak? What is on his head? Perhaps he is masked; if so, is the mask changed?

The final costuming issue, that of coordination of costumes with scenery and lights, might be best solved by a joint production conference between the director and all the design artists. Such a conference will assign to the costumer those properties which are logically part of the costume. It will also allow the costumer and the scene designer to develop a mutually helpful and attractive color and texture scheme. It will help to settle for the lighting designers the problems of color filters. And finally, in plays in which the actors are used as the principal vertical design, the costumer and the lighting designer can come to terms on the use and variety of light.

The initial conference completed, the costumer is free to begin his design. Close touch between the director and costumer is helpful in this period. Among other things, frequently in the noncommercial theatre an actor drops out of the cast during the early rehearsals, and the costumer must know of such changes.

When the initial designs are complete, the costumer and the director are ready for a second conference. At this conference, the costumer usually offers sketches of costumes and, if possible, swatches of materials out of which each costume will be built. Issues at the second conference are the same as at the first. Sketches that do not satisfy the director in whole or in part should be tactfully called to the attention of the costumer and specific changes indicated. Choices of material must be made. The director will want to give special study to such matters as skirt length, oversized decoration, headgear, and proposed hand properties. He should keep in mind that these things are often a hindrance to audience vision and a source of awkwardness in the moving of actors. Like the setting, the costumes place certain limits on both the auditory and kinetic theatres.

After a final conference in which requested changes are accepted by the director, the costumer is free to draft patterns and begin construction. Minor changes are possible after this time, but major changes should be avoided if at all possible. Before turning to the problem of lighting design, we might pause to discuss makeup in terms of costumes, because in most theatres makeup is usually the responsibility of the costumer.

The issues in makeup design are identical with those of costume design. The makeup artist and the director should agree on the style and quality of makeup, the number of makeup changes, and the coordination of makeup with costumes, scenery, and lights. The principal caution the director should bear in mind concerning makeup is that outlandish makeup or prostatic additions to the face will frequently tend to make the face less mobile in the same way that outlandish dress or decoration will inhibit general body movement. Moreover, makeup must be adjusted to playing space and lighting. Small arena theatres require less pronounced makeup than do large proscenium ones. Bright light will wash makeup; certain filter colors, particularly amber tints and fully saturated reds, blues, and greens, will also tend to wash makeup or distort its color. Unlike costume and scenery decisions, makeup choices can be easily changed. Consequently, specific consideration of makeup is often postponed until technical rehearsals. However, if special facial treatment is required, such as the construction of masks, these must be decided upon at the initial costume conferences.

THE DIRECTOR AND THE LIGHTING DESIGNER

Frequently the duties of lighting and scene designer are combined, but whether one or two artists are involved, lighting conferences should be separated from design discussions. While it is true that scene design must coordinate with light and vice versa, the director will want to have one or more conferences devoted exclusively to lighting. The basic issues of lighting design are five: (1) the level of visibility, (2) the quality of light, (3) the grouping of light, (4) the control of light, and (5) the coordination of light with the other areas of visual theatre.

In order adequately to solve these issues, the director will need an initial planning conference and a conference when the lighting plot is completed. The lighting conferences should be delayed until the set is accepted and the costumes more or less fixed, although the lighting designer may want to hold a joint conference with costumer and scene designer as they settle on their final plans.

In the initial conference the director and lighting designer take up each of the lighting issues in a general way. First, in terms of level of visibility, the designer will want to know if the director wishes an even and strongly presented light, or if he wants a more shadowy design. Much here will also depend on the costumes and scenery as well as the general quality of the play. *From Morn to Midnight* might be done in shadowy or uneven light; *The Imaginary Invalid* seems to call for bright, perhaps overly bright, and relatively even illumination. The second issue, light quality, involves not only level of visibility but also filter color, direction, and shape of light. Theatrical light filters, commonly called "gels," come in a wide range of colors. Tints are usually used for acting areas, more saturated colors for tonal lighting and background lighting. However, to capture the quality of a scene, highly saturated filters may be used in an acting area. For instance, in order to intensify the subjective viewpoint, highly saturated gels might be employed in the flashbacks in *Salesman*.

Direction of lighting instruments may also affect the quality of light. For a plastic effect, lights in the proscenium usually come from two directions, in the arena from at least three. But for a flatter effect lights may be used from only one direction. Unusual results are produced by lighting from directly above or below.

The shape of light is partially dependent on its direction and partially on the type of instrument. Floodlights throw diffused light; spotlights throw more concentrated shafts. Specialized lights such as beam projectors or color wheels throw highly visible shafts or disrupted shafts of light. Projections of realistic or abstract design are also possible. The director and lighting designer should agree on what is needed for a given production. For instance, the oblique line is a frequent motif in Expressionism, and the director might want to use oblique shafts of strongly saturated light for some scenes in *Morn to Midnight*.

The third lighting issue is both technical and aesthetic. In settling upon an appropriate grouping of light, the director and designer must adjust such grouping to the capabilities of the dimming and patching facilities of their theatre. The director tells the lighting designer what areas he wishes isolated and controlled separately; the lighting designer tells the director what is possible in terms of his needs. If the technical problems of grouping can be solved, then the director is free to approach the aesthetic ones. Grouping of light allows the director to concentrate attention on one or more spaces. It may allow him to suggest such things as a room being lit by a single lamp; it may permit him to have greater freedom in traffic control. The lighting groups are usually called areas, and in the initial conference the director will mark off the rough areas on a copy of the floor plan.

The issue of lighting control is closely related to grouping. Control enables the director to intensify or shadow a given light area at will, to turn on or off all areas, to regulate the intensity of light, and to introduce special lighting effects. In the initial conference, the director should ascertain the amount of control he can reasonably expect, and he should indicate his general need for control. In particular, he should list the areas most frequently changed, the degree of change required, the number of special lights he will need, as well as their general placement, and the kind and frequency of such special effects as projections, blackouts, lightning, or explosions.

In terms of the final issue, coordination with the other areas of visual theatre, the director and the lighting designer should consult with the costumer and the scene designer. A special note might be taken of light's ability to reshape a set. Often the designer of a unit or platform setting is entirely dependent on lighting to give the set form and interest. He may also be dependent on the lighting to provide entrances and exits. In this regard, the director and scene designer must not expect more than lights can do. While it is true that actors in the dark are no longer on stage, it often works out that the theoretical dark is much lighter in actual practice. Light beams bounce and spill. The smaller the stage, the harder it is actually to isolate one area from another. Most directors find that light is more of a positive factor than a negative one. That is, it is easier to use light to give emphasis to a scene or playing area than it is to use it to exclude a playing area.

When the initial conference is over, the lighting designer begins to prepare a light plot. When the plot is ready, a second conference is scheduled. The good light plot shows the various playing areas, the grouping of light in those areas, the kinds of instruments used, the direction of the instruments, and the location and direction of throw of each "special" light, such as a special to light old Hamlet's Ghost, or a special naked bulb to suggest Willy Loman's kitchen. As with makeup, the adjustment of the setting and focusing of lights in most theatres is a relatively easy matter, at least in terms of a few isolated instruments. Therefore, acceptance of a light plot is not as final an act as the acceptance of a scene design. However, in order to avoid wholesale resetting of instruments with the resulting shortness of tempers, the director should study the light plot with considerable care. The placement and type of special lighting should be given particular attention. He should understand the boundaries of each lighting area. The matter of color filters should not be neglected. And finally, the director and designer should settle on a nomenclature that both will use. For example, confusion results when the director talks of the "Oedipus special" while the designer talks of "special number one." When the lighting plot is accepted, the director has completed his initial decisions in the visual theatre. He will now turn his attention to initial problems in the kinetic theatre.

INITIAL PROBLEMS IN THE THEATRE-VISUAL: A SUMMARY

There are five primary design areas in the visual theatre: the theatre building, the scenery, the costumes, the makeup, and the lights. One or more artists may handle these several areas. The director must be knowledgeable in each area in order to communicate his needs and understand the methods, limitations, and desires of each contributing artist. Each area has its special issues and one or more conferences must be scheduled to solve the problems raised by these issues. When the problems are solved, the director should have obtained a form of theatre, secured a rendering and floor plan or model of the scenery, have a set of costume designs including proposed materials, formed an idea of the makeup design, and collected a lighting plot.

CHAPTER 6

initial decisions
in the theatre-kinetic

The Director, the Actors, and the
Theatrical Designers

After he evaluates and selects a play script, the director immediately
begins his continuing process of analysis of the play. Before he can
complete this analysis, he must have a set, costumes, and actors, because many questions of time, place, incident, and character can only
be answered with a specific set and costumed actors in mind. Chapter 5
examined the process a director normally follows in obtaining scenery,
costume, makeup, and lighting designs. The present chapter will be
devoted to a consideration of the contributions of the theatrical de-

signers and of the actors in the initial phase of the director's work in the kinetic theatre.

The chief kinetic implications of the play script are dramatic character, action, story, and theatrical space, lights, and costumes. Dramatic character, action, and story require the presence of the actor, and therefore the director's first task is the assembling of an acting company.

CASTING THE ACTORS: PUBLICIZING THE TRYOUTS

The first step in casting is to attract prospective actors to tryouts. Directors use various methods of communication and persuasion. An announcement should be placed in all the means of mass communication available to the director—newspaper, television, and radio. Announcements to groups such as classes and clubs will also help. Tryout posters are a traditional means, as are personal contact and word of mouth. Public announcements should contain the play title, the place, and the times of tryouts. Some directors want every available prospect, whether experienced or not. If this is the case, the announcement should stress the fact that experience is not necessary. If the name of the playwright will encourage attendance at tryouts, it should by all means be included in the announcement. Shakespeare, for instance, is a good drawing card for prospective actors. Finally, any additional information the director might feel necessary should be included, such as the need for a dancer, a flute player, or a juggler.

Timing of tryout notices is important. Announcements made too early tend to make people forget the date; those made too late do not allow for the prospective actors to plan schedules. In the average noncommercial theatre situation, the peak of the pretryout campaign should come about one to two days before the first tryouts.

CASTING THE ACTORS: PREPARING FOR TRYOUTS

Directors must make both a technical and an artistic preparation for tryouts. Technically, the director must schedule space and time. He must provide auditioning material, which is usually from the play to be produced; and he must provide a means of identifying the prospective actors and making notes on their skills and appropriateness to the roles being cast. In preparing reading material, the director usually selects from the play script those sections that best express the quality of the character being read for. To identify and remember those trying out, many directors make use of some sort of tryout form. This form will include name and possibly such information as height, weight, and color of hair. Other information requested might be a listing of previous experience or a statement of any special talents such as singing, dancing, playing a musical instrument, or tumbling. It is usually a good idea to ask for a prospective actor's schedule, especially as it affects proposed times of rehearsal. Preparations for tryouts might also include providing for an assistant who could distribute and take up tryout forms and aid the director in other matters of casting.

Artistically, directors prepare for tryouts by studying the script until they have a fairly clear, general concept of each character and an understanding of the relationships of one character to another. Special physical peculiarities necessary to the story should also be noted. For example General St. Pé must have sufficient middle-age characteristics, else the play is pointless. In terms of physical characteristics, the director might particularly note age, height, weight, and sex characteristics. Special vocal needs or unusual skills should be singled out and remembered.

CASTING THE ACTORS: TRYOUTS

Since all the work of every artist in the theatre will ultimately focus on the actor, tryouts are a crucial time in the life of a production. Directors vary in the methods by which they conduct tryouts. No matter what the method, every director wants to be alert, perceptive, and flexible. To be alert, the director comes to tryouts rested and relaxed. To stay alert, he should be able to recognize the approaching signs of listener fatigue—drowsiness, restlessness, inability to focus attention, sudden lapses into daydream; and he should be ready to call a halt to tryouts whenever such symptoms begin to appear. As an aid in avoiding listener fatigue, many directors find it wiser to schedule several short tryout periods rather than one or two long sessions. The scheduling of several tryout sessions at various times of the day and evening also makes it easier for prospective actors to fit tryouts into their schedules.

An alert director has a better chance of being a perceptive director, and a perceptive director is one who at tryouts is able to judge not only the displayed skill and talent but also the potential talent of each auditioner. No director is a perfect judge, and the task of attempting to evaluate both the strengths and the weaknesses of every auditioner is a truly difficult one. When an auditioner is a total stranger to the director, a great burden is placed on the director's training as an actor and as a judge of perspective actors. While most apprentice directors are well trained as actors, many have little experience in auditioning. Beginning directors should take advantage of every opportunity to observe the tryouts of experienced directors and to attempt to match wits with them in the selection of a cast.

When a director has past knowledge of the work of some of the auditioners, his problem is eased somewhat in that he has a base of comparison. But each role is a new set of circumstances and a new challenge and consequently cannot be cast totally on the basis of past performances. Moreover, all actors grow in skill and ability, and in the noncommercial theatre such growth is apt to be quite rapid. Finally, each role may not only call up the hidden talents of an experienced actor but might also reveal unknown weaknesses. To all of these possibilities the director must be alert.

Perhaps the most valuable characteristic of a director at tryouts is his ability to remain flexible. When a director evaluates a play, he naturally forms some fairly definite notions of each of the characters. Almost certainly some of the notions are going to be frustrated by what the director finds at tryouts. After all, the scene designer can always be requested to shift a doorway, or the costumer to select a different type of material, but the actor cannot change such features as height, general looks, or voice quality. Thus the director, particularly in the noncommercial theatre, must cast from the actors at tryouts, and such casting requires flexibility in his concept of what kind of actor should play a certain character.

Flexibility does not imply a "make-do" attitude. It is not always a question of getting the actor who is nearest to the director's ideal. More often than not, a near miss is as good as a mile. Flexibility often means an adjustment on the spot to a new concept of one or more characters; in short, a partial or total reevaluation of the character in terms of the available actors. Flexibility also means the willingness to change tryout procedure to accommodate unforeseen circumstances. There is the painfully shy young actor, the actor that has to be coaxed into reading. There is the actor who has special problems, the actor who wants to read every time, or the actor or actors who create disturbances. Finally, flexibility implies patience and endurance, endurance to hear the same lines poorly read over and over; patience in allowing each actor, no matter how untalented or unskilled, to have his fair share of opportunities to read.

Tryout methods vary so much from director to director that it is impossible to single out a typical tryout procedure. Most directors employ some form of reading as a basis, and usually such reading is taken directly from the play to be cast. Some directors like to read large group scenes so that they can hear as many people as possible in as many relationships as possible. Some directors are inclined to use scenes involving only two or three people so that they can gain an in-depth impression. Mixtures of small and large scenes are also popular. Some directors even prefer private auditions, though in the noncommercial theatre this is generally considered undemocratic. Some directors allow their actors to remain seated; most ask their actors to stand. Some directors ask actors to do a brief pantomime. Some let the actor read once through the role and on later readings give brief directing suggestions to see how the actor responds. Some directors encourage auditioners to prepare a role in advance because they feel that in doing so an insight can be gained into the actor at his skilled best. Other directors discourage advance preparation on the theory that a "cold" reading reveals the natural talent and level of true skill of the actor. Some directors will allow auditioners to indicate the roles in which they are interested, while others discourage role choosing on the basis that it is undemocratic and that it begins the actor-director relationship on the wrong foot. Some directors will read an auditioner only in roles he could possibly play; others will ask the auditioner to read impossible roles so that they can judge his versatility.

Whatever the method or methods used, the aim of the director is not only to get the best possible cast but also to give every auditioner an opportunity to display his acting ability fully. To do this, an air of relaxation, patience, and good humor must be created throughout the auditioning period. Young, inexperienced talent should be encouraged, more experienced talent sustained. To get things off to a relaxed start, most directors make a few remarks about the play in general—the plot, the various characters, and the method to be followed in auditioning. At this time the director might invite questions. Normally, the director will also give information concerning posting of final cast, probable rehearsal schedule, and playing dates of the performances.

In order to hear everybody and yet at the same time to give some attention to a narrower field, a common practice is to have several sessions of general tryouts, then one or two call-back sessions in which particular people are studied more closely. In many theatres, people who are not attending the call-back sessions are encouraged to go to a production meeting where they may join a technical crew in case they are not cast.

When tryouts are completed, the director is ready to face his loneliest and often most dreaded task—casting the roles.

CASTING THE ACTORS: ASSIGNING THE ROLES

Despite all his training, the director will need a good share of luck if he is not to make a mistake in casting, and almost any mistake can be a serious one. There is no way that any audition, no matter how cleverly contrived, can give the director a completely safe insight into how well an actor will work in rehearsals or how effective he will be in performance. Some actors are so nervous in any sort of tryout that they simply do not give a hint of their real potential, while other actors are able to give their all in audition. Sometimes the latter type is cast and, to the director's dismay, never grows beyond his initial reading in tryouts.

Casting means that final limits are now placed on the manners and motive patterns of the play script, and that chief tools of language and movement are now fixed. Thus the director should approach his casting decisions with thought and caution.

The first step in casting is to forget about the "what might have been." Earlier we remarked on the need for flexibility. In assigning roles that flexibility is put to one of its greatest tests. More often than not, the director must reshape his concept of one or more characters or actions in terms of the available cast. Worrying about what he might have wanted is no help in this reshaping. In casting, the director to some extent must suit the role to the available actor, just as later the actor must suit himself to the available role. Such adjusting of role to actor does not imply "typing" either the actor or the role but simply using the elements of the media most effectively. For example, there is some evidence indicating that Miller originally conceived of Willy Loman as a tall, thin man; yet the original actor in the first production production was Lee J. Cobb, a thick, heavy man. Another director might find that his best choice for Willy is a small, wiry actor. To take another example, a traditional view of Gertrude in *Hamlet* is as a large imposing, slightly matronly figure; yet in a given circumstance, the director might well elect to go with a slight, vibrant, slightly nervous but startlingly attractive actress.

In casting the single role, much depends on the total ensemble. It wouldn't do to have a very tall Gertude if the only available talent for Claudius were middle-sized to short. On the other hand, just such a husband–wife combination might be ideal for *The Imaginary Invalid*. Thus in terms of both the single role and the ensemble, the director must remain flexible.

The director must consider auditory, visual, and kinetic factors in his choice of a single role and of an entire company. He must consider the voice quality of each actor and its relation to the total ensemble of voices; he must take into account the actor's skill in oral interpretation, and the range and volume of his voice. In some plays the ability to sing might also be important. In visual terms the director will want not only someone who looks good but someone who looks good in terms of the role. Whoever plays Willy Loman must first of all seem mature physically, and he must be able to project an air of physical exhaustion. The actor playing Oedipus might be young or old, but he must look powerful or at least dignified. A director might not be concerned about the height or weight of the Cashier in *From Morn to Midnight*, so long as he does not appear too powerful or too imposing. Vocal and visual factors must be balanced with kinetic ones. An actor might give an excellent oral interpretation of Argan, but he might also be young, powerfully built, and handsome and move with too much youth and grace. Another actor might look comic enough and move with the jerky frenzy of an old rascal, but his reading might leave much to be desired. Between the two the director must decide.

Plays often present specialized vocal, visual, and kinetic problems. For instance, the chorus in *Oedipus* is a matter that can cause a great deal of trouble. How many should be in the chorus? How will they move? Will they have to have special dancing skills? Will they speak in unison or will the odes be divided among the chorus members? Such decisions can be postponed until casting time, but no later. A director who was planning on a special type of dancing for the chorus, but who can find no dancers, might have to revise his plans; one who was anticipating a large chorus might have to adjust to a much smaller one.

Thus casting is at best a process of compromises and adjustments, requiring attention simultaneously to the auditory, visual, and kinetic theatres. It rests upon flexibility of approach and a willingness to adjust the role to the actor as well as adjusting the available actors to the roles. The ensemble as well as the individual actor must be considered. Above all, the director must be positive. He should not look back to an ideal established before tryouts. Casting an actor because he is the closest to the existing ideal may make for frustrations in rehearsal and disappointment in performance. Actors normally should be cast for their positive values. Moreover, a director frequently has his concepts happily stimulated and improved by what he finds at tryouts. Not all changes in character evaluation are for the worse.

CASTING THE ACTORS: THE CAST LIST

Announcing the cast is both a joy and a burden. There is fun and excitment in at last having assembled the acting company. There is also relief that for better or for worse the casting decisions have been made and the artistic work is about to begin. But there is also the burden of having to contend with those who were not cast. Inevitably people are disappointed, and many of the disappointed are good actors who cannot understand why they were not cast. The director must be prepared for questions, conferences, and sometimes long, tearful discussions. Egos are hurt; confidence is shaken. As tactfully as possible the director must handle the problems of the disappointed. Usually it is a matter of explaining how the actor, while talented, did not suit the role or did not work within the total ensemble. At any rate, such conferences are necessary to restore pride and confidence in the total acting group. Doubtless many a director can remember being at the other end of such discussions at least once in his apprentice acting career.

Aside from comforting the disappointed, the director needs to assemble and organize those who were cast. To this end, the cast list should include information about general rehearsal times, a specific date for the first meeting, and such additional information as the director might feel is necessary. Before posting the cast list, roles and names should be carefully proofread in order to avoid changes that later might cause embarrassment or loss of morale. Changes in casting, except for disciplinary or health reasons, are not normal. Before posting, the director should be certain of his cast choices. Changes after casting make the director seem indecisive or arbitrary, with a concurrent loss of respect and cooperation from the cast.

CASTING THE ACTORS: A SUMMARY

Casting begins with the publicizing of tryouts. Preparation for tryouts includes not only a thorough evaluation of the roles to be cast but also such technical arrangements as the scheduling of time and place and the organization of a tryout procedure. Many methods of auditioning are used by directors, but whatever the method the overall aim is for the director to stay relaxed, alert, and perceptive, and for the auditioners to perform in an atmosphere that is calm and relaxed and in which each auditioner knows that he will be given his fair share of opportunity to prove himself. Tryouts over, the director has the lonely task of assigning roles. Because he must weigh so many visual, auditory, and kinetic factors against each other and because he must consider the total ensemble as well as the individual actor, the director must be entirely flexible in casting. He must be ready to reevaluate any given role or roles in terms of his available acting talent. Casting decisions having been reached, the director posts the cast list with its instructions for meeting times. He now has in his possession all elements of the art of theatre. Before making his in-depth analysis of the play script in light of the set, costumes, lights, actors, and the script itself, the director still has some initial considerations in the kinetic theatre.

THE THEATRICAL DESIGNERS AND THE KINETIC THEATRE

Once the director knows his actors, he is better able to study the contributions of the theatrical designers in terms of the kinetic theatre. He has already observed the general traffic ways of the set. For instance, a door placed upstage in the proscenium will mean that all entrances will be toward the audience, all exits away from the audience. But knowing who is coming through that door will now make a great difference. A narrow entrance might be difficult, but if the director has cast an extremely fat actor, the entrance is now impossible. The same might be true of furniture placement. Certainly the size and general mobility of certain actors will have much to do with the softness or hardness of furniture, or of its shape or ease in handling.

Costumes more often than setting are directly affected by the actor as a moving body. In fact, the basic test of a good costume is not how strong is its visual impact but how well the actor wearing the costume can perform necessary physical activities. Necessary activities vary, but one thing is certain: a good costume for one actor in a given role might be a very poor costume for another actor in the same role. Once the costumer knows the specific actor, he and the director are better able to come to a solution as to what kind of costume would benefit the actor both visually and kinetically. Group consideration in costume as movement is also important. The director might wish color, form, or texture varied for the chorus in *Oedipus* so that he could reinforce his movement patterns with visual variety.

Lighting, by changing both the shape and quality of space, must be considered kinetically. Heights of actors are important, as well as placement and probable movement patterns. If there are one or more lighting specials for the Ghost in *Hamlet,* then either the director must adjust his motion patterns to the specials or the specials must be adjusted to the movement. Depending upon the circumstances of the theatre, lighting plots are often delayed until the basic movement patterns have been established. In this way the director and the lighting designer can cooperate in a progresive creative effort.

INITIAL DECISIONS IN THE THEATRE-KINETIC: A SUMMARY

The immediate problem in the kinetic theatre is the selection of the actors who are the primary element of theatre as motion. Casting involves the holding of tryouts and the assignment of roles. With the acting company assembled, the director reexamines the scenery, costumes, and lighting with an eye to their initial kinetic issues and problems. Initial evaluation completed, the director is prepared to create the theatrical metaphor visually, vocally, and kinetically through actor rehearsals, technical rehearsals, and dress rehearsals. To do this, he will, like the playwright in literature, use certain elements and principles of visual, auditory, and kinetic design. The next three chapters will be devoted to an examination of those elements and principles.

CHAPTER 7

the visual theatre

*The Director and the Principles
of Visual Art*

The director's concerns in the visual theatre are not only scenery, lights, and costumes. The actor must also be treated as a significant visual statement to be coordinated with the total spatial design. In some productions the actor is the only major vertical element of the theatre-visual. While responsibility for setting, lighting, and costuming is shared jointly by the director and the appropriate visual artists, the spatial statement made by the actor is the sole responsibility of the director.

In terms of the visible actor, the director has two tasks. First, he must distribute his actors about the stage in such a way that, in combination with the setting, they present at all times an aesthetically satisfying statement. Second, the director must arrange the total image of the theatre-visual so that it makes a comment consistent with the dramatic statement of the play script. The first task is usually called the problem of visual composition; the second is called picturization or design. In order to solve both his compositional and design problems, the director must have a thorough knowledge of the principles of visual art.

THE DIRECTOR: DESIGN AND COMPOSITION

Good design grows out of good visual composition. The elements out of which the director creates successful composition are the same means he uses for his design goals; therefore, an understanding of the means of composition is prerequisite to a discussion of design. Over the last several decades, the question of composing and designing actors and sets was considered only in terms of the proscenium or picture-frame. With the growing popularity of the open stage, the thrust stage, and the full arena, visual problems have become more complex, more interesting, and more difficult. In proscenium staging the director has to be concerned with only one angle of vision, that angle framed by the proscenium arch. The thrust stage forces the director to consider audience members who have various lines of sight. The arena stage further complicates the problems of the thrust stage, for in the thrust stage the director can always retreat to the neutral wall serving as a fixed visual referent for all lines of sight. The arena allows no such compromise. No two viewers get exactly the same visual impression from an arena image, and no place in the arena can serve as an ultimate reference point. Even when an actor stands "dead center" in the arena, his face is to some viewers, his profile to others, and his back to still others. As we take up each of the means of composition, we will examine how they are affected by the various forms of modern staging.

THE MEANS OF COMPOSITION

The six means or elements of composition are the same for director, scene designer, or costumer. The means are line, form, mass, color, space, and texture. These elements are no more mutually exclusive than are the elelents of play structure, but for purposes of analysis they may be isolated and discussed separately. Each means has an independent function, and any one of them is capable of carrying alone the major burden of a visual composition.

LINE AND COMPOSITION

Line is the basic visual element. In addition to straight line, four lines are identified:

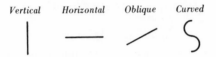

Obviously, oblique and curved lines are more complex than straight vertical or straight oblique. An oblique curved line is the most complex of all line types.

All four lines may be used effectively on the proscenium stage, since they may all be perceived in terms of a fixed referent—the proscenium frame. The oblique line does not exist as such in arena productions, because any oblique line will be seen as a normal vertical or horizontal line by a considerable portion of the audience. In the three-quarter arena or thrust stage, the oblique line may still be used in terms of the neutral or fixed wall, but its impact is somewhat reduced. What the thrust and arena stages lose in oblique line is more than compensated for by the increased vividness of curved and especially vertical lines. There are two apparent reasons for the increased impact of vertical line in arena and thrust stages: (1) the openness of the staging forms, and (2) the fact that the arena floor acts as the major reference point for the arena audience.

The openness or freedom of space in thrust and arena stages is a result of a disappearance of a suggested ceiling in these staging forms. Because the proscenium is arched, there seems to be a sense of upper limit in picture-frame staging. This is not so in the arena, and thus the audience is encouraged the more easily to convert literal vertical line into virtual vertical line, thereby adding impact to the line.

Literal line is what actually exists; *virtual line* is the projection of actual line into space. Such projection is usually suggested by the direction of the literal line. Thus if a man extends his arm and points at a house some yards away, we see not only the actual line of the arm but also the virtual line extended from the fingertip to the house. By the very nature of its frame, left, right, up, and down, virtual lines do not extend beyond the proscenium arch. In the open space of the arena, virtual vertical lines seem to be limitless.

Vertical line is also given impact in the arena from the fact that the floor of the arena is the closest thing to a fixed reference point for all the audience. Since vertical line grows directly out of the stage floor, it would naturally have great immediacy for an arena audience.

Curved line also has increased strength in full arena and many thrust stages as a result of the implied circular form of the arena itself. The more a curved line approaches the circular, the more reinforcement it receives from the circular nature of the arena.

To sum up, line may be of five types—vertical, horizontal, oblique, straight, or curved. There may be curved vertical, curved oblique, and curved horizontal lines or partial combinations thereof. All types of line may be used with equal effect in the proscenium theatre, while in the arena theatre the oblique line does not exist. Oblique lines may be used with some effect in thrust staging. The loss of oblique line is compensated for in the arena by the increased vividness of vertical and curved lines. Part of this vividness results from the ability of vertical lines to convert from literal to virtual line. Virtual line is the metaphorical extension of actual line into space. Part of the vividness results from the form of the arena itself. Line is the most vital and basic aspect of the second element of visual composition—form.

THE ELEMENT OF FORM

Lines describe form; form is that which both punctuates and shapes space. In effect, whenever we are speaking of line we are also speaking of the most rudimentary kinds of form. Thus there are straight and curved forms; vertical, horizontal, and oblique forms; and various combinations thereof. Another way of classifying form is to divide it into natural and artificial form. A third classification is geometric and organic. Natural forms are those existing in nature or close imitations thereof. The actor as a human body is a natural form. Artificial forms are those not yet observed in nature, or more frequently extreme modification of natural forms. Thus when a gardener trims a hedge or shrub into a boxlike or oval shape, he has converted a natural form into an artificial form. Artificial forms are the work of man.

Many artificial forms are geometric; others are organic. Geometric forms are those approaching the rectangular, the circular, the triangular, or the conical in overall shape. Glasses, dishes, furniture, and most houses are good examples of geometric forms.

Organic forms have no typical configuration but are usually the result of accident or functional design. Most organic forms are natural—a leaf, the specific shape of an oak tree, the form of the human hand. Some, such as boats, airplanes, and some types of furniture and architecture, are artificial. For example, the so-called "kidney" shape popular for some types of table tops is an artificial, nongeometric form.

Because of their long use and familiarity, many artificial forms are taken by most audiences as natural forms. A chair or a sofa, though actually artificial, may be treated as if it were a natural form. Some natural, organic forms can be reworked by man into artificial forms. Our example of the pruning of garden hedges is a case in point. In terms of the theatre, the director may shape the organic form of a group of actors into a geometric one, or the costumer may shape the organic form of a single actor into a more geometric figure.

Form, then, described by line, is that element which punctuates and gives shape to space. Form may be classified as straight or curved, horizontal, vertical, or oblique. It may also be classified as geometric or organic, and further classified as natural or artificial.

The most important and most basic form in the theatre is the actor. Taken as an individual, the actor is a natural, organic form that can be molded into vertical, horizontal, straight, curved, or oblique lines or combinations thereof. Through control by the director, the costumer, or the actor himself, the actor's form may be changed from organic to geometric.

When more than one actor is present, the problem of form is complicated by and directly related to the type of staging used. The actor as a theatrical form has innate direction; that is, he has a front and a back. This obvious difference is important in all types of staging. In the proscenium, front and back are understood in relation to the proscenium opening and give rise to certain standard body positions which will be discussed in detail later. In the arena theatre, the body positions are relative; that is, they are understood in relation to other actors or units of the setting. In thrust staging, body positions are relative when the actor is far out upon the thrust platform, and fixed when the actor is close to the neutral wall.

When more than one actor is present, the problem of form is complicated by both the number of actors and the type of staging. Whether two or more actors are understood as a single form or as separate forms will depend greatly upon the director's use of the element of space. When the space between two or more actors, in whatever type of staging, is decreased beyond an arm's length, the actors are usually seen as combined parts of a single form.

The type of staging greatly influences actors used to create larger forms. In the proscenium theatre, the basic form used for multiple actors is the triangle, because this is the basic form of the proscenium.

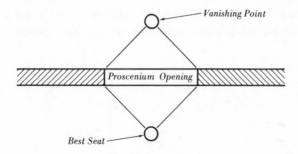

The triangle may be standard, inverted, or distorted in one of several acute shapes. One or more parts of the triangle may be varied horizontally or vertically:

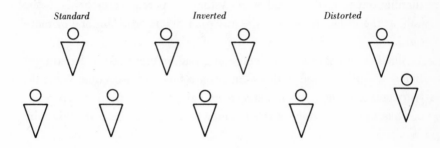

99

Curves, semicircles, and oblique masses are also used in the proscenium stage. Straight horizontal forms are sometimes used, as are gradually ascending vertical forms. Forms composed of several actors of the same vertical height, running from the proscenium arch toward upstage, are perceivable only as the single form of the foremost actor.

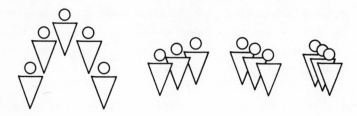

In arena staging, the triangle is not perceivable because of the changes of viewpoint from one audience member to the next. Therefore although the triangle may be used, it will make no compositional or design statement. The circle is the basic and most frequent form in arena staging, because the circle is the basic form of the arena. This is so even when the arena seems to have a rectangular configuration:

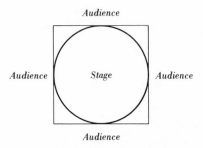

The arena is a circle with center stage as the hub and countless radii running out toward the audience. Actors are perceived as being at the hub, at the circumference of the circle, or arranged along one or more radii.

Since actors may be arranged along one or more radii, the straight line is frequently used in the arena, as are forms of ascending verticals. Horizontals are less easy to perceive and are used less frequently.

Thus the form which a single actor assumes, or the form taken by

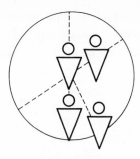

two or more actors, is greatly influenced by the type of staging. Space plays a significant role in the perception of form, and equally significant is the function of the third element of visual composition—mass.

THE ELEMENT OF MASS

Line describes form; mass measures form. The measurement is accomplished by three means: weight, density, and volume. Weight and volume have both a literal and a virtual value, but since the audience does not directly experience mass in the theatre, only its virtual value, or what it seems to be, is of major concern to the director. Weight may be light or heavy; volume may be large or small. Mass may also be viewed as compressed or expanded. Five actors standing next to each other are a compressed mass; the same actors, each separated by three feet, are an expanded mass. Both masses have the same literal weight, but the addition of space not only lessens the density but increases the volume. However, in terms of appearance, the loss of density may give a sense of loss of weight.

Volume is measured in height, width, and depth; weight is measured in apparent compression or density of contributing forms; and compression is measured in terms of space between contributing forms in relation to the outline of the total mass.

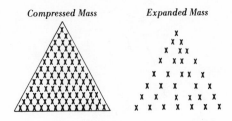

Compressed Mass   *Expanded Mass*

All others things being equal, a high-volume, high-density mass is heavier than a high-volume, greatly expanded mass. A low-volume, dense mass is heavier than a high-volume, expanded mass.

Heavy Mass   *Lighter Mass*

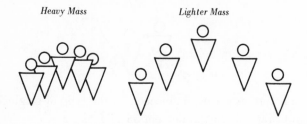

The basic unit of theatrical mass, as the basic unit of form, is the actor. In terms of his own body, he has a more or less fixed weight, density, and volume; but by the manipulation of light, costume, and space, particularly vertical space, the volume of the actor's body can be changed. For instance, a highly textured costume will change the effect of density in the direction of expansion, while a dark, monochromatic costume will lower the volume and increase the effect of compression of the actor's body.

In addition to the single actor, the director has at his disposal several actors to create mass. As with the other elements of visual art, much depends upon the type of staging. In the proscenium, both the form and the density of the mass are crucial. Dense, nontriangular masses tend to be perceived as organic shapes.

The handling of the downstage portions of a mass is critical. If the mass is to be given any dimension, the downstage portion must be more expanded than the upstage portion of the mass. If the downstage expansion is not desirable, the director must increase the vertical direction (through the use of platforms) of the upstage portion of the mass. Hence the stage floor is usually higher at the back of the procenium

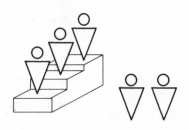

stage than at the front. In short, unless there is a change in volume, density, or vertical distribution, a downstage mass makes for extreme difficulties in sightlines. From the viewpoint of weight, it is very difficult to express weight through compression in the proscenium unless a change is made in the height of the various components. Consequently, line and space play an important role in both weight and volume.

In the ideal arena theatre, where the audience is elevated above the stage, the expression of volume in mass is not a difficult problem. But the director must take care that the prevailing heights of the mass do not block the perception of the total mass. While the proscenium director must be concerned mainly with downstage height, the arena director must watch both peripheral and interior heights. Moreover, too great an expansion in the arena will tend to eliminate the impression of mass much more quickly than in proscenium staging. The use of mass in thrust staging must be adjusted to whether the thrust is more like an ideal arena, or more akin to a traditional proscenium stage.

In summary, mass is the measurement of form in terms of weight, volume, and compression or expansion of components. Thus mass relates form to gravity. To be perceived at all, mass must have sufficient form to set it off from other masses. Perceiving form requires the presence of the fourth element of visual composition—space.

THE ELEMENT OF SPACE

In its basic state, space is the absence of all form. But when any form is present, space is that element which contrasts with form and relates one form to another. Because it is displaced by mass, space adds dimensionality to mass. Because some space is trapped within both mass and form, space is also that element which relates the interior lines of form one to another and which measures the density of mass (i.e., the relational distance in height, width, and depth of each of the component forms of a given mass).

Space can be considered both negatively and positively. Negative space is unaffected by any other element of visual art. For instance, the dark background of many portrait paintings may be considered as negative space. A totally empty, evenly lighted stage might be considered negative space in terms of the theatre. Theatrical space is, however, rarely negative. Any change in the color or distribution of light will add some positive value to space. The presence of an actor or several actors will punctuate, break up, or in some other way activate theatrical space. A setting will also make space more active. The traditional box set of the proscenium makes space quite positive. Thus the measure of the negative or positive nature of space is a relative one. The more positive a given space is, the more difficult it is to perceive line, form, mass, color, or texture.

Space, at least in the theatre, may also be judged in terms of its availability. In the proscenium theatre, the size of the opening in height, width, and depth limits the available space. Moreover, there is a relationship between width and height of the opening. The wider the opening, the higher should be the level of the arch in order not to give the impression of a short spatial ceiling. In the handling of masses, available space must be secured so that height can be varied within sightlines. Depth of stage is also necessary in order adequately to distribute masses of actors.

In the arena, spatial height is not as important as circumferential measurements. Unless the ceiling is so low that the actors are standing among the lights, vertical space seems limitless in the arena, but the audience can quickly measure total floor footage. Sufficient horizontal space is necessary to provide for differentiation of forms and masses in the arena.

Considerable attention must be given to the degree of positive or negative space provided by the stage setting. In the proscenium, the vertical elements of the set are most important in this regard. In the arena, where the actors are the chief vertical element, the treatment of the floor—horizontal space—must be considered. However, in the proscenium theatre with a balcony, and in the thrust stage with an impressive neutral wall, attention must be given to both vertical and horizontal space. Finally, in any type of staging the scenic treatment of the floor in terms of platforms which will change the vertical and horizontal relations of actors to space must be studied closely.

Space, then, is an all-pervading element of composition. It is punctuated by line and form and displaced by mass. It can be measured both negatively and positively. Most theatrical space is positive to some degree because most theatrical space is lighted, and light is usually influenced by the fifth element of visual composition—color.

THE ELEMENT OF COLOR

Any of the previously discussed elements of composition may be, and usually are, treated with color. When line, form, mass, and space are so treated, their statements and properties are greatly affected. Color has four properties: hue, value, saturation, and temperature.

Hue is the unique, inherent quality of each individual color. There are three primary pigment hues: red, blue, and yellow; and three primary light hues: red, blue, and green. All other colors are mixtures of two or more primaries. For purposes of study, hues are often placed on a wheel as follows:

The mixture of two primaries creates a secondary. Secondaries in pigment are orange, violet, and green; secondaries in light are violet, yellow, and blue-green. Each secondary has as its complement the primary color opposite it on the color wheel. Orange, a mixture of red and yellow, is the complement of blue; green, a mixture of blue and yellow, is the complement of red; and violet is the complement of yellow. When two complements, violet and yellow for instance, are combined in equal amounts, the result is a neutral color.

In addition to its hue, each color possesses value. Value is the amount of white or black in a color, or the amount of light a color seems to possess. Value can most easily be discerned when hue is removed, as in black and white photography. What is seen in a black and white photograph are varying shades of gray, shades ranging from almost black to almost white. Note, for example, Plate One. Those grays that tend toward white are high in value; those that tend toward black are low in value.

While value is the measure of black and white in a color, saturation is the measure of the intensity of the hue itself. In other words, some reds are redder than others. A pure red is completely saturated, while a pink is not saturated. Highly saturated colors tend toward mid-range in

PLATE ONE   *A scene from* The Imaginary Invalid *produced at the University of South Florida, Tampa, Florida.*

Director: Jack D. Clay   Designer: Russel G. Whaley

value. As white is added, value increases and saturation decreases; as black is added, value and saturation both decrease. The following chart demonstrates how value and saturation become functions of each other:

High Value	Pink	Low Saturation
Middle Value	Red	High Saturation
Low Value	Maroon	Low Saturation

Not only are value and saturation functions of one another, but hue is also part of this interchange. Certain hues have intrinsic value. Fully saturated yellow has a higher actual value than fully saturated red. Fully saturated blue has a lower actual value than fully saturated yellow or red. Consequently, a high-value blue hue may appear in black and white photography as a shade of gray identical to that of a middle-value red.

Color's fourth property is more psychological than technical. Certain colors are traditionally considered warm, such as reds and yellows; others traditionally regarded as cool, such as blues and greens. However, any individual hue may be rated on a temperature scale. A red to which some blue has been added is a cooler hue than a red to which some yellow has been added. There are warm yellows (butter yellows) and cool yellows (lime yellows); warm blues (purples) and cool blues (aquamarines). Since colors are rarely fully saturated single hues, temperature is often as necessary as value and saturation for descriptive and analytical purposes.

Color has an effect upon every other element of visual art. Color will add to or detract from the vividness of line. It will clarify or complicate the outline of form, and it may be used to show the interrelationships of the various components of an individual form. A change in color may effectively change a natural form to an artificial one; as a single example we might take the coloring of human flesh with green or purple or blue makeup. Color may also be used to make distinctions between closely related forms or to demonstrate a similarity between seemingly unrelated forms.

Color has a profound effect on mass, especially upon the virtual characteristics of mass. For example, masses of high value will seem to have greater volume; the same masses in a low-value color will seem to have less volume. The higher the color value of a mass, all other things being equal, the lighter the apparent weight of that mass. Saturation will also affect weight, volume, and density. All other things being equal, highly saturated masses will seem more compressed and therefore heavier than less-saturated masses. Whether or not saturation adds virtual weight to a mass depends on a comparison to value. Highly saturated, mid-value masses are virtually heavier than high-value masses, but seem to be lighter than low-value masses. On the other hand, highly saturated masses, because of the intensity of color, seem to be larger than low-value masses.

Color temperature further affects mass. Masses colored with a warm hue seem larger and lighter and less dense than masses of a cooler hue. However, each of these rules of thumb must be weighed one against another. A mass may be in a strongly saturated yellow, and because of yellow's intrinsically high value, the mass may actually seem larger, lighter, and more expanded than a similar mass in a rather high value of red.

Color's influence on space is also important. Any space that is colored is more positive space than that which is colorless. When the intensity of the color increases, space becomes even more positive; hence, the importance of lighting in terms of colored space in the theatre. Some highly saturated filters light theatrical space in such intense reds, greens, or blues that the actors can hardly be seen. In short, the space has become almost completely color-positive. By changing in value, color can increase or decrease the apparent size of available space. Thus brightly lighted stages seem larger than darker stages. In the theatre, the increase of the light value is very practical in that an excess of light in a given space will actually cause an overflow or spill and further increase the size of the space.

Temperature will also influence space in that warmly lighted theatrical space will seem more positive than coolly lighted. All things being equal, warmly lighted space will seem less compressed and limited than coolly lighted space.

Aside from coloring of space through lights and scenery, the director's main color element in the theatre is the costumed actor. Thus because he will later use that element for his own visual composition, the director should give considerable attention to the color qualities of each individual costume and to the overall colors of the total costume ensemble. Color is a major means of making an actor larger or smaller, heavier or lighter, taller or shorter, more or less natural or artificial, more distinct or less distinct in line, and more or less complicated in form. Color is further a means of relating one actor to other actors, or of isolating one actor from a mass.

Color, therefore, like the other elements of visual composition, both supports and is supported by line, form, mass, and space. Space provides an area in which color may exist; line and form give shape, direction, and distribution to color. Mass gives depth, height, and weight to color. As a separate element, color has four distinct qualities: hue, value, saturation, and temperature. The interaction of all four qualities is what differentiates one color from another.

THE ELEMENT OF TEXTURE

The sixth element of visual art is texture, the surface quality of any visual element. A surface may be judged as rough or smooth, hard or soft, complex or simple. Each of these three evaluations may be made in terms of literal or virtual surfaces, but since audiences rarely touch an actor or a set in the theatre, the director's only concern is with virtual or apparent texture. The initial surface quality of any visual component is drawn from the material used in creating the component. Thus wood seems hard and cloth seems soft. Unsanded wood is rough; sanded wood is smooth. The bark surface of a tree trunk is more complex in pattern than the surface of a steel post. However, by the use of one or more of the elements of visual composition, the original texture of any material can be altered to seem totally different. Painting a rough surface with a single color will give that surface a smoother quality. Scoring a smooth surface with different types of colors or lines will give it a rough character. Thus a soft, smooth material, through the use of intersecting lines and colors, is made into a plaid, a seemingly rough material. Changes in surface form or mass will also influence texture. Thus by changing the dimensionality of concrete's smooth surface we obtain stucco. By adding forms to a flat surface, for example, a pattern of flowers, we change a smooth material into a complex print. Color itself can be used to gain not only an even, smooth, and simple surface but a rough, complex surface by frequent changes. Varying the temperature or value of a color will often change the apparent hardness or softness of a surface.

Scene designers are quite concerned with texture, and most books on scene design devote considerable discussion to both the theory and technique of texture. The director needs to be aware of texture for two reasons: first, because he must adjust his actors to the texture of the scenery; and second, and more importantly, because he must take advantage of the surface texture provided for the actor through costume and makeup.

In summary, texture is the surface quality of a visual component. It influences each visual element and is in turn influenced by other visual elements. Texture has three measurements: hard or soft, rough or smooth, complex or simple.

THE ELEMENTS OF VISUAL COMPOSITION: A SUMMARY

There are six elements of visual composition: line, form, mass, space, color, and texture. These elements correspond to the six dramaturgic elements of language, story, character, exposition, point of view, and action. As with the dramaturgic elements, the visual elements are not mutually exclusive. Each element both supports the remaining elements and is informed by those elements. In the well executed composition, the elements are so interwoven that it is difficult to distinguish one from the other.

VISUAL ELEMENTS AND THE GOALS OF VISUAL COMPOSITION

When the visual elements are used to obtain an aesthetically pleasing visual work, we may say that the art is well composed. A successful visual composition achieves the five goals of composition: unity, balance, emphasis, variety, and rhythm. These goals are almost identical to the compositional goals of drama. Yet because of the differences in visual and dramatic elements, the goals of visual composition vary in makeup and quality.

VISUAL UNITY

As with dramatic unity, visual unity is the sense of singleness of purpose that results from the total composition. Unity may be gained from one, two, or all the visual elements. When several elements contribute toward unity, we have complex unity. Compare Plates Two and Three. Both are well-unified compositions. Note the complexity of Plate Three and the simplicity of Plate Two. While complex unity is more difficult to achieve than simple unity, neither is absolutely preferable.

Unity may be gained through singleness of hue, a condition usually called a monochromatic color harmony. Unity could be obtained through line. Note how in Plate Four the repetition of line provides a unifying force. In the theatre a certain amount of unity is always present in form, since the human form of the actor is the chief formal element of the stage. Because any stage is itself always a fixed space, the theatre always possesses a certain unity of space. Mass and texture are also unifying devices. For instance, most productions of *Oedipus* will have the mass of the chorus as a means of continuing unity. Moreover, treatment of the surface of the clothing of the chorus will provide textural unity. Observe in this regard Plate Five. The other goals of composition will also contribute to unity: rhythm, through pattern; balance, through resolution; emphasis, through organization; and variety, through changing the means of unity.

Since unity is the sense of oneness of a visual composition, the director must be aware of and concerned with every element of the visual theatre. Anything that appears before the eyes of the audience is either contributing to unity or weakening unity by not making a contribution.

VISUAL EMPHASIS

Emphasis is a key contributor to compositional unity. In both the visual and dramatic arts, emphasis is the fixing of points of attention. It may be simple, divided, or diffused. Simple emphasis fixes one point of spectator attention; divided emphasis establishes two or more points of attention, some of which may have secondary or tertiary importance. Diffused emphasis distributes attention equally over the entire composition. Plate Six is a good example of simple emphasis, Plate Seven presents divided emphasis, and Plate Eight is an approach to diffused emphasis. The best example of diffused emphasis is the typical pattern in an oriental rug. Such patterns give us the feeling that emphasis and subordination do exist, but it is difficult to put our finger on where emphasis begins and ends. Two things mitigate frequent use of diffused emphasis in the theatre. First, most dramatic compositions gain their unity through simple or divided emphasis. Second, Western visual taste is not cultivated toward diffused emphasis.

Emphasis may be gained through the use of any or all of the elements of visual composition and through either actual or virtual line. In the latter regard, a special type of virtual line created by the direction in which actors are looking, commonly called *focus*, is frequently used for emphatic purposes.

Literal Line   *Virtual Line*

The line may be of any shape:

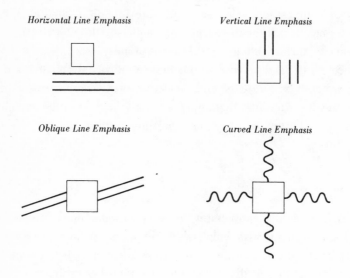

Horizontal Line Emphasis   *Vertical Line Emphasis*

Oblique Line Emphasis   *Curved Line Emphasis*

Vertical and horizontal lines in the theatre must always be considered in terms of the stage floor. Emphasis through horizontal line presupposes that all the lines are the same height or that they are equidistant from the stage floor. Emphasis through vertical line implies differences in line heights or the use of lines that extend unequal distances from the stage floor. Practically speaking, the director must remember that any higher height takes emphasis over a lower height, but where all heights are equal, a horizontal line will take emphasis over a vertical line. Plates Nine, Ten, and Eleven may be profitably studied in regard to use of line in emphasis. Note the use of curved line in Plate Nine. Compare this practice of the use of vertical line in Plate Ten to Plate Eleven's employment of virtual horizontal line or visual focus.

Form also contributes to emphasis. The more regular and precisely outlined a form is, the more emphatic is its statement. The greater the difference between a form and its surroundings, the greater is the emphasis placed on that form. The most common form in the theatre is the human body, and that body has a special relation to emphasis. Since the human body has a front and a back, both these features must be considered in terms of emphasis. All other things being equal, a view of the full-front or full-back of a human body is more emphatic than various angles. Much, however, depends on the type of staging. In the proscenium, five body positions are recognized: full-front, one-quarter, profile, three-quarter, and full-back. These positions are understood in relation to the proscenium arch. All other things being equal, full-front and full-back are most emphatic. One-quarter is next in value, followed by profile. Three-quarter is considered least emphatic. However, if a contrast exists—one actor is three-quarter, and all others are full-front—then the contrasting position is most emphatic.

Body positions in the arena are relative; full-front for one portion of the audience is full-back for another. Here the positions must be understood in relation to fixed units of the set or in relation to other actors. There are really only four arena positions: full-front, full-back, profile, and quarter. Full-front and full-back to another actor or to a fixed unit of scenery are the most emphatic positions, all other things being equal. Profile is the next in emphatic strength; a quarter turn away is least emphatic.

PLATE TWO *A scene from* Oedipus Rex *produced at the University of Washington, Seattle, Washington.*

Director: Vosco Call   Designer: John Ashby Conway   Costumer: James R. Crider

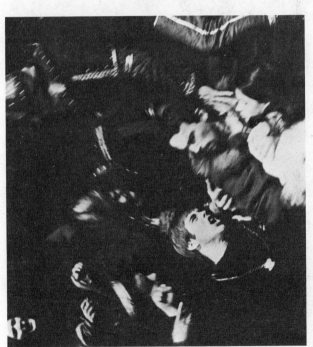

PLATE THREE *A scene from Hamlet produced by the Department of Dramatic Art, University of California, Berkeley, California.*

Director: William I. Oliver

Designer: Henry May

Costumer: Kathleen Buday

115

PLATE FOUR   *A scene from* Oedipus Rex *produced at Cornell University, Ithaca, New York*

Director: Marvin Carlson   Designer: Marvin Carlson   Costumer: Barbara Cox

116

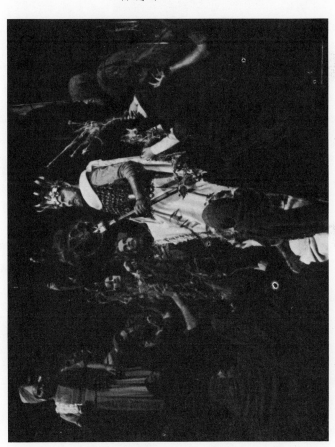

PLATE FIVE *A scene from* Oedipus Rex *produced at Wayne State University, Detroit, Michigan.*

Director: Richard Spear
Designer: Richard Spear
Costumer: Judith Haugan

117

PLATE SIX *A scene from* Oedipus Rex *produced at Miami University, Oxford, Ohio.*

Director: Ronald C. Kein

Designer: Charles Baber

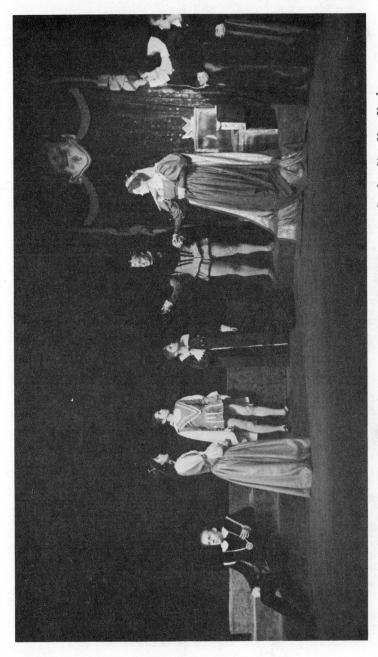

PLATE SEVEN *A scene from Hamlet produced at Adelphi University, Garden City, New York.*
Directors: Mary Lou Plugge and Richard Cleme
Designer: Victor E. Jacoby   Costumer: Victor E. Jacoby

119

PLATE EIGHT *A scene from Hamlet produced at the University of Minnesota, Minneapolis, Minnesota.*
Director: Frank M. Whiting   Designer: Lyle Hendricks   Costumer: Robert Moulton

PLATE NINE *A scene from* The Waltz of the Toreadors *produced at the University of Oregon, Eugene, Oregon.*
Director: Jean V. Cutler   Designer: Ronal M. Reed   Costumer: Peter M. Jamison

121

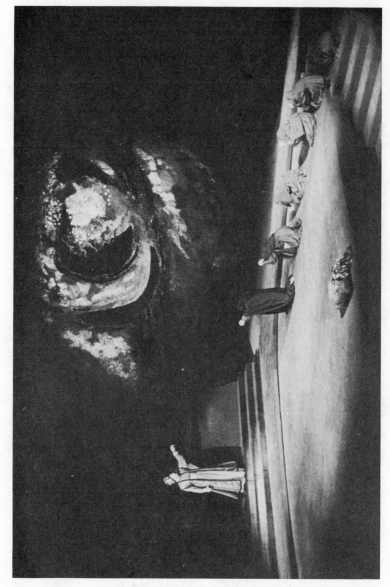

PLATE TEN   *A scene from Oedipus Rex produced at the University of Hawaii, Honolulu, Hawaii.*
Director: Earle Ernst   Designer: Richard Mason   Costumer: Richard Mason

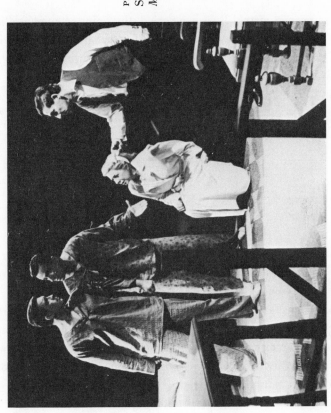

PLATE ELEVEN *A scene from* Death of a Salesman *produced at Tufts University, Medford, Massachusetts.*

Director: Sherwood Collins
Designer: Donald Mullin
Lighting Designer: Frederick Jackson

When several actors are combined in a composition, larger forms and masses also contribute to emphasis. In the proscenium the principal larger form has been identified as the triangle. The actor occupying the focal point of a triangle usually takes emphasis in a proscenium production. Note the following illustrations:

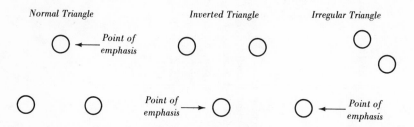

When the normal virtual lines are varied, the point of emphasis in the triangle shifts. This process of shifting the normal direction of virtual line we may call changing focus. Note in the following diagrams how emphasis shifts as focus shifts:

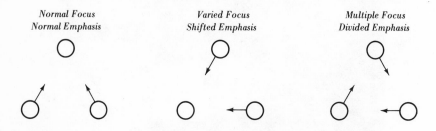

Because of the single angle of audience vision, the triangle is invaluable in proscenium productions, but it has little emphatic value in full-arena staging where the shape of the triangle will vary greatly from spectator to spectator. On the other hand, the circle, having little positive emphatic worth in the proscenium, is the basic emphatic form in the arena. The circle is a somewhat more complex shape whose emphatic potentialities must be sought through the functions of the center, the radii, and the perimeter. Objects on the perimeter of a circle take less emphasis than those on the radii. As points on a radius approach center, they make a concurrent gain in emphasis. Center-circle has strongest emphasis. Consider the following diagrams.

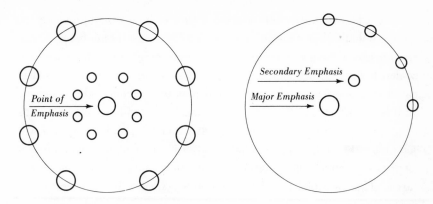

As with the triangle, changes of focus in the circle will produce changes in the normal emphatic pattern. Consider changes of focus and emphasis in the following diagram:

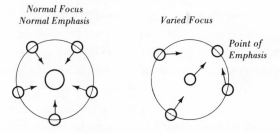

Naturally, the director is not limited to the triangle in proscenium productions and variations of the circle in arena staging, but in all likelihood most forms that tend away from the basic triangle or circle will be more useful to the director in terms of variety than as fundamental visual shapes for an entire production.

Mass also affects emphasis, primarily because anything that possesses mass is more emphatic than something that does not. Additionally, masses of greater volume are more emphatic, as are masses of greater weight and density. Since line and form are implied by mass, masses of certain forms (the triangle in the proscenium, for example) and masses composed of certain lines (those with great vertical height, for instance) will take emphasis over other linear and formal masses.

Color provides additional emphatic values. All other things being equal, a mass of a highly saturated hue will be more emphatic than a mass of a less saturated hue. Masses, forms, or lines of a high value are more emphatic than those of a low value; all other things being equal, elements of a warmer temperature are more emphatic than those of a cooler temperature. Contrast plays a major role in color emphasis patterns. Contrasts in value add emphasis to the contrasting element. In this regard, study Plate Five. Contrasts in hue will also contribute to emphasis. Any hue is a contrast to any other hue, and these hues will set each other off in an emphatic pattern. Particularly conducive to emphasis through color contrast are the combinations of complementaries. Thus a small red line on a green form will give enormous contrast to the line.

Texture is a further source of emphasis. When all other things are equal, rough textures are more emphatic than smooth; hard textures more emphatic than soft; complex texture more emphatic than simple. But if all textures are complex, then a simple texture will be more emphatic; if all textures are rough, a smooth texture will be emphatic. In short, a synonym for any kind of emphasis is contrast.

Assuming that the body of the actor is the basic unit of form in the theatre, the element of space often becomes the most significant means of gaining theatrical emphasis. Since all that is absolutely necessary for theatre is a space and an actor, the simplest means of obtaining emphasis for an actor is to place him in negative space. However, space in the theatre is never entirely negative. Aside from the way in which colored light influences the emphatic value of space, the various kinds of staging distribute emphatic patterns throughout the stage space. In the proscenium, anything close to the audience tends to be more emphatic than that which is farther away. Thus anything downstage is more emphatic than anything upstage, all other factors begin equal. Since the sightlines of the proscenium tend to attract attention to the center of the stage, anything closer to center tends to be more emphatic than that which is farther away from center. On the facing diagram, the nine traditional space areas of the proscenium stage (down-left, down-center, down-right; left, center, right; up-left, up-center, up-right) are indicated in both placement and relative emphatic value.

In arena theatre, the rule of thumb concerning closeness to audience does not hold, since an actor who is close to one segment of the audience is quite distant from another segment. Thus the arena stage space

UR *Not* *Emphatic*	UC *Less* *Emphatic*	UL *Not* *Emphatic*
R *Less* *Emphatic*	C *Emphatic*	L *Less* *Emphatic*
DR *Emphatic*	DC *Most* *Emphatic*	DL *Emphatic*

must be viewed more relatively. Arena space has less intrinsic emphatic value deriving from the form itself and is more dependent on the other visual elements to create emphatic positions. However, the circular form of the arena does provide one more or less fixed position of emphasis, the hub of the circle. All other things being equal, anything that moves away from the hub lessens in emphasis. However, unlike center-stage in the proscenium, the hub of the arena circle can be easily displaced; thus it does not provide nearly as absolute a degree of emphasis. Already remarked is the fact that vertical line in all forms of staging can add emphasis by being increased in length (i.e., height). Also previously noted is the increased vividness of the vertical line in the arena stage. Thus we might say that while in all forms of staging extensions into vertical space will increase emphasis, this condition is most impressive in the arena theatre.

The thrust stage, as a combination of both arena and proscenium, usually offers two equally important areas of spatial emphasis—the center hub of the thrust platform and the center area of the neutral wall. Moreover, the thrust retains much of the vivid emphatic value of vertical space inherent in the arena theatre.

No matter what the type of staging, space has additional emphatic uses. Reduction of space around a line, form, or mass decreases the perceptibility of that mass, line, or form and thus reduces its emphasis. Changes in the positive or negative nature of surrounding space will also affect the emphatic value of a line, form, or mass.

In summary, emphasis may be achieved through a single element or a combination of elements. As with any work in a visual art, the director will have to balance one element against the other to gain the desired emphasis. Specific rules are possible only in terms of individual problems. For example, if *Oedipus* is staged with a large chorus on a small stage space, the director must realize that unless he takes the chorus offstage from time to time, he will never have large amounts of negative space available to him. Moreover, unless he moves his chorus about adroitly or unless he "stores" them always on the sides of the stage, he will not always have available to him such inherently emphatic areas as up-center or down-left. To take another example, if the director accepts a proscenium scene design with a single upstage entrance, his actors will always enter in an emphatic position and tend to move toward more emphatic ones, but by the same token his actors will always move toward and exit from less emphatic space.

As an aesthetic goal, emphasis is not only valuable in itself; it also contributes to unity in that it gives points of organization and importance and tends to make less important elements less apparent and thereby less diverting.

VISUAL BALANCE

In theory, visual balance is a matter of weight and volume. Equal weights of equal volume in an equal space are balanced. In practice, visual balance must also be considered aesthetically and psychologically, that is, in terms of the emotional and aesthetic values of the composition being balanced.

There are several forms of balance. The most elementary type is formal balance, or the equal distribution of weight and volume on both sides of a fixed center. Note the following diagram:

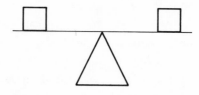

Space plays an especially important role in balance. From our childhood experiences with a seesaw we know that space often influences weight. A small mass, farther from the fulcrum or fixed center, will balance a larger mass closer to the fulcrum. In other words, a smaller mass with more surrounding space will balance a larger mass with less surrounding space. Such a balancing condition is known as asymmetric balance.

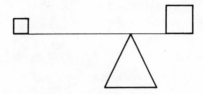

More often than not, aesthetic and psychological factors play a larger role in compositional balance than does simple weight. We know that color value, saturation, and hue will affect the apparent weight of a mass. For instance, a mass of a highly saturated color will seem to have more weight and thus will be able to balance a larger mass of less saturated color or of very high value. A form upon which major emphasis is placed will have great psychological weight and will be able to balance a large but nonemphatic mass. The diagram below demonstrates the influence of color value in aesthetic or psychological balance:

The kinds of balance and the factors influencing them can be employed by the director to gain unity and emphasis for his composition. See, for example, how formal balance gives unity to Plate Twelve. This same plate also demonstrates an emphasis principle of formal balance. The center or fulcrum of a formal balance is normally the point of greatest emphasis.

Asymmetric balance will help the director gain more interesting and complex kinds of unity and emphasis. For instance, put Oedipus in the proper color or surround him with an adequate amount of space and

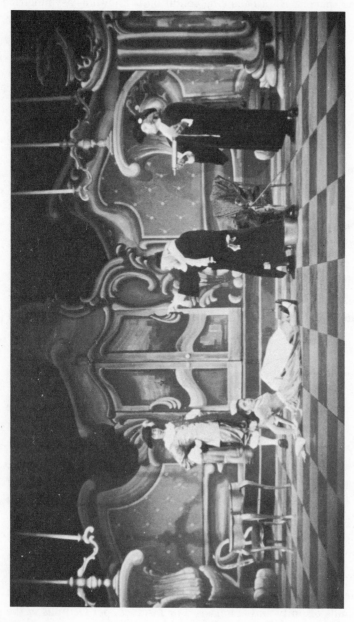

PLATE TWELVE *A scene from* The Imaginary Invalid *produced at the University of Connecticut, Storrs, Connecticut.*

Director: John W. Hallauer   Designer: Jerry Rojo

Lighting Designer: Edward Madden   Costume Designer: Burton Bell

the single character will balance the whole mass of the chorus. By so balancing a larger mass, the single character gains emphasis through contrast. Just such a balance-emphasis pattern is found in Plate Five.

As with space, line plays a special role in balance. Basically, line's primary function is to describe the forms and masses that work in balance, but line has the specific task of pointing out the *force* directions of the major balancing elements. A force direction is the direction in which the weight seems to move. Hence two masses whose lines indicate that both are tending in the same direction may not be balanced, even though their respective weights are identical and are distributed equally from a fixed center. Compare the balance and the imbalance in the following diagrams:

Actually the illustrations above introduce yet another form of balance—dynamic balance. Dynamic balance is more properly referred to as dynamic tension, for it is not a true balance. Dynamic tension's full significance is best discussed in terms of motion or theatre-kinetic, but even in static visual compositions its presence must be recognized. All other forms of balance grow out of *equipoise,* the resolution of motion. Dynamic tension is a balance achieved by moving objects.

Sometimes when masses are in motion they attain a particular arrangement—in space, time, weight, and the factors of motion—that seems to resemble the other forms of balance. Just such a relationship is achieved by the earth and the moon. When our space scientists send up an artificial satellite, if all calculations are accurate that satellite will reach a point in space where dynamic tension or orbit is gained. If the tensions are "perfect," the satellite will remain in orbit forever; if not, the larger mass of the earth will exert enough pull to draw the satellite out of space. At such time the dynamic tension is broken.

The lines of force in the balanced diagram above create a dynamic tension; the lines in the unbalanced diagram do not.

The element of form contributes to all types of balance, particularly psychological balance. To begin with, all completed forms are by definition balanced; when geometric forms are incomplete, an imbalance is present. Organic forms are another matter. Familiar organic forms are treated as balanced by an audience. This is particularly true with familiar organic natural forms. Thus an audience is not likely to question the aesthetic balance of the human body, which is the most familiar organic form in the theatre. Hence a hand is assumed to be balanced. If a finger is missing from that hand, the audience feels that an imbalance exists. Very familiar artificial forms are also reacted to in a similar manner by an audience. Thus a chair with a broken arm will seem unbalanced.

Changes in form will frequently change the virtual weight, volume, or density of mass. The result will be a change in the balance of the composition.

As with form, the element of texture influences the balance of a composition. By changing surface qualities of a mass, texture changes the virtual weight and density of mass. Consequently, two masses of equal volume existing in space at equal distances from a fixed center may not be in balance because of the difference in texture. Such difference may make one mass seem much heavier or more dense than the other mass.

Balance contributes heavily to visual unity because a balanced composition is a work with a strong sense of unity. Balance further aids unity by bringing an organization to the emphatic patterns of the composition. In order to obtain balance, emphatic elements must be supported by subordinate elements.

What unity and emphasis draw from balance they repay in fair measure. The need for unity usually limits the number of factors that have to be balanced in any given visual composition. The presence of emphasized elements in a composition means that the artist has at his disposal one or more centers of real or psychological weight that can serve as major balancing mechanisms.

RHYTHM AND COMPOSITION

Rhythm has been defined as patterned change. Strictly speaking, since visual composition does not occur in time, there is no literal rhythm in composition. Virtual or apparent rhythm does, however, exist. Visual rhythm is the apparent or implied flow of compositional parts one into the other in a recognized pattern. Quite naturally, pattern plays a more important role than does change. Pattern is obtained chiefly through repetition of any or all elements of composition. Note in Plate Thirteen how the repetition of line creates a linear rhythm whose virtual flow is complex but steady. Compare this rhythm to the staccato effect of Plate Ten.

Rhythm may be complex or simple. Complex rhythm makes use of two or more compositional elements as counterpoints. Simple rhythm is developed with a single element. Compare the counterpoint of line and form in Plate Fourteen to the simple rhythm of Plate Fifteen. Complex rhythms are naturally more difficult and more interesting, but satisfactory choice of rhythm depends upon the goals for which the rhythm is composed. Simple rhythm, for example, is an excellent device for creating strong emphasis. Examine Plate Fifteen, noting how the lines themselves and the simple rhythm they create make a powerful emphatic statement. Note also how this simple rhythm is the chief factor in unifying and balancing the composition.

Finally, even in situations where complex rhythms might be more suitable, the director may select simple rhythm to obtain the final goal of composition—variety.

VARIETY AND COMPOSITION

Variety is the difference that adds interest. Any compositional pattern, no matter how pleasing, can become dull if repeated too frequently. The director as visual artist is always seeking new ways to make old visual statements. Consequently, much of our discussion of the other goals of composition has really been a discussion of variety. But the director must be cautious; variety may be an all-pervading goal of composition, but it is not the only goal. Visual statements strong in variety but weak in unity, emphasis, rhythm, and balance are poor compositions.

Variety means variations simultaneously in the elements and in the goals of composition. Variety in the elements of composition suggests that the director should seek to change, fairly constantly, his use of line, form, and texture; his employment of positive and negative space; his interplay of value, saturation, hue, and temperature; and his

PLATE THIRTEEN *A scene from* Oedipus at Thebes *produced at the University of North Carolina, Chapel Hill, North Carolina.*

Director: Kai Jurgenson   Designer: Tommy Rezzuto   Lighting Designer: Bill Hannah
Costumer: Irene Smart Rains   Makeup Designer: Robert Thornburg

PLATE FOURTEEN *A scene from The Waltz of the Toreadors produced at the University of Saskatchewan, Saskatoon, Canada.*

Director: Corliss Phillabaum   Desiner: J. H. Bledsoe

PLATE FIFTEEN *A scene from* Death of a Salesman *produced at the University of Hawaii, Honolulu, Hawaii.*

Director: Robert Sellor
Designer: Robert Sellor
Costumer: Frances Ellison

arrangement of weight and dimensionality of mass. Variety in the goals of composition means that a director who tends to achieve unity primarily through line or rhythm should make a concerted effort to obtain unity through form or balance. If the director habitually uses simple rhythm, then he should seek out opportunities to introduce complex rhythm. Again, if the director's visual balance is normally formal, he should experiment with less formal balances. Conversely, asymmetric balance and psychological balance gain strength from occasional departures into formal balance.

The cardinal rule of variety concerns surprise. Whenever the director feels that the audience knows exactly what to expect of his visual composition, he should surprise them with a logical but unexpected variation. It is through this sort of surprise that emphasis is gained most effectively. In fact, a single instance of variety or contrast can create more emphasis than any other method or device.

THE TOTAL COMPOSITION

In the total composition there are no separate elements. Means become goals and goals become means to other goals. So long as a composition is aesthetically satisfying, there is no need to determine how and why it succeeds. An understanding of the compositional process is necessary, however, if one wishes to remedy an unsatisfactory compositional condition or to enhance the impact of an already strong image.

To write about visual problems is never satisfactory, for words can never express the full implications and complexities of a visual composition. Years of trial and error are necessary for a full understanding of the factors and goals of composition. Even after considerable practical experience, the director will find that each new theatrical situation creates problems of visual relationships that he had never anticipated. Acceptable solutions to such problems are the result of the director's understanding of and experience with the elements and goals of composition.

DESIGN IN THE THEATRE-VISUAL

If the director's task were only composition, his problems would be difficult enough; but the director must design as well as compose. We have defined design as the utilitarian function of an art. In terms of the theatre-visual, design means the joining of the play script with the theatrical picture so that both arts simultaneously comment on the human experience. In brief, visual design—or picturization, as it is often called in the theatre—is the emotional and intellectual meaning of composition. The obtaining of such meaning is complicated, first by the limitations enforced by the play script, and second by the difficulty of coordinating both the elements and goals of composition into a single design statement, while at the same time retaining beauty of composition.

THE GOALS OF VISUAL DESIGN

Design in the visual theatre, particularly as it concerns the director, has three goals: (1) coordination of the visual and dramaturgic elements, (2) coordination of visual and dramaturgic composition, and (3) coordination of visual and dramatic theme.

On the most basic level, the first goal of visual design begins with story line. The visual theatre must reveal the time, place, locale, and some of the expository facts of the play script. Some of this is accomplished in scenery, lights, makeup, and costume. The remainder must be done through the actors. A visual concomitant of language must also be created. Character, viewpoint, and action will also need a visual display.

The second goal of visual design entails the seeking of visual unity which reflects the dramatic unity, the establishment of visual emphasis on those things in the play to which the dramatist has given emphasis, the construction of balance based upon the proportional organization of the play script, the creation of rhythm patterns that sustain the dramatic rhythm, and the use of visual variety to add interest not only to the visual theatre but to the auditory theatre as well.

The third goal of design means that whatever comment is made in the visual theatre it must either clarify the statements of the play script or enlarge and enrich those statements.

To achieve the goals of visual design, the director must understand his script. The exhaustive analysis necessary to such an understanding will be discussed in Chapter 9. In addition to an understanding of the play script, the director should know the design capabilities of the visual theatre. An examination of such capabilities will form the remainder of this chapter.

VISUAL DESIGN AND THE ELEMENT OF LINE

When line is understood as an intellectual or emotional factor, a number of meanings are traditionally assigned to each type of line. These meanings vary according to social customs and according to line's relation to other visual factors. But when all other things are equal, the director can assume that the average audience will attach the following values to the various types of line. A straight line, whether vertical, oblique, or horizontal, implies simplicity, honesty, willfulness, singleness of purpose, and courage. A curved line suggests complexity, sophistication, craftiness, lack of purpose, and fear. A vertical line creates an impression of strength, power, vigor, austerity, conservation, and triumph. A horizontal line usually means repose, serenity, loss of will, and acceptance of fate. An oblique line suggests complexity, indirection, and craftiness. As the oblique line approaches the vertical it acquires the vertical's characteristics.

Various combinations of lines add depth and breadth to linear design. Thus a curved, vertical line would suggest both strength and confusion, or power and sophistication. On the other hand, a curved horizontal line would not be as serene as a straight horizontal. Moreover, lines may be varied within themselves. Thus a vertical line might begin as a straight line and conclude as a curve. This condition would imply that the line is strong but getting weaker. Conversely, a vertical line that began as a curve and finished as a straight line would mean that an initial weakness is being resolved in strength.

With reference to the theatre, the basic meanings of line can be seen in the following examples. Study Plate Six. Notice how the vertical line of the emphatic figure makes a comment on his strength and vigor. Compare this plate to Plate Ten. Observe how the horizontal lines of the subordinate figures tell us about their weakness and complexity.

Line comments not only on character as in the plates cited above, but on any aspect of play. Thus in *From Morn to Midnight* many proscenium directors will make frequent use of oblique line. Such line tells us that the viewpoint is not straightforward but is rather that of the subjective vision of the Cashier. To take another example, if in the scene in *Invalid* when Argan introduces his daughter to the young doctor, Argan's basic line is curved while that of his daughter is straight, we not only observe a conflict but have a good idea of how that conflict will be resolved.

VISUAL DESIGN AND THE ELEMENT OF FORM

Since line and form are mutually dependent, all the meanings of line are also implied in the form described by that line. Further meanings also accrue to form. The basic theatrical form is human, and its most elemental meaning is itself. This obvious fact is important, because the presence of a human carries with it all the profound and complex meanings of humanity. As with the human form, any natural form in the theatre means itself. Thus a chicken means a chicken, a lion a lion. And a human costumed as a lion also means a lion, but with implied human characteristics. Quite obviously, the most important function of the human form in the theatre is the comment it makes on the manners and motive patterns of characters.

Human forms belong to the category of organic forms. In the theatre, organic forms carry the meaning of their function. Thus an organically shaped group of people would mean disorder, a crowd. The presence or suggestion of a tree on stage would mean an outdoor locale. Many organic forms are artificial. Thus a kidney-shaped table would carry the meaning of a locale that was modern, perhaps ultramodern. A pistol would imply danger.

Some artificial forms are geometric. As opposed to organic forms, geometric forms suggest order, composure, simplicity, and strength. Circular geometric forms are more sophisticated, complex, and less strong than rectangular forms. A triangle lies between the circle and the rectangle. It is more complex than the rectangle and stronger than the circle.

As with line, combinations of forms will increase depth of meaning. Thus a rectangle with one semicircular leg creates an impression of overall strength with an underlying complexity. A pistol used as a makeshift hammer combines danger with domestic architecture.

Finally, we have already noted how a human costumed as a lion would combine the meaning of both the animal and the human. We might observe in this regard that costume has an enormous effect upon basic human form. Note how in Plate Sixteen the costume of the chorus, a single, loose robe, makes the form more curved, while the costume of Oedipus increases his vertical quality.

While the actor through his form comments particularly on manners and motives of the character he is playing, form in the visual theatre is not restricted to statements of character. Let us take an example of form as an aid to exposition. In the opening scene in *Hamlet*, the soldier on the battlement—by his clothes, his weapons, by the artificially military and probably geometric manner in which he stands or moves—tells us, even before a word is spoken, that we are at a guarded outpost in a different time and place than the present.

VISUAL DESIGN AND THE ELEMENT OF MASS

Since mass involves both line and form, the meanings of both will also be included in the comments made by mass. Mass, however, brings additional design implications. In the first place, mass has weight. All other things being equal, weight means that strength increases as weight increases; but as weight increases, mobility (the power to stop, start, or change direction) decreases. When volume is added, mass gains complexity. The amount of complexity gained depends upon the form the volume takes. No matter what the form, high-volume, heavy masses are stronger and less mobile than low-volume, light masses. The less complex the form of the volume, the stronger and more mobile the mass. Heavy, large, and simple masses suggest austerity. Masses that are light and have complexity in the shape of their volume suggest sophistication. Compression and expansion contribute additional meanings. Compressed masses are simple, powerful, honest, and strong-willed; expanded masses are complex, weak, difficult to understand, and uncertain as to purpose.

In the theatre, mass is most obvious and impressive in groups or crowds of actors. When considering groups of actors, some implications of the meanings discussed above come immediately to mind. A compact, large crowd distributed in a triangular volume would, at least

PLATE SIXTEEN   *A scene from Oedipus Rex produced at Louisiana State University, New Orleans, Louisiana.*

Director: August W. Staub
Costumer: James M. Ragland
Designer: W. Patrick Harrigan
Lighting: George A. Wood

in the proscenium theatre, imply strength, purpose, power, control, and mobility. A lesser number of actors, distributed randomly in an organically shaped volume, would suggest disorder, lack of direction, and weakness. But a single actor can be considered also as a formal mass. Thus the actor who is standing rigidly at attention is compact, strong, and purposeful, while an actor who leans, arms akimbo, against a mantlepiece is less strong, less purposeful, because his volume is less uniform and his density is less compressed.

While mass may be combined with any element of dramaturgy, it is particularly valuable in revealing the nature of action. Let us take as an example the scene in *Hamlet* when Claudius informs Hamlet that he must go to England. In order to demonstrate who will win this particular conflict, the director might have Claudius flanked by two soldiers as he talks to Hamlet. The Prince could be located below Claudius with one foot on a slightly higher platform. The design of the masses would make a clear comment on the nature of the conflict and the resolution of the crisis. Hamlet's smaller, less-compressed mass would indicate his basic complexity as well as his weakness in facing Claudius. The King's larger mass, increased in weight and volume by the flanking soldiers, would comment on his position of strength and firmness of purpose.

DESIGN AND THE ELEMENT OF COLOR

Color, by being applied to the other elements of visual art, will change both their compositional effect and their thematic meaning. Color has no inherent intellectual meaning, but all societies have assigned meanings to color, and ours is no exception. These meanings are vague, general, and subject to change through the influence of time or local sociological customs, but their general implications may be used by the director.

Color hue has the vaguest of meanings, but we may say, with many reservations, that red often implies courage, boldness, power, and dash. Yellow suggests gaiety, youth, simplicity, innocence. Blue is often taken to mean quietness, resignation, sadness, firmness, serenity. The secondary colors—orange, green, and violet—are combinations of the primaries and take on a complexity of meanings according to the amount of primaries in the mixture. Thus a blue-green is more serene, less joyful than a yellow-green. White and black also have traditional meanings in our society. White usually suggests purity; black implies sorrow and death. Restrictions of color to white and black usually create an impression of simplicity, austerity, strength, while the addition of hues adds complexity, brightness, and liberality to the visual design.

Hue is greatly affected in meaning by color value. Hues of a high value are gayer but weaker; hues of a lower value are more somber and stronger. Saturation also has an effect upon color meaning. Highly saturated colors carry an impression of strength and boldness, less-saturated colors an impression of vagueness and loss of direction. Finally, temperature also has its implications. Warm colors indicate assurance, friendliness, and a generally outgoing quality, whereas cool colors convey reticence, fear, and a generally withdrawn quality.

Combinations of all sorts are possible. Oedipus may wear a generally cool costume (to demonstrate his exalted and withdrawn state as a king), trimmed in warm colors (to indicate his assurance). The basic costume may be highly saturated (to indicate his courage), and the trim may be red (to indicate his boldness). Hamlet is traditionally costumed in black or low-value blue, but accents of a highly saturated warm color might be sparingly used in order to give variety to the costume and also to suggest his capability for warmth toward his friends.

DESIGN AND THE ELEMENT OF SPACE

Space pervades all of visual art, as language does all of literary art. Thus when we talk about form, we are really talking about a certain amount of captured space in two dimensions; when we talk about mass, we are talking about captured space in three dimensions. When we discuss color, we are talking about colored space. Hence everything said so far can apply to space. But aside from mass, line, color, and form, we may discuss space as positive and negative, and the meanings therein. Negative space gives an impression that is at once open, airy, simple, and lonely. Positive space suggests friendship, tightness, and complexity.

Space also has important relationships to the concepts of strong and weak, dominant and subordinate, which will be discussed later in this chapter. Space is not only influenced in meaning by line, form, color, and mass, but also given meaning through the final element: texture.

DESIGN AND THE ELEMENT OF TEXTURE

As surface quality, texture changes the meaning of all visual elements. Texture may be rough or smooth. All other factors excluded, rough texture implies ruggedness and complexity; smooth texture suggests simplicity, polished sophistication. Texture is also hard or soft. Aside from the obvious implications of hard and soft, the two may mean power and purpose on the one hand, weakness and indecision on the other. Complex or simple are the third qualities of texture. Complex textures indicate sophistication, gaiety; simple textures indicate reservation, austerity.

Since as far as the director is concerned texture comes chiefly through costume, he probably will view texture principally as a means of stating manners and motive patterns. However, by playing the texture of one costume against the texture of others, he can increase its design value. Thus by dressing the Cashier in *From Morn to Midnight* in a soft, smooth, simple texture and by having all adversaries in hard, rough, complex textures, the director could heighten the sense of loneliness and isolation, make vivid the subjective viewpoint, and sharpen the basic conflict of the Cashier with all of society.

DESIGN AND THE VISUAL ELEMENTS

By understanding the intrinsic intellectual and emotional values of each of the elements of visual art, the director can increase his design capability and meet the first goal of design in the visual theatre—the coordination of visual and dramaturgic elements. Since the elements of visual art are mutually interacting, directors can gain enormous depth, breadth, and complexity by combining meanings inherent in the various elements. Finally, by understanding the design implications of the visual elements, the director is aided in his second design goal—the uniting of the compositions of visual and auditory theatre. To do this, the director must consider each of the compositional goals of visual theatre in light of the comparable literary goals.

VISUAL DESIGN: UNITY

Visual unity may be simple (gained through one or two elements) or complex (gained through most or all elements). In terms of composition, neither is more acceptable; but design will always force a choice. What that choice is depends upon the play script as understood by the director. For example, unity in *Waltz of the Toreadors* is simple: St. Pé is the major and almost exclusive unifying device. Consequently, the visual design of unity should also be simple. A highly complex visual pattern which sought unity now through line, now through form, now through color would endanger the unity of the script and the cooperating unities of the visual and literary theatres. Of course, in settling on a simple unity, the director is helped by the presence of St. Pé's actual form on stage almost all the time. He will probably want to extend this unity of form by seeking unity of color in costumes and scenery. This does not mean that variety will be excluded, but it might imply that St. Pé wear a highly saturated, mid-value hue, while all others wear less saturated colors. The same might be true of scenery. Perhaps the director might call for a single color scheme, with few and very pronounced furnishings and properties.

On the other hand, *Death of a Salesman* has a more complex unity, one that gains its oneness through counterpoint. Willy's viewpoint is counterpointed by an objective one. Past time is counterpointed by present time. Willy is counterpointed by Biff, Biff by Happy and Bernard, and Willy by his brother and his neighbor. In light of this structure, a director might elect a complex visual unity which featured, as did the Broadway production of *Salesman,* a setting composed of many places, locales, and furnishings in one house. He might elect always to have someone else present in another part of the stage, even when Willy is not playing a scene with that person. He might want to obtain unity in costume through the style and cut of the clothing but retain complexity through variety in color and texture.

As a summary to the problem of design unity, we might note how in Plate Seventeen the unity is obtained through simple uses of form and

PLATE SEVENTEEN *A scene from* The Imaginary Invalid *produced at Wayne State University, Detroit, Michigan.*
Director: Robert T. Hazzard
Designer: Judith Haugan
Costumer: Judith Haugan

how in Plate Three the design of actors counterpoints one mass, form, line, and space against other masses, forms, lines, and spaces to obtain a complex unity of design. The one image tells the audience that the scene is simple and direct, the other that highly complex events are transpiring.

VISUAL DESIGN: EMPHASIS

Emphasis adds visual design by seeking out the dominant elements that operate in unity. The problem in emphasis is to discover in the play script those factors which must be emphasized visually. When the factor to be emphasized is isolated, the director as designer must decide whether the emphasis is to be simple, divided, or diffused. Simple emphasis is easily obtained through the use of line, form (including body position), mass, color, space, or texture. If simple unity is desired, then a simple or single emphatic means is probably preferable.

Complex unity or divided or diffused emphatic demands are more difficult. Take, for example, the Salvation Army Hall sequence in *From Morn to Midnight*. There are four factors calling for differing degrees of emphasis. The Cashier should probably take primary emphasis throughout the scene, but the speakers must also be emphasized. Furthermore, there is the crowd who must become more and more emphatic as the scene progresses. Lastly, there is the Salvation Army Lass who takes a strong secondary emphasis throughout. While many of the emphatic problems will be solved through the auditory and kinetic theatres, the theatre-visual has some burdens. Many solutions are possible; let us suggest one. Refer to the setting in Plate Eighteen and assume that that setting is the one on which the scene will be played. On the high platform down-left, the Cashier could be located. On the small platform below the Cashier, the girl could be placed. The speaker's stand might be on the up-center-right platform. The crowd could be principally center- and right-stage. Thus by using stage space, an emphatic pattern is produced. By including variations in light color, costume color, and texture, and by changing the mass, line, and form of the crowd, variety of emphasis could be arranged throughout the scene.

PLATE EIGHTEEN *Set design for the final scene in* From Morn to Midnight.
Designer: Patricia Staub

This emphatic pattern gives meaning to the scene by isolating the Cashier in his lonely space, while at the same time relating him to the crowd through the intermediate position of the Salvation Army Lass. Moreover, like the crowd the Cashier is drawn to face the speakers. Whenever he does so, the virtual line created by his focus might seem to draw him down the ramp and toward the speaker's stand, an action he will eventually undertake. Finally, the visual design of the emphasis pattern also solves the problem of uniting visual balance with dramatic proportion.

VISUAL DESIGN: BALANCE AND PROPORTION

While they are correlates, visual balance and dramatic proportion are not as nearly alike as are visual and dramatic unity and emphasis. Balance is a fixed, single image; proportion is a matter of progression. Hence there is a barrier between the two which is usually bridged by the use of dynamic tension from the kinetic theatre. A discussion of this issue will be found in the following chapter. Suffice it to say for now that a true visual balance at all times in the theatre will give the lie to the living progression of the play script, since what is balanced is fixed and cannot progress. However, there are moments, particularly near the ends of major scenes, or at the beginning and end of a play or act, when the director might desire a balanced visual image. This will depend upon the specific play script. A balanced design might be struck whenever the director feels that some dramaturgic factor— exposition, story, language, viewpoint, or character—has been arrested or permanently halted in its progression. For example, after Oedipus puts out his eyes, the stage picture might be balanced and remain balanced to indicate that the major action of the play is over. Again, when St. Pé seizes his wife around the throat, the director might freeze the image in a balance to indicate that the characters and this part of their story will progress no more. The question of "to balance or not to balance" is followed by the question of what type of balance is needed to make clear the meaning of the play. For instance, is the balance at the end of *Oedipus* a formal balance to indicate that all factors have been neutralized and put at rest and that all is now right in Thebes? Or should the balance be less formal, more asymmetrical or

psychological, to indicate that while things are fine for the time being more trouble can be expected for Oedipus, his family, and his city? The choice is up to the director, as he is guided by his insights both into the play and to the statements he wishes to draw from the play.

Whatever his decision in terms of balance, the director must resolve the proportional problems of the play script either through balance or through distribution of emphasis, for proportion is both a progression and an organization of that progression. When balance is not a good choice for visually reflecting the organization of the factors of dramaturgy, then the director might use secondary or tertiary emphasis. He may also make use of visual rhythm.

VISUAL DESIGN: RHYTHM

While emphasis and balance supply larger visual organization, rhythm sustains the basis of the pattern and provides for nuances of meaning and decoration. Visual rhythm's chief characteristic is repetition of pattern. Any element that is repeated gains a certain emphasis and a certain stability or tendency toward balance. Look at Plate Thirteen. Notice how the whole composition is made up of repetitive lines and forms. Observe how most of the lines and forms are rising (i.e., composed of extended and extending vertical lines). The rising lines converge on the single upright figure. All the strength, power, intensity, forcefulness, and dignity of the rising lines are passed on to the single figure. Although a single mass, he acquires through rhythmic design all the implications of the contributing mass below him.

By using variations of the rhythmic design found in Plate Thirteen, the director can change the shades of implied meaning without altering the unity, balance, or emphatic structure.

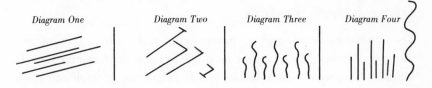

Diagram One   *Diagram Two*   *Diagram Three*   *Diagram Four*

If we assumed that the illustrations above represented Oedipus and the chorus, we might draw the following meanings from the rhythms. (1)

151

The chorus's attitude toward Oedipus is ambivalent. They are subjugated but are rising to offer possible resistance. (2) The chorus resists Oedipus but to no avail. (3) The chorus supports Oedipus but they are too weak-willed to take action. (4) Oedipus still dominates the chorus, but they are stronger-willed than he. Rhythm not only makes its own statements but must be coordinated with the dramatic rhythm at any given moment in the play. As the patterns of dramatic rhythm grow tenser, visual rhythm increases in complexity and repetitiveness of pattern; as dramatic rhythm relaxes, visual rhythm becomes looser in its patterns. Or as dramatic rhythm gathers to a single final tension or crisis, visual rhythm might be reduced from a pattern of masses to a pattern of forms or to a pattern of lines. The space between repetitions might be increased or decreased.

If the dramatic rhythm is complex, the visual rhythm should be complex, using several elements in a pattern of repetition. If the dramatic rhythm is counterpointed, the visual rhythm should be correspondingly counterpointed. For instance, Hamlet has a relation to his mother and a counterpointed relation to Ophelia. Hamlet might be dressed in *black* and accented in *light blue*, his mother might be dressed in *red* and accented in *black*, Ophelia in *light blue* accented in *black*. All those who related to Hamlet through his mother—his uncle, Horatio, Rosencrantz, and Guildenstern—might follow the red–black rhythm; those related through Ophelia—Polonius and Laertes—might follow the light blue–black rhythm. In the play-within-the-play scene, the director might use such color rhythms to reflect the current rhythms of the action as they relate Hamlet to Ophelia and Hamlet to Gertrude. What the director may accomplish through rhythmic nuance depends on his adroit use of variety in design.

VISUAL DESIGN: VARIETY

The purpose of variety in both drama and visual art is to give interest through difference and to gain meaning by change. Anything that is different from what existed before is both interesting in itself and gives meaning through a change in circumstance. We have seen how variety in the use of rhythmic line added meaning to a visual composition. Such meaning can be gained through adding variety to any of the elements of visual art.

The following illustrations reveal how variety of line, form, and texture can change both the emphatic pattern and the meaning of a composition.

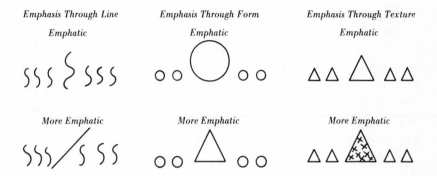

If we look for a meaning in the first pair of illustrations, we might say that every one was initially complex, aimless, sophisticated. With variation, the emphatic line is less complex, less sophisticated, more purposeful. However, in terms of the total composition, a much more complex, even conflicting, situation exists after the variation. In the second pair of illustrations, all figures are stable and content. After variation, the emphatic figure has purpose, drive, and more complexity. In addition, some conflict has been added to the situation. In the third situation, little change has taken place in the complexity of conflict of the total composition, but the emphatic figure has grown in complexity and conflict within itself.

As with the other design goals, the director must turn to the play script in order to discover those moments when variety is most necessary—whether it be variety of unity, emphasis, balance, and rhythm; or variety of line, form, mass, color, space, and texture.

If we return to the illustrations just studied and apply them to a dramatic situation, we can get some insight into the coordination of visual and dramatic variety. In the first illustration we might have the situation of Hamlet with the soldiers just before seeing the Ghost and just after. Before the Ghost's appearance, all are generally uneasy and unhappy. The will to act and a meaning and purpose for acting are not there. They are together but not in conflict. After seeing the Ghost, the soldiers are not affected in their general motives, but Hamlet is now galvanized. He has both the manners and the motive for action. What action is not yet clear to him, hence the oblique line. He is immediately in conflict with the soldiers, who do not want him to follow the Ghost. He overcomes them, and his ability to do so is implied in the opposition of his straight, strong line with their weak, curved lines.

What type of variety and when are decisions the director must make based upon the play script. In the discussion of *Hamlet* above, the variety was a strong, vivid change in line. Perhaps the third pair of illustrations of variety would make a better choice for presenting the scene in *Waltz* when Ghislaine first appears. St. Pé is changed, complexity is added to his internal state; but it is neither a strong change nor one significant enough to produce an external conflict.

Whenever using variety, the director should remember that any change, however slight, in visual design will change the meaning of the total design. Therefore, variety for its own sake is an excellent compositional goal but is a poor design goal. All design variety should be meaningful in the manner the director and playwright intend.

DESIGN AND THE GOALS OF VISUAL AND DRAMATIC COMPOSITION: A SUMMARY

The second purpose of design is to combine and amalgamate the goals of visual and dramatic composition. In this function, the director is different from such visual artists as the painter and the sculptor. While they design their compositions for meaning, those compositions have no burden to refer to another art. On the other hand, no matter how visually pleasing and meaningful his work may be, the director must always design to support and enrich the work of the dramatic author. Consequently, each of the goals of visual art must be coordinated with their counterpart in dramatic art.

VISUAL DESIGN AND DRAMATIC THEME

The final end of visual art in the theatre is the coordination of visual and dramatic theme. The end is not mutually exclusive of the other aims of visual design; hence, much of the discussion of visual design has been in terms of dramatic design or theme. This final section will deal with certain overall problems present at any phase of visual design. Dramatic design grows out of the combination of all elements and goals of dramaturgy, but it rests on the element of action. Action is conflict–crisis–resolution. All other elements, including language, are caught up in this pattern. In such a pattern, three conditions are usually present. (1) There are contrasting forces. (2) Some forces are stronger, some weaker. (3) Some forces are dominant, some subordinate. These three conditions are not always straightforward and simple. In many plays the contrast is not strong. In other plays, the stronger forces do not overcome the weaker. In many plays the dominant forces are not always the stronger forces. In almost all plays, forces frequently exchange strong–weak, dominant–subordinate positions, and the resolutions either eliminate contrast or shift the base of contrast. How these forces or conditions are handled by the playwright will reveal his view of life or his theme. The function of the director as visual designer is to analyze the handling of the conditions of dramatic theme and to so arrange his design that the conditions are made clear and rich visually.

VISUAL DESIGN AND CONTRAST IN DRAMATIC FORCES

The first problem in contrast is to isolate it wherever it might exist. Sharp contrasts are easy, but many subtle contrasts also exist in most plays. Moreover, the subtle contrast may prove to be more significant and important than the obvious and sharp contrast. For instance, there is a sharp contrast between Oedipus and Creon, but there are less sharp but more important ones between Oedipus and Jocasta. The contrast between Oedipus and Creon can be handled visually through color, mass, or line, but how to handle the one between Oedipus and Jocasta? They are alike in as many ways as they are different. Certainly their ages must contrast; but if the director elects to stress this visual element, will he not stretch the credulity of most modern audiences who will wonder why a young man would marry such an old woman? Perhaps physical difference in hair color might be the answer; but they must seem to be of the same family, especially by the end of the story. Some more subtle means must be found to establish such a contrast. Surface texture of costume would be one answer. Another might be vertical line—Oedipus would always be higher than Jocasta. Space

Creeping to CS, Crouching

BERNARDO   Who's there?
FRANCISCO Nay, answer me.   Stand and unfold yourself.

Straightening up —

BERNARDO   Long live the king!   *(still tense)*
FRANCISCO Bernardo?
BERNARDO   He.

Crossing to him

FRANCISCO You come most carefully upon your hour.

Arms about each other, back slapping

BER.   'Tis now struck twelve; get thee to bed, Francisco.
FRANCISCO For this relief much thanks: 'tis bitter cold, And I am sick at heart.
BER.   Have you had quiet guard?
FRANCISCO Not a mouse stirring.

BERNARDO   Well, good night:
If you do meet Horatio and Marcellus,
The rivals of my watch, bid them make haste.

Starting out

FRAN.   I think I hear them.   Stand, ho!   Who is there?

Xing to him entering from R

HOR.   Friends to this ground.
MARCELLUS   And liegemen to the Dane.
FRAN.   Give you good night.
MARCELLUS   O, farewell, honest soldier: Who hath relieved you?
FRANCISCO   Bernardo hath my place;
Give you good night.

Exit ↗

MARCELLUS   Holla, Bernardo!

Props: Spears for Bernardo & Francisco, Battleaxe for Marcellus

PLATE NINETEEN   *A page from a prompt book for a production of Hamlet.*

156

might be another answer—Oedipus would always be alone in space, always separated from Jocasta.

Whatever might be the solution, the director must seek out contrast and present it. Some contrast is so strong that it needs the merest kind of visual base; other contrast is subtle and must be presented with significant visual help. Visual cooperation in terms of contrast is just that—cooperation. Giving the play script too much help is just as detrimental as giving it too little. A subtle contrast can be made coarse and blatant by too much visual help.

Contrast can create compositional problems. While sharp contrast is in itself emphatic both dramatically and visually, it also tends to disrupt unity and cause imbalance. Thus contrast must be worked into the overall visual composition and contained within that composition.

VISUAL DESIGN AND THE PROBLEM OF STRONG AND WEAK

The concept of strong and weak grows directly out of dramatic conflict. If contrast exists and generates conflict, then the agents of conflict are either stronger than their opponents, weaker than their opponents, or somewhere in between. The director must examine the play script with an eye to measuring the relative strengths and weaknesses of all conflicting forces at any moment in the play. Throughout the visual design, this strong and weak relationship must be so presented that at any given moment, if the play were halted, the audience could explain the conflict and the relative positions of all the forces. Presenting strong and weak does not mean presenting good or bad. It is good art for a strong character to appear weak when conditions demand, or for a weak character to appear strong at a certain point in the conflict. All will depend on the wishes of the playwright. Usually forces vary in strengths and weaknesses as story and action develop.

Strong and weak may be revealed through any of the visual elements. Straight lines are strong; curved, weak. Vertical lines are stronger than nonvertical lines. Horizontal lines are weakest. Geometric forms are generally stronger than organic forms; natural forms are usually stronger than artificial forms. Heavier, denser, more-voluminous masses are stronger than lighter, expanded, and less-voluminous ones. Red is usually regarded as the strongest of hues, yellow as the weakest. Higher value colors are weaker than low-value ones. Less-saturated colors are weaker than more-saturated colors. Warm colors are stronger than cool colors. Rough textures are stronger than smooth textures; hard textures stronger than soft; simple textures stronger than complex ones. Positive space is strong space; negative space is weak space.

A special problem exists with theatrical space and with the human body as a visual form. These are the two most common elements of directorial design, and they need consideration in terms of strong and weak. To begin with, while positive stage space is strong, it will naturally weaken a body existing within it. Therefore, most stage space is kept relatively negative unless the intention is to weaken the actor. In this negative space, the actor may assume certain body positions. Of the five proscenium body positions, full-front and full-back are the strongest. One-quarter is strong, profile is neutral, three-quarter is weak. Of the four arena body positions, full-front or full-back to another person is strong, profile is strong or neutral, quarter is weak. No matter what the theatrical form, some body positions tend to change value the longer they are held. This is especially true of full-front and full-back. Perhaps because of the lack of visual variety, or perhaps because the impact is too vivid to last, full-front and full-back will tend to become weaker. In the arena full-front and full-back seem to hold strength longer than in the proscenium, where one-quarter will retain strength a very long time.

The location of a body in theatrical space will greatly influence strength. In both the arena and the proscenium, the farther an actor extends into vertical space the stronger he seems. This is especially true in the arena. Horizontally, the actor in the proscenium is stronger when he is closest to the audience. Therefore downstage areas are stronger than upstage areas. The actor is also strongest when he is at a natural focal point; therefore, center-stage areas are stronger than left or right. In the arena, the hub of the arena is stronger than the radii. The actor gets weaker as he approaches the periphery of the stage. The thrust stage has three points of strength: downstage-center, center-stage, and up-center on the neutral wall. All other areas are equally weak.

As is obvious from the above discussion, natural points of emphasis are points of strength. However, emphasis is not the only manner in which strength is given to a dramatic force. Unity, particularly simple unity, by removing distractions, provides strength. Balance is also a source of strength. Any force located at the fulcrum in a formal balance is a strong force. Any force which through space asymmetrically balances a larger force seems to gain strength thereby. Rhythm provides strength through repetition. Variety provides strength through contrast. In regard to strength and weakness, it might be profitable to review all the illustrations in this chapter with an eye to the strong and weak statements made in each of the compositions.

VISUAL DESIGN AND THE PROBLEM OF DOMINANT AND SUBORDINATE

If contrasting forces and strong–weak relationships were the only thematic problems, the director would have a difficult enough time; but he must also incorporate dominant–subordinate relationships. This immediately complicates some seemingly simple solutions. For instance, the Cashier in *From Morn to Midnight* is in contrast to society; he is weak in relation to society, but his viewpoint dominates most of the play. The director now has the problem: if he gives emphasis to the dominant viewpoint, he will give strength to the Cashier. If he gives strength to the Cashier, the contrast between the Cashier and society is lessened. If he does not give dominance to the viewpoint of the Cashier, then no contrast at all exists between society and the Cashier, at least not in the fashion intended by the playwright. Thus the director must play one element against another. The Cashier's viewpoint may be given dominance through the use of line and form—oblique line and highly distorted, geometric form. At the same time, the Cashier may be weakened by opposing him against huge masses, or by putting him in soft, neutral clothing.

As with strong and weak, dominant-subordinate relationships are constantly changing. A strong person may dominate one scene, a weak character the next. A very significant character such as Hamlet may be momentarily equaled by or dominated by a Rosencrantz. The director must study his script and be careful to give dominance to those to whom it is due at any given moment and relegate to subordinance even the most important character in certain scenes.

A final example might suffice. In the second scene in *Hamlet,* the

King opens with a speech. Hamlet is also on stage. Certain stars of the past have elected to give Hamlet some emphasis and, therefore, dominance from the beginning of the scene. Clearly, however, chief dominance must go to the King. What exactly should a director do?

Any element of dramaturgy may require dominance—a soliloquy, the viewpoint of Willy Loman, the internal struggle of St. Pé, the important message from Corinth, the fact that we are in a Salvation Army Hall. Dominance can be gained from any element or goal of visual art. The same elements that give strength give dominance. Emphasis is the most obvious method; but balance, variety, and rhythm are also excellent means. Any point of balance is also a point of dominance; any repetition will provide dominance, as will any difference in line, form, mass, color, space, or texture.

The problem with dominate–subordinate relationships is that they must be balanced against the need to express both contrast and strong-weak relationships. More frequently than not, a weak factor must be given dominance. Oedipus at the end of the play; Argan, Willy Loman, and the Cashier, throughout their plays; and St. Pé when he confronts his wife are all examples of a weaker character who must be given dominance. At such times the director may have to play one element against another—line against color, space against mass—in order to obtain the coordination of all thematic statements.

STYLE IN THE THEATRE-VISUAL

The special manner in which the artists of the visual theatre—together with the director—use the elements of visual art to reach compositional and design goals may be termed the visual style of a production. This style should be consistent with the style of the auditory theatre as both a reflection and extension of the auditory statement. The visual style should also complement the kinetic style of the production.

THE VISUAL THEATRE: A SUMMARY

The theatre-visual consists of the setting, the lighting, the costumes, the makeup, and the actors. Although the director may have to make decisions in all phases of visual theatre, with the actors as basic form, he directly creates a work of visual art. The aims of visual theatre are composition and design. The elements by which the aims are achieved are line, form, mass, space, color, and texture. These elements are used to obtain the goals of composition—unity, emphasis, balance, rhythm, and variety. Both the goals and the elements are used to gain visual design, which is the use of visual art to make an intellectual and emotional statement. There is a threefold purpose of design in the visual theatre: (1) to unite the visual and dramaturgic elements, (2) to reflect the composition of the play in the composition of the visual theatre, and (3) to unite the thematic or design goals of the playwright and the kinetic artists with those of the visual theatre. In terms of the latter, the director must understand the concepts of contrast of forces, strong–weak relationships, and dominant–subordinate relationships.

CHAPTER 8

the kinetic theatre

The Director and the Principles
of Kinetic Theatre

Just as he does in the theatre-visual, the director composes and designs
in the kinetic theatre. In visual or spatial art the director seeks the
major cooperation of several designers in addition to the actors; in
kinetic art, the actor, the dancer, and the choreographer are the director's major collaborators. Visual art is concerned with the fixed
image in space, literary art with that same image in time. Kinetic art
presents the image simultaneously in space and time, so that it is an
art of space-time. Each art has its distinct factors or elements. Spatial art

162

employs line, form, mass, color, texture, and space itself. Literary art employs exposition, agent, story, action, point of view, and language itself. The elements of kinetic art are body-in-space, direction, rate, energy, control, and movement itself. As with the other arts, the elements of kinesis are not mutually exclusive, for one element builds and shapes another; and just as the element of space pervades all visual art and the element of language all literary art, so the element of movement pervades all kinetic art.

The factors of kinesis are used by the director to compose an aesthetically pleasing pattern of motion and to design an emotionally and intellectually meaningful mobile image.

THE ELEMENT OF MOVEMENT

Motion is any progression that happens simultaneously in space and time. In terms of theatre, motion is any shift in space-time made by a perceivable body. Usually such shifts are accomplished through the mobile body of the human actor. In this regard, the director should keep in mind that any gesture, however tiny, perceived by the audience is motion. Thus the rolling or blinking of an eye may be as important as a run across the stage.

Motion is akin to space in that both elements possess positive and negative qualities. Negative motion is rest, equipoise, or balance. As balance becomes less formal, more asymmetric, or psychological, negative motion becomes more positive. Simple positive motion requires only a mobile body in space, but as other visual and kinetic elements are added—more bodies moving in varying directions at varying rates—motion becomes more charged and positive. As with highly positive space, some negative motion must be present as a base of comparison if highly positive motion is to be perceived at all. Therefore, rest is a necessary part of artistic motion.

As in visual art, motion may be either literal or virtual. Thus while a literal motion is the actual displacement of a body in time and space, a virtual motion is the seeming change, whether the change is actual or not. For example, if the audience sees the beginning and the end of a motion, they will normally react as if the whole motion had been virtually present. Specifically, if Hamlet draws his dagger to stab

Polonius, rushes at him, covers Polonius' body with his own, then draws away as Polonius falls, the audience will accept the pattern as virtual killing. To take another example, if an actor rushes to the lip of the apron and stops suddenly, the audience will react as if his movement continued into their very laps.

Since motion is a function of both space and time, kinetic theatre is limited by the specific spatial dimensions of the stage and the specific playing time of the produced script. In practical terms, such limitations mean that if a mobile body is to be perceived by an audience, there must be sufficient time for the body to move and sufficient space in which it can move. What are sufficient time and space will depend upon the use of the other elements of mobile art.

THE ELEMENT OF BODY-IN-SPACE

The element of body-in-space is shared by both kinetic and visual art; thus, this element unites the two arts. Body may be composed of line, form, mass, or all three combined. Body may be colored or textured. Whenever visual art affects kinetic body, all elements of motion are influenced. For example, a body of dense, weighty mass is more difficult to move from rest to motion and from motion to rest than a light body. Such a body will tend to change direction less easily and with greater loss of energy. But the apparent weight of a body can be changed through color; so that regardless of actual weight, a body colored in high-value yellow will seem much lighter and more intrinsically mobile. The basic body in theatre is the actor, which has the form of the human. It is capable of linear change from straight to curved, from vertical to oblique to horizontal. It may combine different lines in its different parts. The form is capable of internal motion—the movement of its various parts; it is also capable of total motion—the movement of the entire mass at one time.

The body has weight and volume which can be adjusted. It can be combined with other human bodies to make larger masses. The human body has an intrinsic front and rear, or intrinsic direction. It is capable of being adjusted in the rate of its motion. It has its own intrinsic energy and is capable of controlling that energy. In short, the human form is a perfect basis for kinetic art. Other forms are used, particularly in the cinema, but none are as versatile as the human body.

In order for a body to move, there must be space. In the theatre, this space must be perceived as space by an audience. Negative space is always perceived as a potential field for mobility. The perceptibility of motion in positive space depends upon the degree of positiveness and upon the contrast between the positive space and the mobile body. Both visual and kinetic factors may be used to increase such contrast. A change in color between the body and surrounding space, or a change in rate of the body's motion through space, are both examples of means of increasing contrast between a body and surrounding positive space. A major function of makeup is to provide color contrasts between the moving parts of the human face and the positive space of the face itself. The human face is a good example of another aspect of positive space. Familiar positive spaces, such as the human face, are regarded more or less as negative by an audience. But when familiar spaces are treated in an unfamiliar manner—a strange makeup pattern on the face, a weirdly distorted and asymmetrically balanced stage set—they are regarded as positive by an audience, at least until that audience becomes familiar with the new treatment. Until the audience does familiarize itself with the newly positive space, minor movements are not perceived and major movements are lessened in impact.

The element of body-in-space is shared by both the visual and kinetic theatres and introduces all the elements of visual design into the kinetic design. Moreover, since the body-in-space is usually a human or humanlike form, the element extends into the auditory threatre and introduces all the elements of auditory design into the theatre-kinetic.

Movement of a body in theatrical space is related directly to the theatre form. This matter is perhaps best discussed in terms of the third element of kinesis—direction.

THE ELEMENT OF DIRECTION

Any mobile body has direction; that is, it is moving toward one point in space and away from others. Direction is measured by both the total progress of motion (where it begins and where it ends) and the kind and number of changes within the progress. For example, Oedipus may move from Creon at center-stage to the door of his palace. His direction was to the door and away from Creon. In doing so, he may have changed direction by going first to stage-left and then to stage-right.

Endgame by Samuel Beckett. University Theatre, Virginia Polytechnic Institute and State University.

Director: Paul Antonie Distler

Designer: Donald A. Drapeau

In simple, two-actor scenes intensity may be gained by having both actors repeat the same visual element. In this case, both actors are facing the same direction and both are in the same style and quality of costume. Variety is obtained by varying length of vertical line and increasing the mass of the seated actor.

Thus his direction was broken. If the break were curved, we might say that he moved toward the door in a curved motion.

The direction of a mobile body is influenced by its line, form, and mass. For instance, both the lines and the form of the human body tend to give it a forward and a rear direction, and an upward and a downward direction. Other forms have even more pronounced intrinsic direction. A two-dimensional triangle has an extremely strong forward and backward direction but little vertical direction. A three-dimensional triangle has strong intrinsic vertical direction but no horizontal direction. A ball or a square box has no intrinsic direction.

The distribution of weight in a mass may greatly influence its intrinsic direction. Masses in which the weight is concentrated in one spot will tend to move in the direction of weight, all other things being equal. Since weight, line, and form are all influenced by color and texture, we may say that any visual element may influence and shape kinetic direction. Thus a body whose color value is low at the bottom will tend toward falling; one whose value is high at the top will tend toward rising.

As pointed out earlier, the relationship between space and direction of motion must be understood in terms of the type of theatre being used. In any type of theatre, vertical space will provide for vertical direction—thus movement may be up or down, rising or falling, standing and jumping, or sitting, kneeling, and lying down. Horizontal space will vary in value from proscenium to arena. In proscenium space, direction of movement is understood primarily in relation to the audience and to stage center. Movements in the direction of the audience are downstage movements; those away from the audience are upstage. There are also movements toward center and movements away from center. There are movements to stage-right and stage-left that are parallel to the audience; that is, the body moves from up-right to up-left, remaining always in the same plane. There are also movements that are at once toward or away and left or right. There are the diagonal proscenium movements such as moving from up-center to down-right or from up-right to down-left.

Hence the proscenium directions are upstage (away from the audience), downstage (toward the audience), left and right (parallel to the audience), and various diagonals. In the proscenium, curved crosses that are essentially parallel to the audience are usually not perceived by the audience as any variation in direction. Even gentle curves that are up or down or on a diagonal are not usually perceived as curves by a proscenium audience. Consequently, the gently curved movement (i.e., a movement with very slight change in overall direction) is used in the proscenium by actors and directors to adjust body positions and facilitate traffic flow.

In the arena, direction of movement is far more relative. Since the audience surrounds the stage on more than one side, there are no upstage or downstage directions. However, the center of the arena is perceived, though not equally, by all members of the audience so that movements may be toward center or away from center.

The one area of the arena perceived equally by all audience members is the stage floor. Thus a movement can be up or down. Rising and falling movements have greater effect on direction in the arena because of the fixed stage floor and the seemingly unlimited vertical space. Moreover, a rising and falling movement is shared equally by all audience members, whereas a movement toward the center of the arena is always a movement away from some members of the audience and toward others. Other movements in the arena are understood in terms of toward or away from other actors or articles of scenery or furniture. Some directors divide the arena according to compass directions, and some approach it as if it were a clock, so that the actor is told to move south or cross at nine o'clock. Since these directions tend to place a burden on the actor's memory, most directors simply use "up," "down," "to," and "away from" center or some other reference point.

When more than one actor moves, multiple directions are possible. Thus two or more movements may be parallel, appositional (toward the same point from different starting positions or angles), or counter. Counter-movements are known as "countering" or "dressing the stage." In the proscenium, the main function of counter-movement is to keep sightlines clear. That is, when one actor moves, others counter so that they both balance the stage and remain in good sight lines. In the arena, counter-movement is more important as a means of establishing primary direction, and a secondary counter-movement tells the arena audience where the primary movement is *not* going. Moreover, by varying the elements of rate, energy, and control, counter-movement can make even more vivid the direction of the primary motion. A special form of counter-movement is rest—no other movement in any direction. Obviously, the direction of a single, positive movement is made more distinct by having all other movement negative. Finally, the joining of several movements in the same direction will add weight and volume to the moving body and thus tend to aid it in maintaining direction. However, too many movements of too many bodies in the same direction may make the motion too positive to be easily perceived by the audience.

THE ELEMENT OF RATE

Rate is the measure of the velocity of a moving body and has a temporal and a spatial aspect. Spatial rate is the amount of horizontal or vertical space transgressed by a body during the progress of its movement. Obviously, direction will greatly influence spatial rate. Let us suppose that there is a chair and a table placed ten feet apart. If an actor moves directly from the chair to the table so that his movement is exactly ten feet long, then he has moved at the fastest possible spatial rate. His movement is direct and short. If, however, the actor walks around the back of the chair before crossing to the table, his rate is spatially slower, his movement indirect and longer.

Rate is also measured in time. The temporal speed of a movement is the amount of seconds and minutes it takes an actor to transgress horizontal or vertical space. Temporal rate is one of those elements that ties the kinetic art of theatre directly to the temporal art of drama. If we return to our example of a chair and table, we can say that the actor who *runs* between the chair and table is taking a shorter cross than the one who *walks* at a slow and measured pace.

Obviously, spatial and temporal rate are interrelated. In the normal course, a short spatial cross will also be a short temporal cross. But the two measures can be manipulated separately. The use of direction will be important in the separation of temporal and spatial rate. A quick temporal rate, with many changes of direction, will usually produce a longer spatial rate. A slow temporal rate, with no change of direction, will usually produce a short spatial rate. Let us take again our example of the chair and the table. If the actor who went behind the chair before crossing to the table did so at a run, his temporal rate might well have been quicker than the actor who crossed directly to the table. Thus both actors might have reached the table at the same moment, so that both would have the same overall rate.

Current directing terminology for rate is varied and sometimes misleading. Temporal rate is usually described as fast or slow, quick or long. Spatial rate is usually referred to as long or short, direct or indirect. However, all the terms are sometimes used interchangeably.

A final aspect of rate should be noted. As with many other elements of art, rate has both a literal and a virtual dimension. Depending upon other factors, rate may be actually much faster or slower, longer or shorter than it seems. Rate is affected by all the spatial elements of visual art and all the temporal elements of dramatic art. Thus, when an old, fat character in a low-value tweed suit crosses from a chair to a table, he may seem to take more time than a young, slender character in a high-value yellow dress. The psychological implications of the play, as well as the mass, color, and texture of the moving body in each case, change the virtual rate of movement.

THE ELEMENT OF ENERGY

The initiation or cessation of motion, the maintenance or change of direction, and the increase or decrease of rate all require energy. Energy may be defined as the force necessary to sustain motion. Since the human body is the basic moving unit of kinetic theatre, theatrical energy is measured in terms of that body. A human body moves by a process of contraction and release; that is, energy is compressed through the muscles and then released. Thus energy as a kinetic element is either concentrated energy or released energy. Two more inclusive terms might be *potential energy* and *expended energy*. Potential energy is measured in terms of the force necessary to execute one or more anticipated movements. Expended energy is measured in terms of the force released in initiating, maintaining, or completing one or more motions. At any given moment a body can be described in regard to the relation between its potential energy and its expended energy.

By its very presence, the human body has considerable potential energy. Other bodies—an empty boat, for instance—have little or no potential energy. But place a man with oars inside the boat and it has obtained the potential energy of the man. This example illustrates a principle of energy in kinetic art: Energy is transferable from one body to another and from one portion of a form or mass to another portion of that same form or mass. Thus an actor can transfer energy from his arm to his head, or he can transfer his own energy to another actor. For example, when one actor hits another actor, the energy involved in the punch is transferred from the assaulter to the assaulted. Most forms have a logical physical place where potential energy is conserved and other places where energy is expended. In the human body, the center of potential energy is the central trunk of the body. Energy is normally expended through the extremities—arms, legs, hands, feet, and head.

When kinetic art is considered alone, sources of energy are derived directly from the potential of the body. Thus natural bodies have the energy normally granted to such bodies. An average actor would have the energy normally attributed to an average male; an actress the energy an audience normally attributes to the average female. A lion would have the energy normally granted such a large wild beast. The energy value of artificial forms, whether organic or geometric, would depend upon a number of other factors including the audience's past experience with such forms. In general, organic natural forms seem to possess more inherent energy than geometric forms, but most geometric forms have more energy than artificial organic forms.

In the theatre, kinetic art is combined with both visual and dramatic art, so that the sources of potential energy are greatly increased. In terms of visual elements, straight lines have more potential energy than curved lines; vertical and oblique lines more potential energy than horizontal lines. We previously discussed the effect of form on potential energy. Mass adds additional values. Compressed masses have more potential energy than expanded masses; heavier masses more potential than lighter masses. Masses of large volume have greater energy than those of lesser volume. In regard to color, red and orange hues have more potential energy than blue, green, and yellow hues. White is a stronger source of energy than black, so that higher color values have more potential energy than lower ones. More-saturated colors are more energetic than less-saturated colors; warm colors more energetic than cool colors. Positive space has more potential energy than negative

365 Days from the book by Ron Glasser. Shevlin Hall Arena Theatre, University of Minnesota.

Director: H. Wesley Balk

Note how all the energy of surrounding actors is pressed into the central figure and released through his mouth. Note also the fact that visual composition in the arena is based upon the hub, radii, and circumference of the circular form.

172

space, but negative space makes the bodies occupying it seem to have more energy than bodies occupying positive space. Rough, hard, and complex textures have more energy than smooth, soft, or simple textures.

The play script provides other sources of energy. Through exposition, the script will tell us where to look for sources of energy. If we are told that a certain knife has the magical power or energy to fly through the air, then within limits we usually grant that source of energy to an apparently inert object. Through character, a kinetic body obtains other sources of energy. Claudius has more potential energy than Polonius because he is younger than Polonius. However, Claudius has more potential energy than Horatio not because he is younger but because he is a king, and the fact of kingship gives him a source of great potential energy. Linguistic style may also provide a source of energy. Language that is strong and concise in image and syntax may impart that strength and concision to the speaker in terms of energy. Time, place, and incident also generate potential energy. Note how the opening scene of *Hamlet*, at night on a lonely battlement, with the imminent appearance of a ghost, generates a considerable amount of potential energy. This scene is also a good example of action as a source of potential energy. Any dramatic crisis will impart the energy of that crisis directly to the participants in the crisis. Finally, even point of view becomes a source of energy. By selecting a subjective point of view, the playwright can increase the energy of certain characters. A good example of this is *Death of a Salesman*. When we compare the potential energy of Willy during his subjective visions to that of Willy portrayed in third-person objective, we see how much more forceful is the subjective viewpoint.

Point of view brings up yet another aspect of energy. Energy is both an internal and an external quality; that is, there is both physical and psychic energy. In the physical art of the theatre, psychic energy must find some physical outlet, be it motion or sound. Hamlet, for instance, has the normal physical energy of any man his age. He will have the further physical energy of the actor who portrays him in weight and volume. But Hamlet has more than usual psychic energy—created by the death of his father and the hasty marriage of his mother. This potential internal energy must be revealed. Shakespeare does so in a number of ways, but one of his chief methods is transferring interior energy into the special speech form known as the soliloquy.

Potential energy is conserved by rest and controlled movement and expended by moving and speaking (speaking being, after all, a highly specialized type of motion). Literary, visual, and kinetic factors all influence the expending of energy. To begin with, all positive movement requires the expense of energy. Some special states of rest require an expense of energy: for example, if a character wishes to remain seated and to do so involves resisting persuasion of other characters. In addition to mobility, the expense of energy is influenced by the original direction of the motion and by the number and kinds of changes of direction. Every change of direction involves expense of energy. Complete reversals of direction usually involve enormous expense of energy. Rate of movement is also important. High speeds in either time or space require more energy than slow speeds. Finally, energy influences itself. Frequently, bodies with high energy reserve will simply expend more energy because that energy is available. In this regard, much depends on the factor of kinetic control. On the other hand, some bodies, especially extremely heavy bodies with little potential energy, will require more energy to move than bodies with greater energy reserves.

Visual elements also influence the expending of energy. For instance, a curved line expends more energy in motion than does a straight line. Form plays a major role. A ball moves with more ease than a box; a man moves with more ease on his legs than on his hands and knees. Mass is particularly important. The heavier a mass, all other factors being equal, the more energy is required to move that mass. Moreover, mass moves with the least expense of energy in the direction in which its weight is concentrated. Thus human weight being concentrated in the center and lower parts of the body, it is less expensive in terms of energy for an actor to go down stairs than up; less expensive to sit, kneel, or fall than it is to rise. Finally, it takes less energy to move the arms and legs toward the center of the body than away from the center of the body.

The volume of mass is yet another factor. High-volume masses require more energy to move than low-volume masses. So, too, with density: Dense masses require more energy for motion than expanded masses. By their effect on the apparent weight of mass, color and texture also influence the paying-out of energy.

Space is the final visual element affecting energy. Movement through any type of negative space requires less energy than motion through positive space. The more positive the space, the more energy is required to move through that space. For example, if Oedipus were to cross from stage-left to stage-right, the cross would require less energy if Oedipus did not have to move through the mass of the chorus. If, however, at the same time that Oedipus made the cross the stage lighting changed from a tint to a highly saturated green, it would take more apparent energy to move through that space.

Dramaturgic elements also affect the expending of energy. In terms of language, it obviously takes more energy to give a long speech than a short one. But length alone is not the only concern. Volume, pitch, rate, and phrasing of a speech will also influence energy expenditures. More energy could be expended in one or two high-pitched shouts than in a whole paragraph said slowly and quietly. Consider in this regard how much more energy is expended during the speech in which Claudius prays than in his speech at the opening of Act I, Scene 2. Yet both speeches are about the same length.

Perhaps the greatest expense of energy caused by literary influence is energy expended in conflict—whether that conflict be internal or external, whether it be between character and character, character and story, character and viewpoint, or manners and motives. Notice the extreme expense of energy involved whenever Willy and Biff confront each other, whenever Hamlet and Claudius are together on the stage, and whenever General St. Pé remembers himself as Lieutenant St. Pé. What energy is expended in conflict is sometimes recouped in crisis, but this recovery is often only temporary. For the resolution of crisis many times drains all the energy reserves from one force and redistributes those reserves among other forces. For instance, relations between Oedipus and Jocasta are finally brought to a head in the scene in which Jocasta begs Oedipus not to send for the shepherd. As the scene comes to a crisis, both characters gain in potential energy, but when Oedipus resolves the crisis by refusing her request, Jocasta flees the stage, her potential energy depleted. What energy remains from the crisis is passed on to Oedipus.

The progression of incidents in a story, the shift in time and place, and even the relating of exposition, make energy drains on agents involved in the drama. A shift in point of view might make an energy drain. For instance, we have already observed how Willy Loman gained in potential energy whenever the viewpoint shifted into his own subjective vision. By the same token, whenever the point of view returned to third-person objective, Willy Loman lost potential energy.

When all potential energy is expended from a body, that body is no longer capable of positive motion. For instance, the dying Hamlet is not able to move; Oedipus with his eyes destroyed is barely capable of motion. These two examples occur at the ends of plays. However, *Death of a Salesman* offers an excellent example of total energy drain at the end of the washroom scene. When Willy has relived his memory of Biff, the woman, and the hotel room, he is completely void of energy. He is discovered sobbing on the floor of the washroom and is helped off by a waiter. Then Miller tells us that Willy is in bed resting. From the rest he recovers a little energy, but it is barely enough to take him through the play.

New potential energy can be recovered from exposition or story line, as in the example above. It can, however, be obtained from any of the elements of visual, kinetic, or dramaturgic art. For example, a costume or lighting change from a cool to a warm color may add energy. An increase in mass can provide energy—Horatio's clapping a hand on Hamlet's shoulder as the Prince confronts the King after the killing of Polonius will add to Hamlet's mass and his energy potential. A movement from sitting to standing, while it costs energy, may repay the investment by the potential energy gained from an increase in height or vertical line. The placing of visual emphasis on a body will often tend to increase that body's potential energy. If the body moves in a certain direction—for instance, if Willy moves from stage-left to center-stage—it will gain in potential energy from the strength of stage space; if Willy turns his body from three-quarter to full-front, he will obtain potential energy from the new formal arrangement.

At any point in the progression of a play, new sources of potential energy are available. After Oedipus tells Jocasta about how he killed a stranger on the road, the fact that they both have terrible fears that that stranger was Laius leaves them both depleted of energy. But the messenger from Corinth with the news of the king's death—a man Oedipus believes to be his father—raises new potential energy in both Oedipus and Jocasta. A sudden exposition, a shift in point of view, a change in direction of movement, or a crisis can all provide new energy as well as call for expenditure of energy.

To sum up, the pattern of conservation and expenditure of energy provides the basis for motion in kinetic art. This pattern is influenced in the theatre by kinetic, visual, and dramaturgic elements. It is, however, essentially shaped by the sixth element of kinetic art—control. control.

THE ELEMENT OF CONTROL

Control in kinetic art is directly wedded to character in dramatic art. That is, a character is the way he is because of what he must do (his manners) and what he wishes to do (his motives). A body moves because it must move (involuntary control) and because it wishes to move (voluntary control). In the finished theatrical product, the manners and motives of character invoke voluntary and involuntary control of motion. *Control*, then, may be defined as the regulation of movement in terms of body, space, direction, rate, and energy either through the desires of the body executing movement or through external, involuntary forces. Control is a kinetic element that unites the auditory and kinetic theatres.

Let us take an example of voluntary control. Hamlet sees the King at his prayers. He draws his sword and prepares to kill the King. His motives not to kill intervene. Hamlet halts his motion toward the King, reverses direction, moves away at a different rate, and returns his sword to its sheath. The changes of direction, quality of motion, and rate of motion were all caused by voluntary control. On the other hand, if in his motion toward the King, Hamlet's way had been blocked by a steep staircase, then part of the change in motion and direction would have resulted from involuntary control.

A clearer example of involuntary control might be found in the scene in *Oedipus* where the old shepherd reveals his dreadful secret. In that scene the shepherd might attempt to run away. The running would be the result of voluntary control. If, as he attempted to escape, the chorus caught the shepherd and forced him to return to the king, the change in direction would be the result of involuntary control.

Most movement is a mixture of voluntary and involuntary control. For instance, although Hamlet wishes to kill, he does not wish to kill Polonius. However, his manners as a young prince in danger prompt him to initiate and continue the direction of his motion no matter who is the recipient of his deadly thrust.

Just as with the other elements of kinesis, control is affected by all the factors of visual, dramatic, and kinetic art. A heavy body moving in a downward direction along a raked platform may have voluntarily initiated the motion, but once started the motion is maintained involuntarily. Moreover, the rate of downward motion will increase involuntarily unless control is exercised on rate. So, too, that same body meeting another body at the foot of the ramp will bump into the second body unless voluntary control is exercised to change direction or unless motion is initiated in the second body. Visual and kinetic art elements have the greatest influence in involuntary control; dramatic art, by providing human motives, has the greatest influence in voluntary control.

Control's most important impact is not in change of motion, rate, or direction but in the establishment of energy patterns. All things being equal, any exercise of voluntary control will expend greater energy than the exercise of involuntary control. In some circumstances involuntary control will expend no energy at all. For instance, when a man is pushed or carried from one location to another, he loses none of his own energy in accomplishing the motion. In special conditions the exercise of voluntary control will save energy. If a man capable of walking fast deliberately walks slowly, the control exercised on rate actually conserves his energy. However, if the walk is abnormally slow—if the man, for instance, is walking extremely slowly down a steep ramp—then the voluntary control of energy is also causing an expense of energy. In short, it takes energy to control energy.

THE ELEMENTS OF KINETIC ART: A SUMMARY

There are six elements of kinetic art: body-in-space, motion, rate, direction, energy, and control. Body-in-space unites kinetic art directly to visual art; temporal rate, energy, and control unite kinetic art directly to the time art of literature. None of the elements of mobile art are mutually exclusive. In the completed product all participate in a single union. The elements of kinesis are used by the director to obtain an aesthetically pleasing mobile composition. In order to provide aesthetic pleasure in kinetic composition, the director must realize five compositional goals: sequence or integrity of motion, emphasis, dynamic tension, rhythm, and variety.

KINETIC COMPOSITION: SEQUENCE OR INTEGRITY OF MOTION

Sequence is the counterpart of visual and dramatic unity. But while unity in visual and literary arts can be judged in terms of the finished product, kinetic art is never a complete form. Kinetic art is a process. When the process is finished, the art is not complete; it is merely done. Thus kinetic art must be understood in terms of its process. Consequently, kinesis gives pleasure not through unity but through a sense of mobile integrity or sequence. When kinesis has integrity there is an experience of logical flow of movements one into another, an impression that every past movement has contributed to the present movement in an inevitable sequence.

There are three principles upon which integrity of motion is built: (1) the tendency of bodies to maintain their state of motion, (2) the tendency of bodies to attract other bodies, and (3) the tendency of vacuums to draw matter.

Concerning the first principle, we can elaborate by saying that a body in motion will tend to stay in motion unless acted upon by another force. Conversely, a body at rest will tend to stay at rest unless acted upon by another force. Moreover, a body in motion will tend to retain the same speed, direction, expenditure of energy, and exercise of control unless acted upon by another force.

Thus an actor who moves across the stage from left to right will continue walking until some agent stops his motion. An actor who is sitting will remain sitting unless an agent causes him to move. Such agency may be obtained from kinetic, visual, or dramatic art. For example, furniture (mass obtained from the theatre-visual) placed directly in the path of a moving actor will cause that actor to change the direction of his movement or stop motion altogether. Exactly what influence a mass has upon a moving body will depend upon the size of the obstructing mass and upon the form, rate, direction, potential energy, and control of the moving body. Some characters might merely stop; some may alter direction. Some characters, running at high speed and having no alternative space, may fall against the furniture before stopping.

Other visual elements may affect the tendency to maintain motion. Lack of space in which to move is the most obvious example. Highly positive space will create an apparent friction and thus change the quality of the motion. A change from a high-value color to a low-value color on the moving body will increase the apparent weight of the body. Such weight increase might slow the rate of motion, accelerate the expense of energy, and even cause the motion to come to rest. Changes from a low-value color to a high-value one might well have the reverse effect. Texture changes usually affect the integrity of motion in much the same fashion as does color. Differences in line or form will also influence mobile sequence. A body moving down an incline, all other things being equal, will increase its rate and decrease its expenditure of energy; but if the form of the incline is reversed, and the body is forced to move upward, a decrease in rate and an increase in energy expenditure are likely to occur.

Kinesis affects its own sequence. In terms of a single moving body, any increase in rate will step up the expenditure of energy and cause an eventual change in the state of motion. A decrease in rate will produce an opposite result. Sudden increases in potential energy, or sudden, great expenditures of potential energy will influence rate, direction, and very often control of motion. Control itself can cause a change in direction, speed, rate, and even the size of the body's mass. For example, if General St. Pé is moving away from his wife's door, he may by exercising control change his direction and walk rapidly toward her door.

When more than one moving body is involved, these bodies not only act as visual masses which influence kinesis, but also will affect other bodies by their very motions in terms of varied speeds, directions, and energy. For example, a heavy body moving at high speed in a fixed direction is, if it strikes a resting body, likely to cause a second body to pass from rest to motion. Moreover, the energy of the blow will pass from the moving body to the resting body. Thus if one actor gives another actor a gentle push, the second actor will move a step or two without expending any of his own potential energy. If the first actor gives the second a vigorous shove, the latter might move several steps without expending his own energy. The effect of one moving body upon another must be adjusted to all the factors of mass, space, direction, rate, energy, and control. If a very small actor pushes a very large actor, all other factors being equal, integrity of motion will be violated if the large actor falls down. However, such violation of sequence may be used for comic effect. When such violation *is* employed for comedy, the violation should be consistent; that is, the violation should be used throughout so that an unexpected but artistically logical integrity is established.

Dramatic art also influences the principle of consistency of motion by providing agencies that will alter motion. Exposition, story, or language may provide forces equal to a large visual mass. A man shouting "stop," an unexpected bit of news, a shift in locale or time may all force a moving body to change from motion to rest, from rest to motion, from one rate to another, from moving upstage to downstage, from a state of great potential energy to a state of little potential energy.

Through either manners or motives characters will cause a change in the factors of mobility. An old man will not run as far or as fast as a young man. An old man who starts a motion by running will soon deplete his energy and thus change his rate from a run to a walk. A man who fears another man will alter the direction of his movement if the feared man is in the line of motion.

Action will also revise consistency of a mobile state. Conflict causes expenditure of energy, with the probable resultant alteration in the state of motion. Resolution usually conserves energy, with a concurrent change in the uniform state of motion. Finally, and possibly most importantly, all the elements of dramaturgy relate directly to control. Point of view, character, action, story, language, and exposition will all cause a moving body to exercise the control necessary to change direction, rate, and expenditure of energy.

Hello, Dolly! *by Michael Stewart and Jerry Herman, based on* The Matchmaker *by Thornton Wilder. Creative Arts Center, Division of Drama, University of West Virginia.*

Director: Charles D. Neel
Designer: Frederick Ullrich

Note how it is necessary to increase the vertical line of actors who are to be seen beyond a large downstage mass. Note also that despite the location of the actress at the center of the formal composition, the large downstage mass tends to reduce her strength and dominance.

The second principle of sequence is that bodies exercise attraction upon each other. Thus two or more bodies occupying the same space will be attracted toward each other. Much depends initially on the size of the separating space. If the space is small, the attraction between bodies is great. The old rule of all actors' keeping an arm's length away from the star has a basis in this principle. To come any closer means that the attraction between two bodies is so great that if they do not move together, the audience will do the moving for them by treating the two bodies as a single mass. If the space is great, the attraction between the two bodies is small. Much here depends on line. If the two bodies are facing each other or looking at each other, the direction of their virtual line increases the attraction.

Mass is also important. Two equal masses attract equally, but larger masses exercise great attraction on smaller masses. Small masses exert little pull on great masses. By influencing the apparent size of mass, color and texture are also important in the attraction of bodies. Moreover, in themselves color and texture have attractive powers. A body of rough, hard, and complex texture tends to attract bodies of smoother, softer, and simpler texture. A body high in color value, saturation, and temperature tends to attract bodies that are low in color value, saturation, and temperature.

The attraction of masses means that if all other things are equal, a body in motion will alter its motion if attracted by another mass. A body at rest will move if sufficiently attracted by another mass. Thus if two actors are crossing upstage when they are passed by four actors in bright yellow crossing downstage, a perfectly logical sequence would require that the actors crossing upstage adjust to the attraction of the large yellow mass by changing the direction, rate, or energy of their motion.

Kinetic factors also influence the attraction of masses. Two bodies moving toward each other in the same direction increase their attraction as they approach one another. When the same bodies move away from each other they decrease in attraction. Rate is important. A large mass at rest will exercise strong pull on a small body moving past it. If that small body is passing slowly, it may be attracted into the body of the resting mass; but if that same body is moving past the mass at fairly high speed, it may have its direction altered but may still continue as an independent body. Finally, a small body moving swiftly past a large stationary mass may receive a very slight pull, so slight that the pull merely slows the passing body momentarily. Thus a small boy racing past a company of red-coated guards may slow down slightly and turn his head. The same boy walking past the guards might stop and walk toward the company.

Energy and control are also operative. The more potential energy possessed by a body, the better able it is to resist the attraction of other bodies. This is particularly true if control is exercised to expend such energy in resisting attraction. Let us return to our small boy. He has been told by his mother not to stop on the way home from school. A small boy by nature has great potential energy. Let us suppose that energy has been increased by his mother's promise that if he gets home early enough she will have a surprise for him. When the boy runs past the company of guards, he is naturally attracted. He slows down to a walk. Then he exercises control. He looks away. He walks faster. He begins to run again. If the exercise of control has cost him all his potential energy, he may slow down once again. If not, he runs home.

The director must carefully gauge all factors in the attraction of masses in order to measure the exact amount of attraction, the exact amount of impulse to a certain type of motion.

Through such elements as character, action, language, or viewpoint the play script must also be considered in terms of attraction of masses. Two large masses attract each other in space, but the play script indicates that the two are in conflict. Thus if they do unite, it might well be at a run in order to fight. Two other bodies, a young man and a young woman in love, are also attracted to each other. As they approach each other, they do so slowly, in order to embrace.

The third principle of integrity of motion is that vacuums attract matter. Nature abhors a vacuum; emptiness cries out to be filled. Thus vacuums promote and shape motion. Some vacuums are more motion-inducing or more compelling than others. Negative space attracts more bodies than positive space. The most negative space—thus the most compelling vacuum—is space that has been recently positive. Thus new vacuums are more compelling than older ones. Moreover, the attractive powers of negative space are seemingly in direct ratio to its previous positiveness. Hence a space suddenly vacated by a large mass is more compelling than one vacated by a smaller mass.

All the elements of visual and kinetic art influence the creation and controlling of theatrical vacuums. To begin with, space itself is the most crucial element, since a vacuum is created from more or less negative space. No matter what the form of staging, the more stage space available, the easier is the creation of vacuums. Extremely tiny stages present the most difficulty; however, extremely large stages may offer so much negative space that control of vacuums created is difficult.

In addition to space, line and form are vital elements in the control of vacuums. Any incomplete line creates a vacuum at the point of incompletion. This point may occur within the line or at the terminus of the line. Study the examples below:

Since all line is rudimentary form, we may say that incomplete forms create vacuums at the point or points of incompletion. These forms may be organic, artificial, geometric, or natural, but in all cases they must be familiar to the audience. An unfamiliar shape will seem neither complete nor incomplete to an audience. Consider the examples below in terms of vacuums created by incomplete forms:

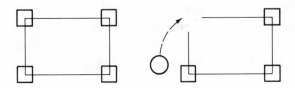

The influence of mass on vacuum is twofold. First, by displacing space, mass fills and destroys some existing vacuums; but as we have observed earlier, when mass moves from space to space, it leaves behind it a new vacuum whose attraction is measured by the size of the vacating mass. The second influence of mass on vacuum is in terms of the configuration of the mass. As with line and form, incomplete masses tend to create vacuums at their points of incompletion. For example, a mass whose implied volume is not complete possesses a vacuum at the point of incompletion; so, too, a mass whose implied weight is less than normal tends to seem empty and to attract additional matter. In a two-dimensional diagram, these particular vacuums are difficult to illustrate. But if we assume that the first figure below is a pyramid and the second a rounded balloon, we may observe the vacuums created.

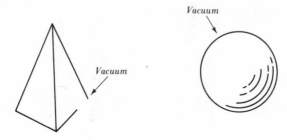

The illustrations above also indicate the influence that color or texture may exercise on vacuums. By changing the quality of all elements of visual art, color and texture also change the quality of vacuums. Through stage lighting, color can create vacuums, destroy existing vacuums, and increase or decrease the attractive power of vacuums.

Since the vacuum or negative space is an integral part of kinetic sequence, it is natural for the elements of motion to influence vacuums. Initially vacuums are created or filled by the movement of mass from space to space. Such a movement will usually fill one vacuum as it creates others. In this regard, study the top diagram on page 187. Note that the initial impulse to motion was caused by an incomplete geometric form.

This illustration also demonstrates how direction, rate, and energy influence vacuums. Note that the direction of approach of the new body caused energy to be imparted to the stationary body at the lower left of the formation. Just how much energy was imparted

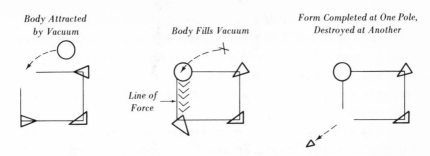

Body Attracted by Vacuum

Body Fills Vacuum

Line of Force

Form Completed at One Pole, Destroyed at Another

depended upon the speed of the approaching body. The higher the speed, the greater the expending energy. This expending energy was passed for the most part on to the lower-left body. The rest was distributed throughout the rectangle.

Assuming, as we did in the illustration, that enough energy was passed from the one body to the other to cause the resting body to go into motion, then even as the approaching body fills the old vacuum and completes the rectangle it is simultaneously creating a new vacuum elsewhere and destroying the rectangle.

In the opening and closing of vacuums, much depends on all bodies related to the vacuum and on the newly approaching body. Thus the force lines or the implied or actual motion, speed, direction, and control of all affected bodies must be considered. For example, in the illustration above, if the three triangles are three actors whose dramatic situation gives them great potential energy, they may not react as indicated. Instead, they may exercise control and expend just enough energy to maintain their positions even in the face of the newly approaching body. In such a case, no new vacuum would be created. On the other hand, the actual or virtual direction of bodies might

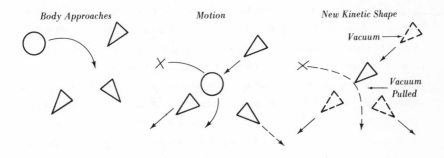

Body Approaches

Motion

New Kinetic Shape

Vacuum

Vacuum Pulled

severely affect new formations of negative space. Study the diagram at the bottom of page 187. Note how the form of the bodies gives each a virtual direction which it will naturally follow as the new body approaches. If we imagine that the triangles are actors facing in the direction of the apex, we can understand how the diagram would apply to the theatre.

As with energy, the element of motion also has a unique relationship to stage vacuums. Motion of any type promotes the creation of vacuums but motion in a particular direction creates a peculiar vacuum —the trailing vacuum. Stated another way, any moving mass will create a negative space directly to its rear. The attraction of this trailing vacuum will be determined by the size of the mass, the speed at which the mass is moving, and the energy expended by the mass. However, all other things being equal, a trailing vacuum is always more compelling than a vacuum caused by incomplete stationary forms. Hence a single actor moving at high speed will create a more compelling trailing vacuum than will a large, incomplete stationary mass of actors. The following diagram will help illustrate this principle:

Body Moving At High Speed   *Attraction of Moving Body*   *Moving Body Captures*
Approaches Bodies At Rest   *Causes All Bodies to Move*   *Another Body*

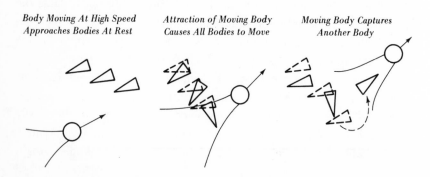

Energy has several applications in terms of stage vacuums. We have already observed how it can be passed from one body to another in order to create a vacuum, or how it can be used to resist the creation of a new vacuum. However, its most significant feature, perhaps, is how it can affect the attractive powers of a given vacuum. As you recall, a space that has just been recently vacated by a mass has considerable attraction. Most of this attraction is because of the energy residing in that space. Whenever a mass moves it expends energy, and some of that expended energy remains in the prior location of the mass. The more sudden the movement of the mass, the greater the expended energy, and the more residue of energy is left in the new vacuum. The most sudden and energetic motion a mass may accomplish is the immediate disintegration of its form. This disintegration is often caused by the mass being bombarded by a moving body. In theory, the bombarding body may be a small body, moving at high speed, attracted to a larger mass. In dramatic practice, we might imagine the situation diagramed below as a scene from *Oedipus*, a scene in which Oedipus moves toward a portion of the chorus, while three other members of the chorus form a mass in the lower-right portion of the stage. When the mass is bombarded, it disintegrates. However, Oedipus is moving at such high speed that although the impact serves to change his direction, he is not held by the vacuum. But a vacuum is formed, a vacuum charged with great attraction because all the energy of both the previous mass and the recent impact remains in the vacuum. The resulting attractive power is so great that the stationary mass of the three chorus members is pulled into motion by the vacuum.

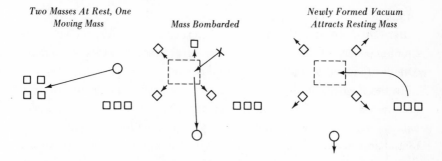

Two Masses At Rest, One Moving Mass   Mass Bombarded   Newly Formed Vacuum Attracts Resting Mass

Trailing vacuums are, of course, a special way of looking at the principle that masses attract. As a final aspect of stage vacuums, we might remind ourselves that as bodies fill a vacuum, form is being made or changed. If a new form is being created, then the potential energy of the form will be the sum of energy contributed by each of its parts, plus any energy growing out of the total form. However, if an already existing form changes its internal configuration no potential energy is gained, but at the same time energy is expended to complete the motion. Consider this fact in regard to the illustration above.

SEQUENCE: A SUMMARY

We have dealt in more detail with integrity of motion than with dramatic or visual unity. Kinetic sequence is no more or less complex than other unities, but little has been written concerning the phenomenon, hence the length of our discussion. In brief, sequence is the impression of the concise and logical flow in the processes of motion. It rests upon three principles: (1) A body tends to retain a uniform state of motion or rest unless influenced by some other force; (2) bodies attract other bodies; and (3) vacuums exert attractions on bodies. The principles all interact and are influenced by visual, auditory, and kinetic factors. All three principles may be combined to achieve sequence, or a single principle may be employed. When a single principle is used, we have simple sequence; when two or more are present, we have complex sequence. Whatever the integrity of motion created, the director will want to avoid the violation of any principle because to do so destroys the impression of oneness of sequence.

KINETIC COMPOSITION: RHYTHM

Dramatic rhythm is a pattern of change in time; visual rhythm is pattern in space. Kinetic rhythm is patterned change in space and time simultaneously. Thus mobile rhythm is at once broader and more complex than either auditory or visual rhythm.

In the theatre, the keys to the achievement of good kinetic rhythm are the elements of motion and energy. Negative motion conserves energy; positive motion expends energy. The relationship between potential and expended energy is the rhythm of a motion. In other words, rhythm is the measure of movement's pattern of conserving and expending energy. Quite naturally, this pattern of conservation and release is influenced by the remaining kinetic elements. Changes of direction, rate, or control will normally affect the pattern. The line, form, mass, color, texture, and stage space of the moving body will influence both change and pattern. For example, a body that moves in sudden, rapid spurts with many changes of direction may be said to have an aimless, staccato pattern or rhythm; while a large, heavy mass that moves slowly and steadily in a fixed direction will have a measured, sure rhythm.

190

Rhythm may be simple or complex. When one or two factors are used exclusively to obtain rhythm, the rhythm is simple. For instance, if the pattern is to run two steps, change direction, walk three steps, change direction, run two steps—then the pattern of conservation and release of energy is fairly constant and we have a relatively simple rhythm. But if the pattern is walk a step, run three, walk two—we have a more complex rhythm since both rate and the conservation–release of energy are now more varied. With this in mind, consider the illustrations below.

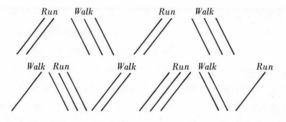

When more than one moving body is involved, complex rhythm may be obtained by counterpoint. The most elemental form of counterpoint is counter-motion. This occurs when bodies move in opposite directions. If the bodies countering also vary in motion, energy, size, space, and rate, then the counterpoint is highly complex. Observe the counterpoint in the following diagrams.

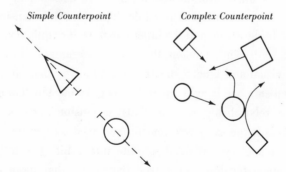

Simple Counterpoint   *Complex Counterpoint*

Mobile rhythm influences and is influenced by kinetic sequence. Obviously the pattern of motion in terms of energy, rate, and control will decide the attractive powers of masses and vacuums and will

191

influence the tendency of bodies to retain a uniform state of movement. On the other hand, the principles of sequence will shape rhythm. A rhythm of walk two, run two is only aesthetically possible if proper forces, masses, and vacuums exist to cause the body to change from one motion rate to another.

Kinetic rhythm, in its conservation and release cycle, should always seek logical proportion. From a lifetime of living and moving, an audience is all too well aware of when energy is logically conserved and when it is logically released. This is especially true in terms of the most theatrical body, the human being. Thus when energy is conserved beyond a logical proportion, the audience becomes restless for release. If release is not forthcoming on stage, the audience may well take matters into their own hands and seek relief by shifting, wiggling, squirming, coughing, and even "laughing in the wrong places." By the same token, overrelease of energy might cause the audience to seek their own methods of conservation. Thus actors are sometimes surprised to discover that the harder they work, the colder and more unresponsive the audience becomes.

KINETIC COMPOSITION: DYNAMIC TENSION

In Chapter 7, dynamic tension was described as the kinetic analogue of visual balance. In the theatre, dynamic tension is much more frequent than visual balance. Motion and balance are antithetical; where true balance exists, no motion is possible. Thus dynamic tension must be substituted in the visual and the kinetic theatre for equipoise.

To achieve dynamic tension, the director organizes all the goals and factors of visual and kinetic theatre in such a way that all moving and resting elements are caught up in a recognizable but temporary relationship, a relationship so fine that all tensions are in a seeming balance. This is the same relationship achieved by our space scientists when they launch an artificial satellite into orbit. The difference between dynamic tension and a true balance is that there are always one or more factors working to destroy the tension.

In the theatre, every good tension will have its logical change factors. These factors grow out of either the elements or the goals of kinetic composition. Since change factors should be evident, we may say that implicit in every tension is the issue of counterpoint, or that every tension is composed of two or more countering forces. Such counterpoint may be simple or highly complex. For example, if two bodies of equal mass approach each other at the same speed and energy level from exactly opposite directions, we have a simple counterpoint or simple tension. Or in terms of sequence, if a free body is attracted in one direction by a large mass and in another direction by a compelling vacuum, a simple tension or simple counterpoint exists. However, if several factors, all varied, create a tension, the counterpoint is highly complex. Reexamine the above diagrams. Note the simple tension in the first. The second diagram shows bodies of differing form and mass moving in different directions. Imagine also that the bodies are moving with differing speeds and expense of energy. The resulting counterpoint becomes highly complex.

Tensions must have sequence; that is, they must be joined logically and dissolved logically. As far as an audience is concerned, the way a tension is created, maintained, and dissolved must meet their expectations. Thus the director should make clear his tension structure. For example, if three bodies approach each other, they will ultimately reach a state in time and space when and where they achieve a tension. If the director wishes body A to break the tension, from the beginning he should have sufficiently varied body A's speed, direction, size, energy, or control so that it would obviously not remain in tension. In this regard, consider the diagram below. Note that the triangle is moving in a slightly different direction from either of the circles. Note also that as the circles move they create a vacuum to their rear. It is immediately obvious to an observer that the vacuum will draw the triangle and thus serve as the tension-dissolving element.

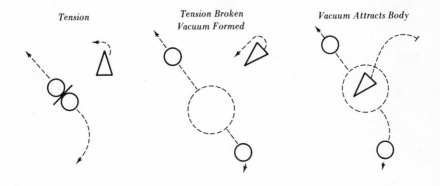

| *Tension* | *Tension Broken*
Vacuum Formed | *Vacuum Attracts Body* |

The director should be always alert for the point at which tension is joined and the point at which it is broken; for unlike balance, tension is a continuing process. As soon as tension is joined, it should begin to be dissolved; as soon as it is dissolved, new tension should take its place. The cycle ends only when the kinetic composition melts finally into the visual, and a state of balance is achieved.

Rhythm is the base upon which tension rests, since rhythm is the pattern of change in kinetic elements and change is the genius of tension. But because identifying the tension-making and tension-destroying factors are so important, the goal of kinetic emphasis is also vital to satisfying tension.

KINETIC COMPOSITION: EMPHASIS

The function of emphasis in kinetic composition is identical to visual and auditory emphasis—to call the audience's attention to the most important motion. Emphasis may be simple, divided, or diversified. Simple emphasis singles out only one movement; divided emphasis gives varying degrees of importance to two or more motions. Diversified emphasis distributes attention over a large pattern of motions and is more common in kinetic theatre than in visual or literary theatre. A good example of diversified emphasis is any large crowd scene in a spectacular motion picture.

Emphasis may be achieved through any one or more of the goals or elements of kinesis. Moreover, since kinetic art involves body-in-space, kinetic emphasis may be achieved in whole or in part through visual emphasis. Again, since auditory theatre is wedded to kinetic art, emphasis may be achieved through auditory means.

Motion is the basic element in kinetic emphasis. Anything that moves is more emphatic than things that are not moving. But since the concept of emphasis implies the concept of contrast, when all bodies are moving, a single resting body is more emphatic. Rate, energy, and control also contribute to emphasis. All other things being equal, energy, either potential or expended, will be a point of emphasis. Thus if two characters are on stage moving at the same rate in the same direction, the character with the greatest potential energy or the character with the greatest expenditure of energy will be more emphatic. However, the emphatic feature of energy will be affected by rate and direction. In general, extremes of rate—very fast or very slow—are usually more emphatic; but since very fast rates expend energy, high speeds will lose emphasis more quickly than low speeds. Changes in direction are more emphatic than a fixed course, but since any change in direction depletes energy, too frequent shifts in direction will quickly lose emphasis. The apparent terminus of a movement's direction will also affect emphasis. In this regard, a review of the discussion of stage space in Chapter 7 will be helpful.

When all other factors are equal, any body-in-space that varies its movement, direction, rate, energy, or control will be emphatic. Thus we may say that rhythm is a major influence in emphasis. Any rhythm that contrasts with other rhythms is a source of emphasis. In theory, simple rhythms are more emphatic than complex rhythms, but simple rhythms lose their emphatic impact faster than more complex ones.

As already observed, emphasis is vital to dynamic tension because in order for the audience to follow the structure of a tension, emphasis must be placed on both the tension-building and the tension-destroying elements. Since tensions always imply counterpoints, dynamic tension requires divided emphasis. Such emphasis is obtained in kinesis in much the same manner as in visual art. For example, the point of principal emphasis might be obtained through slow, sure motion; the point of secondary emphasis through changes of direction. Imagine moving bodies in the following illustration:

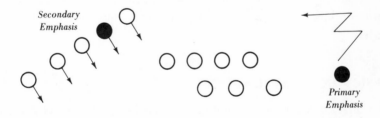

Dynamic tension returns what it borrows from emphasis, for the destructive factor in every tension is by its very nature an emphatic factor.

So, too, with the first goal of kinetic composition—sequence. Emphasis is both a giver and a taker. Emphasis must direct the audience's attention to the principle of sequence which applies in any mobile process. If a vacuum is to be the motive of motion, then the vacuum must be emphasized. If a body is to maintain its previous state of motion, that body must be given emphasis. If one mass is to attract another, that mass is to be emphasized. On the other hand, an attracting body or vacuum will pass secondary emphasis to the attracted body. A body occupying a very compelling vacuum will take the emphasis attached to that vacuum.

KINETIC COMPOSITION: VARIETY

The final goal of kinetic composition is a final goal of all arts—variety. Variety implies differences in the use of all elements and goals of composition. Kinetic variety means that direction, movement, rate, energy, control, sequence, tension, rhythm, and emphasis must all be used with a difference. The difference not only adds interest but also enables the director to achieve his goals. Thus without variety there is no change and hence no rhythm. Without variety in motion there is no tension, only balance; and without variety, direction of audience attention is impossible.

KINETIC COMPOSITION: A SUMMARY

The director uses the elements of kinesis to achieve a pleasing aesthetic composition. In order to achieve this composition, five goals must be realized: kinetic sequence, dynamic tension, emphasis, rhythm, and variety.

DESIGN IN THEATRE-KINETIC

The director has a design purpose as well as compositional goals in kinetic theatre. His design purpose is threefold: (1) to unite visual, dramaturgic, and kinetic elements; (2) to unite visual, dramaturgic, and kinetic composition; and (3) to coordinate visual, dramatic, and kinetic themes. In regard to these goals, a review of the discussion of literary design in Chapter 4 and visual design in Chapter 7 might be very helpful.

The first goal of kinetic design means that the kinetic theatre must reflect the story, the characters, the action, the exposition, the language, and the point of view of the play script. The second goal means that sequence, emphasis, tension, rhythm, and variety must reflect visual unity, emphasis, balance, rhythm, and variety; and dramatic unity, proportion, emphasis, rhythm, and balance. The third goal means that the dramatic and visual themes must be supported and built upon by the kinetic themes.

DESIGN AND THE ELEMENT OF BODY-IN-SPACE

The kinetic element of body-in-space is best understood as embodying the visual elements of line, form, mass, color, space, and texture. The intellectual and emotional meanings inherent therein have been discussed in Chapter 7. Of course, as a body-in-space is influenced by motion, direction, rate, energy, and control, its meanings vary in both the kinetic and visual theatre. Hence a straight line is a strong, austere line; but if that same line is moved from a strong space into a weak one, or if that line is moved at an extremely rapid rate, its visual strength is diminished. So, too, while downstage-center is a strong, dominant space in the proscenium theatre, a moving body in upstage-left will decrease the dominance and strength of downstage-center. The effect of mobility is even greater in the arena. While center is normally a strong, dominant area, any motion elsewhere on the stage will drain almost all strength and dominance from stage-center. Moreover, a moving body has a unique affect upon the strength or weakness, dominance or subordination of any fixed space. A body passing through a strong, dominant area will collect much of the strength and dominance of that area and deposit it elsewhere on stage, all other factors being equal. Thus by passing through down-center and stopping at center-right, a body can transfer the implications of downstage to a place further upstage. So, too, a body passing through a weak stage space will take on the weakness of the area. Thus the strongest possible movement is not from strong position to stronger position but from weak position to strong position, because of the greater contrast. In brief, a strong body passing through a weak stage space acquires a certain weakness. When that same body returns to a position of strength, it seems all the stronger. The reverse is also true. The weakest possible movement is not from weak to weaker but from weak through strong to weaker. The pattern of dominance and subordination will follow the same form. Hence the most dominant movement is a passage through subordinate stage space to dominant stage space.

In terms of body position, physical form is similarly affected. Thus the weakest possible body position is obtained by moving from a weak body position through a strong body position to a weaker body position. For example, to move from one-quarter to full-back to three-quarter is much weaker than to move from one-quarter to profile to three-quarter. Again, to move an extended arm toward the center of the body and then to let it drop is much weaker than to let an extended arm merely fall. Of course, the reverse is also true. It is much stronger to go from a vertical position through a horizontal position and then to a new vertical position than to go from strong vertical to stronger vertical. In this regard, study the following illustration in terms of motion.

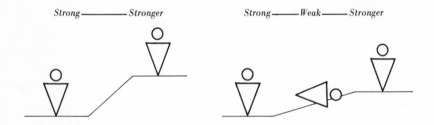

Obviously, what is said about body-in-space must be understood in terms of the other elements of kinetic art. Let us see how they affect design.

KINETIC DESIGN AND THE ELEMENT OF MOTION

All other things being equal, positive motion is at once stronger and more dominant than negative motion. Hence what moves is strong and dominant, what rests is weak and subordinate. Moreover, movement provides the strongest possible means of obtaining contrast with various other visual and auditory elements.

Motion must be adjusted to visual and dramaturgic elements. Visually, some bodies are not capable of the same motion as others. A judge seated behind his bench cannot move with as much freedom as the lawyer on the floor below. Dramatically, an old man cannot move in the same manner as a young man. Adjustments are possible among all three theatrical arts. In purely visual terms, a heavy mass moves less easily than a lighter mass. But a quickly moving mass is usually absolutely lighter than a slower moving mass. Let us take a situation from *Waltz of the Toreadors* to see how these two factors can be played against each other. The Secretary is by dramaturgic definition a young man. He is further by dramaturgic demands a colorless fellow. A young, colorless clerk would logically be dressed in dark, sombre hues, making him heavier and slower. But by moving him quickly and gracefully, we counterbalance the effect of color and return his youth and lighten his weight. Motion, of course, can be used to influence all visual or dramatic elements. Motion increases as conflict increases, perhaps even to the level of actual fighting. Motion usually decreases during resolution. Movement, such as the handling of a letter, can give as much exposition as any line of dialogue. Motion can present viewpoint. For instance, some directors might prefer to have the Cashier in *From Morn to Midnight* move very little while the other characters might be engaged in feverish activity, or other directors might use a reverse approach. Either use of motion would demonstrate a difference in viewpoint between the Cashier and the other characters. To take a final example from visual elements, an organic form that moves is stronger than a geometric form at rest; an artificial form that moves seems closer to a natural form.

KINETIC DESIGN AND THE ELEMENT OF DIRECTION

Our discussion of design in terms of body-in-space also involved many of the issues of direction. Any movement in the direction of strength is strong and dominant; any movement away from strength is weak and subordinate. Motions from strength and dominance through weakness and subordination to strength and dominance are extremely strong.

When all other factors are equal, changes of direction are weak. A complete reversal of direction is usually weak. However, because emphasis gives strength or dominance, a sudden reversal of direction may have strength and dominance. Conversely, singleness of direction is strong; a single, fixed direction is the strongest possible movement. Direction must be adjusted to both visual and dramatic factors. If there is a large bed on the set of *The Imaginary Invalid,* it will influence the direction of all motion. Some people, otherwise quite strong, will change direction simply to avoid the bed; others, who might be quite weak, will climb right over the bed without changing direction. For instance, Argan's wife might detour around the bed when necessary. But during the scene in which Argan spanks his youngest daughter, the child might very well climb over the bed. In this case, the change of direction reflects not only the strength and weakness but also the manners pattern of the characters.

Direction can reflect any dramatic situation. Two characters in conflict might always move in counter-directions; but when that conflict comes to a crisis, they might move to the same area. Note that this is the case in *Hamlet,* where Hamlet and Claudius seem always to be moving toward different locales until the King and Hamlet are brought together in the chapel. This scene is also a good example of how a small change in direction can be highly significant. Note that the playwright has Hamlet draw his sword in the direction of the King, and then with the words "up sword" has the Prince change the direction of his movement, a small change of direction that will affect the whole course of the play.

Of course, change in direction might be tied to time and place or language as well as to character or conflict. Because Oedipus is a king in ancient Greece, the chorus might well change vertical direction when he appears (i.e., they might change from an upright posture to bowing or kneeling). Again, when Hamlet says, "suit the action to the word; the word to the action," there is a change in direction within the line. The director might wish to point up the linguistic change by a change in direction of the actor's movement.

KINETIC DESIGN AND THE ELEMENT OF RATE

Temporal and spatial speed must be coordinated with visual and dramaturgic design. All other factors being equal, normal spatio-temporal rates are stronger than extreme rates. However, normal rates rarely prevail. Perhaps it is better to separate temporal speed from spatial speed for this discussion. If no other elements are used, the quicker the temporal cross, the stronger the cross; the shorter the spatial cross, the stronger the cross. Much depends on other factors. If the spatial distance is long, perhaps the time rate can be stepped up so that the total cross is still short. However, too excessive a temporal rate will appear weak. Sometimes, in order to shorten the spatial distance, a change of direction is necessary. However, if the change of direction is too great, it will cancel the strength obtained by the shortened cross. Speed must be adjusted to the direction of the cross. When dropping in vertical space, a slower drop is stronger and more dominant than a faster one. When rising in vertical space, a faster rise is stronger and more dominant than a slower one. Extremes in any kind of rate are weaker and less dominant.

Both visual and literary elements must be considered. To move a large, heavy mass at high speed often reduces its strength and dominance. In dramatic terms, to have an old, fat man—for instance, General St. Pé—rush about at high speeds makes him weak and subordinate. On the other hand, to have a small, light mass, such as the Secretary to St. Pé, move slowly and deliberately often tends to make that form weak and subordinate.

Rate must always be adjusted to all the auditory and visual elements. For example, a form moving backward will visually move more slowly than one moving forward. To take a literary example, rate may well be adjusted to support point of view. For instance, when we are supposed to see the world through the Cashier's subjective viewpoint, normal rates may be deliberately speeded up or slowed down. The same thing may be true for comic effect. Thus whenever Argan's wife makes an entrance, the director might deliberately have her move at a slower, more deliberate temporal rate than would be considered normal; while Argan, upon seeing her, might speed up his normal spatial or temporal rate.

KINETIC DESIGN AND THE ELEMENT OF ENERGY

The source of any great energy is dominant and strong; thus great potential energy is dominant and strong. A sudden and great expense of energy creates strength and dominance at the moment of expenditure. However, the strength follows the energy, while the body expending the energy grows rapidly weaker. Much depends on all other visual and kinetic factors. Larger masses may expend more energy without growing appreciably weaker. Direction will affect the expense of energy. Large masses moving upward vertically expend more energy than small, light masses moving in the same direction. When descending, large masses expend less energy than light masses and are thus stronger and more dominant. Rate plays its role—the higher the rate, the more energy expended. Thus fast rates are often weaker than slower rates.

Dramaturgic factors are important. Crisis, for example, generates psychic energy, energy that can be borrowed to increase the strength or dominance of a physical body. Thus while she is not powerful, Gertrude is stronger in her scene with Hamlet than she is at any other time in the play. Language itself can increase or decrease potential energy. The very language in which the Ghost tells his story increases Hamlet's psychic energy.

The control of energy is important to actor and director in terms of the play script. This control is often referred to with such terms as *building, overplaying,* and *underplaying.* Building a character means conserving enough potential energy to carry the character through conflict and crisis. Spending energy reserves too rapidly might make the first act exciting, but it often makes the second and third act seem hollow or flat. For instance, if Oedipus is too violent in his reaction to Creon—that is, if he spends too much energy—he will not have sufficient reserves to carry him logically through the terrible crisis awaiting him. Spending too much energy in relation to reserves is usually called overplaying. On the other hand, underplaying is not necessarily a virtue. To have too much reserve energy, or not to spend enough to make the conflict seem to lead to a logical crisis, is as great a fault as overplaying. The control of energy must be geared to both visual, kinetic, and dramatic necessities. Sometimes a body must move no matter what the expense of energy. For example, in kinetic terms a body that does not move toward a highly compelling vacuum is violating an artistic necessity. In visual terms, a small mass must move out of the path of a larger mass. In story terms, it would violate the manners patterns of ordinary men if Horatio did not move out of the path of the Ghost.

KINETIC DESIGN AND THE ELEMENT OF CONTROL

In theory, the exercise of control creates the impression of strength and dominance; the loss of control seems to make a body weak and submissive. Again, a number of factors must be considered relative to control. At its base, control implies the willful conservation or release of energy and the willful change of motion, direction, and rate. Such exercise of will implies strength. However, to exercise will to change direction, rate, or state of motion implies the spending of energy. Hence control may be a weakening as well as a strengthening factor. Much depends upon the conditions under which control is exercised. A large mass moving downward at a high rate must spend considerable energy willfully to change rate and direction. However, the same mass moving horizontally need not expend as much energy to maintain its normal rate.

Dramatic factors are important in terms of control. Oedipus as king, when walking among the members of the chorus, may willfully control his direction without much expense in energy; but a member of the chorus who wishes to remain in the path of the king must expend great energy. The very old and the very young spend greater energy in exercising control than do people of young to middle age. However, all exercise of control is energy-depleting, and consequently control is ultimately a weakening rather than a strengthening agent. Often a director who wishes to show a dominant person becoming weaker will force the actor to use control in order to change direction or rate. But in general, the director should be careful not to ask his actors to rely too heavily upon sheer control in order to move, rest, change direction, modify rate, or adjust energy.

DESIGN AND THE ELEMENTS OF MOTION

When the director adjusts the elements of motion in order to create a meaningful design, he must simultaneously coordinate visual, kinetic, and dramaturgic factors. Unlike the choreographer who may create a meaningful kinetic pattern without reference to any other art, the director must always use his motion design to broaden and enrich the visual and dramaturgic structure of the total production. To do this, he coordinates not only the elements but also the goals of kinetic composition with the goals of visual and dramatic composition.

KINETIC DESIGN: VISUAL, DRAMATIC UNITY AND SEQUENCE

In a broad sense, sequence or integrity of motion must parallel visual and dramatic unity. Thus *The Imaginary Invalid,* a simply unified play dramatically, would call for simple visual unity and relative simplicity of sequence. To this end sequence might develop chiefly through the use of a vacuum or the attraction of masses. On the other hand, a director might see *Oedipus* as a rather complex play. The visual unity would then be more complex, and the kinetic sequence might use all three principles of sequential integrity.

KINETIC DESIGN: PROPORTION, BALANCE, AND DYNAMIC TENSION

Kinetic theatre avoids balance, except when its own statement is ended. Consequently, mobile design does not seek to cooperate with visual balance; instead, it substitutes varieties of dynamic tension. However, as much as possible the kinetic designer will attempt to have his tension reflect the replaced balance. Thus if the balance replaced would have been formal, the tension is kept relatively simple; if the replaced balance would have been assymmetrical, the tension is usually more complex. Therefore, the tensions struck in *Invalid* might be much simpler than those in *Death of a Salesman.* In the first play, for instance, usually no more than one factor would create or dissolve any given tension. In the second play, several factors might both create and dissolve tensions.

Before moving to the relation between tension and dramatic proportion, we might consider one special way in which visual balance, dynamic tension, and sequence are interdependent. An audience tends to treat an incomplete familiar form as possessing a vacuum at the point of incompletion. This vacuum is motion-inducing. Any motion-inducing factor aids in either the creation or the dissolution of a dynamic tension. Another way of looking at an incomplete familiar form is to say that the form is imbalanced. From this we may deduce that the audience tends to regard any unbalanced form as incomplete. Hence unbalanced forms create vacuums, which in turn promote sequence and dynamic tension. Therefore, by avoiding balance, dynamic tension actually enlists at times the aid of visual balance in maintaining itself. In this regard, study the following illustration. Note how the lack of balance is an inducement to motion in a specific direction.

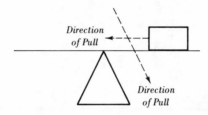

The correlating of dynamic tension and dramatic proportion is perhaps one of the director's most important tasks. In general, the director must see to it that the organization of his tension and of the playwright's proportional pattern are as nearly identical as possible. Since temporal progression is an essential element in both goals, the adjustments in time are not difficult. The director's principal problem is to see that the spatial factors of his tension also reflect the proportional organization of the play script. Let us take an example—the Gravediggers scene in *Hamlet*. In sum, the scene is shared equally by the Gravediggers and Hamlet. However, in temporal progression the proportion varies throughout. The scene opens with total attention given to the Gravediggers, in which both clowns share equal dominance. The dominance then shifts to Hamlet momentarily, then to Hamlet and the First Gravedigger, and finally to Hamlet alone. Throughout all characters are strong; but by the end of the scene, Horatio and the Second Gravedigger have clearly taken subordinate roles. The temporal tensions must be stated in terms of a kinetic pattern which at first holds both Gravediggers in a tension. The original tension is broken by the entrance of Hamlet, who as the tension-breaking element will automatically take dominance. In fact, because Hamlet breaks the tension, some directors might block the scene so that Hamlet is present from the outset. If this course is taken, it involves a spatial statement that must be incorporated into the temporal tension. Other directors might wish to bring Hamlet on stage when the Second Gravedigger exits. In this case, Hamlet would fill the vacuum

Summer and Smoke *by Tennessee Williams.*
Washington University, St. Louis, Mo.

Director: Nelson T. Magill

Designer: W. Harlan Shaw

Note here how effectively an item of scenery, the angel in the park, becomes a major agent visually and psychologically in the scene. The designer's creation of the statue in a pose pregnant with motion makes the angel almost an active participant in the kinetic aspect of theatre.

created by the exit of the Gravedigger. After Hamlet enters, the scene is proportioned or organized about Hamlet and the First Gravedigger, but the director has available the physical presence of Horatio as a subordinate element. Horatio can be manipulated both spatially and temporally so that the tension is kept from slipping into a balance.

KINETIC DESIGN: EMPHASIS

The coordination of visual, kinetic, and dramatic emphasis is a matter of discovering what should be emphasized and then employing the appropriate kinetic, visual, or auditory devices. The matter of what should be emphasized is settled first by an analysis of the play script and then by an understanding of the compositional needs of the visual and kinetic theatres. Hopefully, all three theatres should call for identical emphasis patterns. Employing the appropriate emphatic device is another matter. Frequently the playwright will give emphasis to his characters through language. Then the emphatic function of the visual and kinetic theatres is to provide support for the auditory emphasis. Often, however, the playwright will request, implictly or explictly, emphatic help from the visual or kinetic theatre. For example, after Oedipus learns what he has done, he must *do* something. The emphasis pattern passes from the auditory to the kinetic theatre. Somewhat later, when Oedipus reappears after he has blinded himself, he must show his blindness to the audience. Now the emphasis pattern has passed from the kinetic to the visual theatre. In other situations, the choices may not be so clear-cut. The director must select the appropriate emphasis pattern—auditory, visual, kinetic, or a combination thereof—that he considers most appropriate to the needs of the total production.

In addition, the director must identify the kind of emphasis appropriate to the style of the play or the scene and reflect that appropriateness in both the kinetic and auditory theatres. For example, *Waltz of the Toreadors* is composed mostly of two-character scenes in which the emphasis is simple. Such simple emphasis should also appear in the visual and kinetic theatres. On the other hand, the final scene in *From Morn to Midnight* uses divided emphasis, and this divided emphasis must also occur in the visual and kinetic composition. As we have seen in the preceding chapter, varying types of primary, secondary, and tertiary visual emphases are distributed among the Cashier, the Salvation Army Girl, the speakers, and the crowd by their visual placement on stage. The same emphases may be obtained through kinetic means. The Cashier, for instance, could move about with many changes of direction; the crowd could move slowly and directly. The speakers might move seldom but with great releases of energy, while the Salvation Army Girl might not move at all. Through contrast each would gain a certain kinetic emphasis. The Cashier, through his more frequent movements, would have primary emphasis; the Salvation Army Girl, through her almost negative motion, would have almost equal emphasis; and the crowd and the speakers would have tertiary emphasis. By controlling the movement throughout the temporal sequence of the play, first one agent and then another might be given primary emphasis. For example, if the Cashier moved about with many changes of direction at the same time that the speaker was moving with a great release of energy, there would be a momentary primary emphasis placed on the greatest release of energy—the movement of the speaker.

KINETIC DESIGN: RHYTHM

Since auditory rhythm occurs solely in time and visual rhythm entirely in space, kinetic rhythm—which functions simultaneously in time and space—is the major catalyst in uniting and coordinating all the compositional goals of theatre. The spatial aspects of kinetic rhythm—space, body, direction, and spatial rate—can be used by the director as an analogue to the patterns of visual rhythm. The temporal aspects of kinetic rhythm—motion, energy, temporal rate, and control—can be used to reflect the changes of auditory rhythm. Moreover, since the elements of kinetic rhythm are interrelated in both time and space, they reflect visual and auditory rhythm at one and the same time. Thus a director who has an actor run to a door on stage left, open it, close it rapidly, and walk slowly back to stage-right, has made a visual rhythmic pattern: two straight lines. He has made a kinetic rhythm—motion in one direction, change of motion, motion in another direction. If, as the motion took place, the actor said loudly, "I'm not afraid of what's behind the door," and, after opening and closing the door, he said slowly and thoughtfully, "I should learn to keep my mouth shut," the kinetic, visual, and auditory rhythms would have been united in a single movement.

To unite visual and auditory rhythms adequately, kinetic rhythm should seek from the play script the pattern of change created in the auditory theatre—change in language, agent, story, exposition, point of view, and, above all, action. These changes can be reflected in change of body, space, motion, direction, and rate. They can be most especially reflected in the exercise of control in terms of character, and conservation and release of energy in terms of action. From the visual theatre, kinetic rhythm seeks the patterns of line, form, mass, color, and texture which will affect a moving body.

Finally, kinetic rhythm should be coordinated with dramatic rhythm in terms of its style: Complex dramatic rhythms call for complex kinetic rhythms, which in turn make for complex visual rhythms; simple dramatic rhythms call for simple kinetic and visual rhythms.

KINETIC, AUDITORY, AND VISUAL VARIETY

Problems of variety remain constant in all media; only the specific elements change. A play with a variety of character motives calls for much visual variety in stating that character; the same script will need kinetic variety in stating the same character. *Death of a Salesman* has variety of point of view. Visual variety in color, space, line, or texture will be needed to reflect the dramatic variety; kinetic variety in direction, speed, or energy will also be required to reflect both the visual and dramatic variety.

KINETIC DESIGN: COORDINATING THE GOALS OF KINETIC, VISUAL, AND DRAMATIC COMPOSITION

Coordinating the elements and goals of composition in the visual, auditory, and kinetic theatres is a simultaneous activity, for coordinating the elements means coordinating the goals. Certain goals do not exactly coincide: Kinetic sequence is not exactly equivalent to visual and dramatic unity; visual balance and dynamic tension are truly antithetical. In the case of the former, as close a reflection as possible is the aim; in the case of the latter, the director must make a suitable substitute of the appropriate tension for the discarded balance. Some goals are identical in aim if not in means—dramatic proportion and dynamic tension, for instance; or visual, dramatic, and kinetic variety and emphasis. In the case of one goal, rhythm, the kinetic contribution is the essential catalyst that unites visual, auditory, and kinetic theatre into a single, unique art.

STYLE IN THE THEATRE-KINETIC

The fashion in which the artists of the kinetic theatre—especially the director—employ the elements and goals may be called the kinetic style of a production. Since the theatre-kinetic is the catalytic factor in the entire production, the kinetic style not only complements but unifies and extends the visual and auditory styles of a given production.

THE KINETIC THEATRE: A SUMMARY

The kinetic theatre consists primarily of the moving actor. The director and/or the choreographer employ the actors as basic kinetic instruments; shifting scenery and changing lights may also make kinetic statements. There are six elements of kinesis: body-in-space, direction, rate, energy, control, and motion. Some of these elements are shared with the visual and auditory theatres and thus a statement in the kinetic theatre becomes simultaneously a statement in the auditory or visual theatre.

The elements of kinesis are so combined as to achieve the aims of kinetic theatre: composition and design. Kinetic composition has five goals: sequence, emphasis, dynamic tension, rhythm, and variety. The purposes of kinetic design are: (1) to unite visual, dramaturgic, and kinetic elements; (2) to unite visual, dramaturgic, and kinetic composition; and (3) to express simultaneous visual, kinetic, and auditory themes.

CHAPTER 9

the auditory theatre

*The Director, the Script, and the
Principles of Auditory Art*

In Chapter 4 the elements and goals of dramaturgy were discussed as the basis upon which the director makes his initial decisions in the auditory theatre. As long as the play remains on the page, the director need concern himself only with dramaturgy. However, a produced play script is a simultaneous combination of things shown, done, and spoken. The last two chapters were devoted to vision and motion; this chapter will take up the problem of the theatre as sound.

In creating the theatre of sound, the director must translate the dramaturgic elements of language, agents, exposition, story, point of view, and action into auditory elements; and he must further realize the dramatic goals of unity, proportion, emphasis, rhythm, and variety in and through the auditory goals. To achieve the translation of written script to sound, the director must have a knowledge of the principles of auditory art. He should also understand how sound combines with kinetic and visual art to give a total theatrical treatment to the play script. The auditory elements are sound, tempo, pitch, volume, phrasing, and stress; the auditory goals are unity, harmony, emphasis, rhythm, and variety.

THE ELEMENT OF SOUND

Sound in the theatre has both a negative and a positive property. Positive sound is any audible quantity perceived by an audience; negative sound is rest or pause. Positive sound may range from consonance to dissonance—that is, from noise to music, and from full to thin—from single to multiple sounds. Positive sound is discernible by its contrast with negative sound. Both negative and positive sound have *duration,* the amount of time negative or positive sound lasts. Duration has a literal and a virtual quality. Some sounds seem virtually to last longer than they do in literal time; some pauses seem virtually to be shorter than they are literally.

Most sound in the theatre is, of course, that of the human voice either speaking or singing. Other sounds are possible, from the actual or imitated sounds of nature to the contributions of one or more musical instruments. In creating or organizing sounds other than that of the human voice, the director may want to enlist the aid of technicians or musical directors.

THE ELEMENT OF TEMPO

Sound is a function of time. Time is measured in terms of rate or tempo; that is, time is either fast, slow, or normal. Normal is, of course, an arbitrary matter; but in terms of the theatre, normal tempo is usually related to ordinary human speech. In this regard, however, it might be well to keep in mind that actors should speak more slowly than they do in ordinary conversation. The reason for such slowing down is because the audience cannot ask the actor to repeat, nor can they ask for additional information to aid in understanding.

With slightly slower than ordinary conversational speech as the norm, sound can be increased or decreased in rate. Past a certain point at either extreme, sound changes completely from its original character. Too rapid sound, in either speech or music, may give an overall impression but will tend to destroy individual subunits. Thus in speech, a stream of rapid sound may be heard but words may be indistinguishable. Extremely slow tempo will give great emphasis to the subunits of a sound sequence, so that in speech the words may be distinguished but their relationship in phrases or clauses may be lost. In music, very slow tempos may sound each note but tend to lose the melodic line.

Tempo is, of course, directly related to the negative and positive quality of sound; that is, there are two means of varying tempo. One is to slow down or speed up the production of positive sound, and the other is to increase or decrease the amount of negative sound or rest in a given sound sequence.

THE ELEMENT OF VOLUME

Volume is the measure of the presence of sound from loud to quiet. All positive sound has some volume, but depending on the physical surroundings, a certain level of volume must be reached before an auditor can perceive volume at all. Thus as the size of the theatrical building increases, the average level of speech and music must have a concurrent increase. Often the director must remind the actor who is used to working in a small theatre to increase his volume. On the other hand, actors or musicians accustomed to working in large theatres may have to be reminded to adjust downward their average level of volume. In radio, television, and film, the actor normally does not increase his volume above ordinary conversational levels. The sound engineer adjusts the actor's volume through manipulating recording levels.

Volume is naturally influenced by the breadth of sound. While it is true that a single instrument can run the scale from loud to soft, the greater the number of instruments, the larger the volume of the sound. However, by exercising control, a single instrument can be made to sound considerably louder than several instruments. Although all ele-

213

As You Like It *by William Shakespeare. University Theatre, University of Missouri, Columbia.*
Director: Stephen M. Archer   Designer: Lewis W. Stoerker   Costumer: Hazel Hall

Note particularly how the actors in high-value costumes have immediate and strong emphasis. Note also how the figure at the center of the formal balance acquires emphasis.

ments of sound have a literal and a virtual quality, volume is especially interesting in this regard. Some instruments can be manipulated so that they seem to be louder or softer than they actually are. The most common theatrical example of a loud sound that seems virtually to be soft is the well-known "stage whisper."

THE ELEMENT OF PITCH

Pitch is often confused with volume. Indeed, the two are frequently interrelated, so interrelated, in fact, that the two elements make use of the same descriptive terms. Thus we may speak of low pitch and low volume, high pitch and high volume. Indeed, when we are told to speak lower, we may not be positive whether we are to change volume or pitch. However, pitch is not volume; it is the measure of the value of a sound from high to low no matter what its volume. Thus we may have a high-pitched, loud sound or a low-pitched, loud sound. The first sound might be called a shriek; the second could be termed a bellow.

All other things being equal, however, pitch tends to have certain common relationships with volume. Thus in normal speech, the softer the volume, the lower the pitch; the louder the volume, the higher the pitch. Hence most shouts are higher in pitch than ordinary speech, and most whispers are lower in pitch than ordinary speech.

When all factors are equal, the breadth of sound—the range from full to thin—will have an effect on the quality of pitch. Because of the effect of overtones on pitch, multiple instruments will tend to sound lower in pitch than single instruments. In addition, potential to produce overtones in a single instrument will affect pitch. Thus the male voice with its longer vocal bands tends generally to be lower in pitch than the female voice. In this regard, we should note that pitch has both an absolute and a relative property. A given voice may be absolutely high-pitched, or soprano, and still run the range from high soprano to medium soprano to low soprano.

THE ELEMENT OF STRESS

Stress in auditory terms is analogous to the element of energy in kinetic art. Stress is the measure of force given to the production of an

individual sound. In this sense, language, noise, and music are composed basically of stressed and unstressed sounds, phonemes, or notes.

Since all positive sound is stressed to some degree, stress is a relative
measure which deals in more or less force. In language we usually
speak of sounds that have primary stresses, those that have secondary
stresses, and those that are unstressed (i.e., having very little stress).
Thus in such a word as "before," there is a stressed and an unstressed syllable. By giving equal stress to both syllables we would
change the meaning of the word from a preposition to an imperative
statement not to be three but to "be four." In a word such as "telephone," the primary stress is on the first syllable and a secondary stress
is on the third syllable.

In music the stress pattern is usually referred to as the beat; in verse
the stress pattern is called the meter. In fact, one way to distinguish
verse from prose is by the increased regularity of verse meter over
prose stress. On an elementary level, music may also be distinguished
from noise by music's tendency toward regularity of stress or beat.
Certain common beats—the rock beat, the jazz beat, the waltz, the
flamenco—are recognized in music; and certain standard meters—the
iambic, the trochaic, the anapestic, the dactylic, the spondaic—are
used in verse.

Stress may be natural—that is, what we are used to hearing—or
artificial. Artificial stress would be deliberate variance from the norm
in order to maintain regularity of verse or beat, or merely to produce
some effect such as a foreign accent. However, even in normal or
natural stress, the degree of force may be varied greatly.

Force is closely related to volume, pitch, and tempo. All other things
being equal, stressed sounds tend to be louder, higher, and slower than
unstressed sounds.

THE ELEMENT OF PHRASING

Phrasing is the form-creating element of sound. When we phrase, we
are separating sounds into their related groupings. By phrasing we
change both the composition and the design of sound. Phrasing begins
on the level of notes in music and of phones or individual speech
sounds in language. In music phrasing continues on through measures
up to the movements of a major composition. In language phonemes

combine to make words, and words combine to make clauses or other meaningful linguistic units.

Phrasing may be achieved through the use of one or more of the other auditory elements. We have already observed how a shift in stress changed the preposition *before* to the command *be four*. In this shift in stress, there is also involved a slight change in the rest pattern of sound. Thus in the preposition *before*, there is no rest or pause involved between the syllables, while in the imperative *be four*, there is a slight pause inserted between the *be* and the *four*. In this way, stress and variation in the positive and negative use of sound affect the phrasing pattern, and the phrasing, in turn, affects the emotional and intellectual impact of the language.

Varying volume, pitch, or rate will also affect phrasing. Sounds made at the same general volume, pitch, or rate—all other things being equal—will tend to be regarded as belonging to the same phrase by an audience. Changing the quality of any of the auditory elements will change phrasing. The best exercise in this regard is to select a simple declarative statement and vary phrasing by changing the quality of first one, then another, of the auditory elements. Such a statement as "This red pencil belongs to my old aunt" would make an interesting base for an exercise in phrasing.

THE ELEMENTS OF AUDITORY ART: A SUMMARY

There are six elements of auditory art: sound, tempo, volume, pitch, stress, and phrasing. These elements are the counterparts of the elements of visual art and kinetic art. The elements are not mutually exclusive, and change in the quality of one or more elements will usually change to some extent the quality of all elements. By combining, varying, and contrasting the auditory elements, both the compositional and design goals of auditory art are achieved.

THE GOAL OF AUDITORY UNITY

Auditory unity means that all sounds heard (or unheard) at any given moment in an auditory composition seem to belong together and that they contribute to a singleness of impression. Auditory unity does not mean that heard sounds need be melodious. In fact, a given auditory composition might well consist in part or in whole of noise. A simple example of this kind of composition might be one that presents the noises of a city block from horns to hammers.

Auditory unity may be simple or complex; that is, it may be obtained through one or several elements of sound. Thus an extremely simple auditory unity can be gained from one voice or instrument using only very slight variations in volume. Some rock musicians gain considerable and very simple auditory unity by increasing volume much higher than many members of the older generation seem to think is necessary.

On the other hand, auditory unity can be as highly complex as the integrity of impression achieved by the highly textured sound produced by a large symphony orchestra. For most theatrical situations, auditory unity is neither as complicated as the orchestration of a symphony group nor as simple as a mere increase of volume. Unity depends to a great extent upon the achievement of the other goals of auditory composition. Harmony, in particular, is an auditory goal that contributes heavily to a sense of unity.

THE GOAL OF AUDITORY HARMONY

Harmony is the auditory counterpart of literary proportion, visual balance, and kinetic tension. Harmony is the blending of the elements of sound so that the contribution of each element and each producing instrument has an appropriate and proportionately pleasing place in the entire auditory composition. We traditionally think of harmony in group part singing such as in the barber shop quartet, where voices at different pitch levels are blended. But harmony can also be seen in less stylized or formal circumstances. For example, if two persons are having a heated discussion in a given scene, the director might have one actor speak higher and more rapidly, while having the second actor speak more slowly or with greater volume. In this way the voices are blended, each actor has certain vocal elements through which to express his manners and motives, and the audience may hear and understand both actors.

Harmony is not simply a matter of a single auditory moment. The audience is given a total impression of harmony that prevails over the entire auditory composition from its beginning to its completion. Hence directors often consider the vocal quality of their entire cast as they construct an auditory composition. For example, a director may not cast a given actor because he already has too many members of his cast with exactly that actor's vocal quality. This consideration is especially important in musicals and radio dramas.

As with unity, harmony may be simple or complex. Simple harmonies are achieved through the blending of few instruments and few auditory elements. More complex harmonies require more instruments or more variation in the use of elements. However, without the use of the third element of auditory composition, emphasis, harmony would not be proportional at all. Its effect would merely be a melting of all sounds into a single sound.

THE GOAL OF AUDITORY EMPHASIS

As in other arts, emphasis is the directing of attention to aspects of the auditory composition which are most important at any given moment. Auditory emphasis may be primary, secondary, or tertiary; that is, it may be given to a single aspect of the composition or it may be spread over one or more aspects in varying degrees. Emphasis may be obtained through the use of one or more of the auditory elements. The fewer elements used, the simpler the emphasis pattern; the more elements used, the more complex the emphasis pattern. For example, when in the midst of a major movement the orchestra pauses suddenly and then introduces the sound of a single woodwind, the emphasis is achieved very simply by varying the positive quality of sound itself. On the other hand, the woodwind might have been given emphasis by continuing the sound of the body of the orchestra but increasing the tempo and raising the pitch of the woodwind's statement. At this point, secondary emphasis might have been gained for one of the percussion instruments by also increasing its tempo to match that of the woodwind's.

What is true of an orchestra of musical instruments is equally true of voices speaking; indeed, of a single voice speaking. Thus if we wish to give particular emphasis to a given phrase, we may change the normal tempo of our speech, raise its pitch, or vary the stress pattern. This is exactly what happens when we change such a phrase as "watch your step" from a friendly piece of advice as we leave a bus, to a cry of danger after an earthquake. In dealing with the latter circumstance, we would probably indicate danger by raising our pitch and increasing the speed of our delivery.

When several speakers are talking, the director might give primary emphasis to one speaker by increasing his volume, while giving secondary emphasis to another by changing his phrasing pattern.

By calling attention to what is important, emphasis aids in the construction of harmony and in the sense of unity. In turn, emphasis both supports and is given support from the remaining goals of auditory composition: rhythm and variety.

THE GOAL OF AUDITORY RHYTHM

Rhythm has already been defined as patterned change, and, as pointed out earlier in this chapter, a major basis for pattern in auditory composition is the use of recurring stresses, beats, or meters. However, rhythm is a much larger and more important concept than mere beat or meter, although in auditory compositions in which beat or meter is extremely pronounced, as in some forms of popular music or in certain verse patterns, it is difficult to recognize any other rhythm except that achieved through stress patterns.

However, any and all elements of sound may be used to produce rhythm. If a recognizable pattern of relationships between positive and negative sound is established, then a rhythm has been achieved. Thus if there is patterned change between the tempo of a given speech and its volume, a tempo–volume rhythm has been attained. Hence we may talk about a change in rhythm between two lines of identically structured poetry. Take, for example, the following two lines of blank verse from Shakespeare.

> To be or not to be, that is the question.

and

> If music be the food of love, play on.

In both lines the meter is exactly the same: iambic pentameter. However, the first line has a much more rugged and staccato rhythm than the second line. The variation in rhythm is attained not through change in meter but through variation in pause patterns (note that a major rest takes place about the middle of the first line but not until near the end of the second line), and in tempo (compare for instance the differences in normal pronunciation time between "to be or not" and "if music be").

The two lines cited above, with their use of both strong stress repetition and considerable rhythmic variety, also call to mind the final goal of auditory composition: variety.

THE GOAL OF AUDITORY VARIETY

Auditory variety is the differing of the elements of sound in order to gain interest. It is variety that changes mere repetition into rhythm, that gains emphasis, and that transforms simple unison into textured harmony. However, as has been previously noted, variety has an impact beyond the aesthetic. Every change and every variation, no matter how slight, has an effect not only upon composition but upon the meaning of the auditory theatre. Thus even as the director strives for variety, he will want to be constantly watchful for its effect on the meaning of the auditory composition.

AUDITORY DESIGN

Design is the use of the auditory composition to make a meaningful statement. Several forms of auditory compositions exist, but most of these are not usually the concern of the director. For the most part he will be dealing with auditory compositions based upon play scripts or pieces of literature that attempt in some manner to be dramatic. He will of course use music, either instrumental or vocal, in his production; and to the extent that music is important to a director he should improve his knowledge in that field. Usually dramatic directors seek the aid of a musical director if complicated music is to be a significant part of a given production. If a director works principally in musical comedy or opera, he would do well to become a knowledgeable musician. The same is true of other forms of auditory compositions in the theatre. Hence a director should have some basic knowledge of simple prosody; but if he tends to produce pre–eighteenth-century classics, then he should have a firm knowledge of verse and verse forms.

For the majority of directors, the major need is to know and understand the literature of drama, its structure and variety. This knowledge is necessary because it is the play script that forms the basis or score of the director's auditory composition, and it is the interpreting of the play script that provides the basis for auditory design or meaning. Chapter 4 has already dealt with the general structure of the play script but did not suggest the total function of the director in regard to the play script. That function is the analysis of the individual script in order to construct a basis for design in the auditory theatre and an understanding of how the script provides for the joining of the auditory, kinetic, and visual theatres.

ANALYZING THE PLAY SCRIPT FOR AUDITORY DESIGN

Because of the need to categorize elements and goals for purposes of discussion, it may well seem that script analysis is simply a matter of understanding the script category by category. Unfortunately, the process is far more complicated. Certain realities of theatrical production make it impossible to perform a simple, categorical analysis. For example, before complete analysis can be made of the construction of a script, the analyzer must have in mind a fairly precise idea of the theatrical form (proscenium, cinema, television, thrust, arena), the setting, the costumes, the audience, and the actors. However, before we have a setting, costumes, audience, or performers, there must be some analysis of the script in order to select such things as properties, colors, clothing period, ticket prices, and actors. Thus analysis is a process that chases its own tail, going forward to a certain point and then doubling back upon itself. For example, *Death of a Salesman* may have been analyzed to the point that an arena production was decided upon; now the director will need to return to the script in order to analyze language patterns, let us say, in the intimate atmosphere of the arena.

With most directors, analysis is a continual process that runs right through the final performance. However, for sake of discussion, analysis here will be approached in categorical terms. Let us begin with studying and relating the auditory elements to the dramatic elements of language, agents, exposition, story, and point of view.

LANGUAGE AND THE ELEMENTS OF
AUDITORY COMPOSITION

It is through the element of language that dramatic composition is most often and most directly connected with auditory composition in the theatre. Written language has a visual existence, but spoken language is, of course, sound. And sound is the first element of auditory art. In analyzing language, the director finds himself in much the same relation to a play script as a conductor is to a musical score. However, written language is far less precise than music. Thus the director has at once more freedom and more difficulty than does the musical conductor.

When analyzing language, the director will want to study both its beauty and its meaning, that is, both its structure and its rhetoric. These two aspects of language must be translated into sound, and then that sound must be refined by the use of the other elements of auditory art. On a basic level, the director must decide who speaks, how many speak, and how often a thing is spoken. Obviously much of this decision is already made by the playwright, but if we take as an example the scene in *Hamlet* when the Ghost appears to the soldiers on the battlement, we can easily see that the director must make some choices. First, the soldiers begin to shout. Do they all shout together? How many people talk? Do they repeat their lines? Second, the Ghost is present. Do we want him to make any sound at all? Is there music or background noise? Does a clock strike? Whatever the director decides will have a marked effect upon the auditory composition of the scene and will ultimately affect the entire production style.

Later in this same scene from *Hamlet* the Ghost speaks. Clearly sound is present, but is it consonant or dissonant? Is it full or thin? A director might elect to have more than one ghost so that the figure could appear first one place and then another. Another director may have the ghost's lines be said with an echo to increase the other-worldly impression. Finally, the whole speech need not be spoken. In an attempt to shorten or tighten the scene, a director might cut some of the speech. In essence, cutting results in reducing the presence of sound.

Working with his actors, the director produces language as positive or negative sound. He also makes that sound consonant or dissonant, thin or full. Moreover, the sound may be delivered at a varying tempo. When tempo is varied, both the quality and the meaning of language are altered. Speaking more rapidly than usual will make the speaker seem excited, nervous, hurried, subordinate, and generally weak. Often rapid delivery has a comic effect. Speaking more slowly than normal makes a speaker seem restrained, perhaps disinterested, unhurried, dominant, and generally strong. However, employing extremes of tempo in any direction will tend to result in unnatural and therefore generally weak states.

To return to the Ghost in *Hamlet*, it is traditional to have him speak more slowly than might be considered normal. On the other hand, in a play such as *From Morn to Midnight*, the Cashier might increase the general tempo of his delivery as the play progresses. The director may decide that tempo in both cases should be kept relatively normal but that volume should be varied. Thus the Ghost may speak much more quietly, perhaps even in a whisper, while the Cashier might increase his volume throughout the play so that by the last scene he is literally shrieking in nervous tension. As the Cashier increases his volume, he might also raise his pitch. Thus although increased volume tends, in general, to give dominance and strength to an agent, the higher pitch turns that strength into weakness. By combining pitch and volume in a special way, the Cashier is made dominant and weak.

The foregoing examples demonstrate that, all things being equal, any change in volume or pitch provides dominance. However, raising pitch usually weakens the speaker, while lowering pitch adds strength. Increases in volume add strength and usually show strong passions such as anger or great joy. Decreases in volume may be strong or weak depending on the circumstances of the speaker. Decreases often show fear, tension, and suppressed excitement.

Pitch has a special language function at the termination of phrases. Any meaningful utterance will terminate in an even pitch, a raised pitch, or a lowered pitch. An even pitch indicates that the phrase will be attached to other phrases to form a slightly larger or slightly modified idea. Even pitch at the end signals the audience to keep listening closely. A raised or lowered pitch means that the phrase is finished, the particular idea completed. Raised pitch at the end means a question or an exclamation, but not all questions have raised pitch.

Questions that are clearly understood from grammatical structure alone are usually finished in a lowered pitch. For example:

Did you come home last night?

(lowered pitch at end because the transposition of subject and verb already indicates a question)

You came home last night?

(raised pitch at end because question is not clearly indicated by the grammatical structure)

Thus all phrases that end in a raised pitch are questions or exclamations, but not all questions end in a raised pitch. On the other hand, a lowered pitch might mean a question, a declaration, or an exclamation. In this regard, note might be taken of the fact that the old rule of thumb that one raises one's pitch whenever one sees a question mark is a very poor rule for actors to follow.

The whole issue of punctuation is a major problem when translating written into spoken language. Punctuation is a visual guide for the eye, not the ear. Moreover, the "rules" of punctuation are often arbitrary and meaningless. In general, we are told to pause at a comma and raise our pitch for a question mark. Read the sentence below, following the "rules": "What are we having for supper tomorrow, Mary?" According to the "rules," the speaker is one with cannibalistic tendencies. In truth it might be well for both actor and director to ignore, for the most part, all punctuation marks in the play script. Often two so-called sentences must be read as one unit, while a single word must stand alone as a major thought. Observing punctuation can make for wooden delivery because the actor seems to be "reading" rather than conversing.

Stress and phrasing are the other auditory elements which must be considered when changing written language or music to spoken or played language and music. Note has already been made of how shifting of stress within a single word can change that word from a preposition to a complete two-word sentence with an entirely different meaning. Changing the phrasing or grouping of sounds and words can also accomplish the same result. Consider, for example, the shift in meaning between "nitrate" and "night rate." The sounds are exactly the same, but the phrasing or grouping has been varied.

In understanding the scope and function of stress and phrasing on written language, it might be helpful to return to our sentence, "What are we having for supper tomorrow, Mary?", and vary the stress and phrasing to see how many meanings might be gotten from a single statement. When stress and phrasing have been thoroughly studied in relation to the above sentence, it might be useful to add varieties of pause, pitch, tempo, and volume to see just how many meanings and nuances of meaning can be obtained from a single written sentence. Having different basic voices read the sentence might also prove enlightening. Male voices will provide a different meaning from female, young voices a different meaning from old voices, and tenor voices a different meaning from bass voices.

In summary, language is related directly to sound, and through this relationship the play script is united to the auditory theatre. In analyzing the play script in terms of lanugage, the director considers which language will be spoken, by whom, and at what times. He also attempts to reach decisions concerning the tempo, pitch, and volume of a word, line, or speech. Finally, he studies the use of phrasing and stress so that the composition as well as the meaning of language may be heard by an audience.

DRAMATIC AGENTS AND THE ELEMENTS OF AUDITORY THEATRE

Sound in the theatre is produced by some sort of instrument or agency. At times the agency is virtual and implied rather than literal. Train whistles or bird calls produced offstage or on a soundtrack imply or suggest that birds or trains are actually present. On the other hand, some recorded sound, such as background music, suggests a mood or a feeling possibly representing that which the agent cannot say.

The most common agent producing sound is the actor, and generally the actor represents a human character. Whenever the character makes sound—be it language, noise, or song—he is revealing his manners, his motives, or a combination of both. This revelation takes two forms: specific and general.

Each speech unfolds particular aspects of a character's manners or motives, but the agent's general delivery of language also tells much. For example, an extremely nervous person will speak at a generally faster tempo, a frightened person with a slightly higher pitch, and a stupid person might speak loudly and slowly. In terms of a particular speech, the director must attempt to understand what the speech tells the audience about the speaker and how the factors of sound or pause, tempo, volume, pitch, stress, and phrasing are to be employed to express the speaker's manners and motives.

Directors, of course, know that there is no absolutely right or wrong way to deliver a line. Much depends on the actor and his colleagues. A small, thin actor might wish to express fear by raising the pitch of his speech; a tall, heavy actor might want to display the same emotion by reducing volume to a tense whisper. In analyzing the revelation of manners and motive patterns through vocal delivery, the director will be helped by a strong background in acting and in oral interpretation or reading aloud. In general, he will want to pay particular attention to the beginnings of lines, the ends of lines, the negative modifiers, the verbs, and the abstract connectors or joiners such as prepositions and conjunctions. For example, in the famous line, "if music be the food of love, play on," the key words are "if," "music," "be," and "play on." Out of the four words, two are verbs, "be" and "play on," and one is a preposition. Moreover, the four words are found at the very beginning and end of the line.

In studying the script for its meaning in terms of the agent's manners and motives, the director will be helped by simultaneously considering the dramaturgic factors of exposition, story, and point of view.

EXPOSITION, STORY, AND POINT OF VIEW AND THE ELEMENTS OF AUDITORY THEATRE

Exposition gives us information; story sets time, place, and incident; and point of view sets the total narrative attitude—omniscient, objective, subjective. These elements interact with auditory elements to give design to the total production. For instance, the way a line is delivered in terms of volume or phrasing may tell us a great deal about an agent's manners and motives, and it may also tell us about the time, place, or incidents of the story. In this regard, the very verse quality of *Hamlet* sets it in another time and place than the present. But if the director had in mind a "modern dress" production of *Hamlet,* he might deliberately move away from the meter of the verse, making every attempt to read the lines as if they were modern conversation while letting the verse take care of itself. Another director might strive to make a close analysis of the meter patterns so that he could bring out the verse quality first, with the general informative quality following from there.

Point of view also involves auditory problems. In *Hamlet, From Morn to Midnight, Waltz of the Toreadors,* and *Death of a Salesman* shifts from objective viewpoint are frequent. Whether the shift be in the form of aside, soliloquy, or flashback, the director must decide if it is necessary to employ auditory elements in a special way in order to demonstrate that the viewpoint has been altered. For example, a common practice is to deliver asides in a lower volume than the ordinary. Reduction in general tempo is a traditional method of delivering soliloquies; slowing speech seems to suggest thoughtful interior states. Extreme distortions in any of the auditory elements are sometimes used to suggest highly disordered emotional states from insanity to drunkenness.

Exposition needs to be given special study as the transition from sight to sound is being made. The play script can give information, as, for example, when one character tells another that it is twelve o'clock. On the other hand, the script may request that the auditory theatre provide the information, as, for example, if the stage directions call for a clock to strike twelve. These matters are simple enough, but the problem becomes knotty when the director feels he must cut the play script—that is, reduce the size of the auditory composition.

Cutting or altering a play script may involve anything from the updating of a line or two (for instance, changing references to radio into references to television) to the elimination of significant portions of one or more acts. *Hamlet* is a case in point. Playing of Elizabethan scripts in their entirety is usually not attempted in the modern theatre. Such scripts might run from three to five hours if left unaltered. Often the final scene in *Hamlet* is stopped on the "good night, sweet prince" speech. Other common cuts are the elimination of most of the Rosencrantz and Guildenstern scenes and the altering of the Gravediggers scene to the point of dropping it entirely.

The most acute problem in cutting or altering is that necessary items of story, exposition, agency, and viewpoint cannot be cut without doing severe damage to the entire production. Too often the reviser of the play script attends only to story and exposition without considering agency and viewpoint. What is left may be a narrative without much dramatic impact. On the other hand, when approaching a play such as *Hamlet*, a director may feel that he cannot cut the great and famous soliloquies. Hence he cuts in exposition, story, or character. The result may be isolated examples of good writing but in general a poor overall drama. Consider, for example, that ending *Hamlet* without having Young Fortinbras take over the kingdom does injury to Shakespeare's contrast between the world of action (Young Fortinbras) and the world of contemplation (Young Hamlet). On the other hand, no matter how much it breaks the heart of a man of the theatre, Hamlet's famous "speak the speech, I pray you" may be cut without changing the quality of any part of the dramatic composition.

ACTION AND THE AUDITORY ELEMENTS

Dramatic action is the pattern of conflict, crisis, and resolution which gives drama its basic excitement. Implied action must be discovered in the written script and translated into sound. Action, of course, can be located in any or all of the elements of dramaturgy; but except for a few descriptive stage directions, action in the play script springs essentially from the dialogue. Moreover, action is the dramaturgic element most directly related to kinetic theatre, especially the kinetic element of energy. In general, conflict situations are energy-imploding, crises are at once energy-exploding and energy-sustaining, and resolution situations are energy-releasing.

The director will want to study his script for the action cycles present and for the appropriate auditory devices needed to express these cycles. In this regard, he should realize that all sound production requires some energy, and therefore any talking is weaker than any silence—all other factors being equal. Any approach to negative speech is thus energy-conserving or tension-building. Hence decreased volume is usually more energy-conserving than increased volume. This explains the excitement of tense "underplaying" in speaking and might further account for the failure of most inexperienced actors to realize that decreased volume may have more impact than a loud shout. What a shout gains in dominance from increased volume it loses in strength from expenditure in energy.

Some of the same conditions hold true for other auditory elements. Increases in tempo will normally spend more energy and serve usually as tension-releasing devices, while decreases in speed will serve to conserve energy. Increasing the use of stressing, or giving great emphasis to an already strong stress pattern such as that found in verse, will serve to spend energy; while reducing the attention given to stressing will usually conserve energy. As a general rule, increasing pitch releases energy, whereas decreasing pitch saves energy.

Much, of course, depends upon the exact pattern of increase or decrease of tempo, pitch, or stress. For example, a slowly but steadily increased pitch pattern may actually build tension because tempo—the speed of the increase—is being played off against pitch. Slow speeds conserve energy and increase tension. But as the pitch goes higher and higher, energy will begin to be released no matter what the speed of acceleration. Frequently, as energy begins to be released through rise in pitch, the rate of rise will also be accelerated for final excitement. Consider in this regard the use of a siren. If it suddenly comes on high and loud, we sense an immediate release of great energy; but if the siren commences at a barely perceptible auditory level and increases in pitch and volume very slowly to a medium-high point, the siren will probably seem to be creating tension. Beyond this point, the siren will likely begin to release tension. The rate of acceleration of pitch and volume will determine the exact amount of tension release involved.

Phrasing is especially difficult to discuss in a general manner because it is so closely related to grammar and the informative nature of language. No matter what the aesthetic circumstances, certain phrasings or sound groupings simply cannot be employed, because basic linguistic structure is thereby destroyed and communication is either impossible or is so drastically altered as to have the same effect as a total loss. However, we may say that phrasing's function in relation to dramatic action is determined by the length of the phrase, the tempo of the phrase, the volume, the stress patterns employed, and the linguistic information contained in the phrase. All other things being equal, short phrases conserve more energy than longer phrases and therefore are normally tension-building while long phrases are tension-relaxing.

The Madwoman of Chaillot *by Jean Giraudoux. Department of Speech, University of Florida.*

Director: August W. Staub

Designer: Henry Swanson

Costumes: Mary Stephenson

Note the complexity of composition gained by the excessive texturing of the costumes and the enlargement of their mass through draping, folding, and adding of accessories. Emphasis must be gained in spite of the highly positive space. Emphasis is achieved through repetition of the sharp, simple lines of pointing arms and fingers.

By combining this rule of thumb with the use of volume, we can say that short, normal-to-quiet volume phrases are usually more energy-conserving and tension-building than long, loud volume phrases. By adding tempo, we can also say that quickly delivered phrases are more energy-expending than are slowly delivered ones. Therefore, even though a long phrase is in itself energy-spending, we can counter-balance this by reducing the volume or decreasing the tempo of our delivery. Finally, all phrases will require some sort of stressing or force in delivery. The phrase employing heavy stressing will be domi-nant but will spend energy and thus be more tension-releasing than tension-forming.

Phrasing must be considered not only internally but also externally; that is, the single phrase will have to be understood as it interacts with surrounding phrases. On the written page, this interaction is sequential and grammatical and is affected only by punctuation marks and changes in print quality. Linguistic interaction is basic and conveys certain information. On this level alone, with no other factors intrud-ing, phrasing may be conflict-producing, crisis-containing, or tension-releasing. If a character says, "I'm more relaxed now that you've told me the truth," then there is undoubtedly a release of tension. However, when this linguistic information is translated into an auditory composi-tion, the single phrase "I'm more relaxed . . ." will now have to be joined to the phrases ". . . now that you've told me . . ." and ". . . the truth." The manner of joining, or the manner in which the phrases are made consecutive yet sufficiently independent, will have both an aesthetic and a further thematic effect on the action cycle. If pausing or negative sound is used, energy is conserved through paus-ing, and thus tension may actually be heightened even in a speech indicating a state of relaxation. This may or may not be the desired effect, depending upon the motives and manners of the speaker.

Phrases may be joined or isolated by the use of any of the elements of auditory theatre. Thus if we read our current line as a single, un-paused unit, the phrase ". . . now that you've told me . . ." may be isolated by varying the volume, tempo, pitch, or stress patterns for that phrase only. Each variation, of course, will alter the basic linguistic information conveyed by the line and thus may change a line seem-ingly intended as a crisis-releasing device into one that actually builds tension.

UNITING THE GOALS OF DRAMATURGY WITH THE GOALS OF AUDITORY COMPOSITION

We have seen how the dramaturgic elements—language, agent, story, exposition, action, and point of view—may be united with the auditory agents—sound, tempo, volume, pitch, stress, and phrasing. Of course, these elements exist not for themselves but to achieve compositional goals. Hence, the next step in auditory design is to analyze the play script in light of using dramaturgic and auditory elements to achieve a union of dramatic and auditory goals.

The key issue in this juncture is the union of dramatic and auditory rhythm. This joining is very important because the rhythm of the dramatic structure will be delivered by the human voice, the chief instrument of the auditory theatre. The sound-making human being will at the same time be making the chief statements in the kinetic and visual theatres. Thus a single instrument makes a simultaneous synthesis of all the factors of theatrical art from the play script to the movement design. It is principally upon the shared rhythm of drama and movement that this special synthesis is obtained and secured. In foregoing discussions we have observed the special relationship of dramatic rhythm to the element of action and of kinetic rhythm to the element of energy, as well as the close relationship between action and energy. All these relationships seem in some way to be related to the rhythm of motion and life itself—the rhythm by which we use energy in a variation of a contraction–release cycle in order to move and breathe. In fact, speech is the basic sound agent in the auditory theatre; and speech itself is a physical act dependent upon the contraction and relaxation of various muscles in our breathing and eating apparatus in order to vary the flow of air so that different speech sounds are produced. Because of the continuous and vital link rhythm provides throughout theatre, its presence in drama and its link with auditory composition must be closely analyzed in every play script.

DRAMATIC RHYTHM AND THE GOALS OF AUDITORY THEATRE

Rhythm is patterned change, and in the drama this change takes the form of cycles of tension–crisis–release that are most easily seen in the element of action or the kinetic element of energy. In auditory compositions, rhythm is most closely related to beat or meter, but it usually is a broader concept which includes change as well as pattern.

Dramatic rhythms can be found at a very simple level in every element of the play script; but because language is the most obvious element of a written play, we might more easily study it first in the single line. Let us look once again at the line "To be or not to be, that is the question." A tiny but complete dramatic rhythm is contained therein. Most readers would deliver the line in such a way that tension increases until the pause indicated by the comma. A short crisis follows in the pause, and the release of tension is accomplished in the second half of the line. In terms of action, the two initial phrases, "To be" and "not to be," are joined in intellectual–emotional conflict by the word "not." The phrase "that is the question" provides an intellectual as well as rhythmic and aesthetic resolution.

If we study the line "If music be the food of love, play on," we find that the tension-producing part of the line is longer and develops more slowly, that the crisis is swifter, and that the resolution drops rapidly in the verb phrase "play on." Perhaps this is needed because the conflict is more subtle, implied by the slight doubt contained in the hypothetical "if" rather than in the direct confrontation between being and not being.

Simple, basic, dramatic rhythms exemplified in the lines cited might be called *constituent rhythms* because they are the smallest recognizable rhythmic units. Constituent rhythms need not be as long as a single sentence. They may take place in a short phrase or even be contained within a single pause—a pause beginning in a moment of tension and held until the tension peaks and is released. They may also require several lines to be completed. Take the following speech from *Hamlet*. We have already analyzed the first constituent rhythm. The second constituent rhythm, however, does not attain release until the words "end them."

> To be or not to be, that is the question.
> Whether 'tis nobler in the mind to suffer
> The slings and arrows of outrageous fortune
> Or to take arms against a sea of troubles,
> And by opposing, end them. To die—to sleep.

The two constituent rhythms combine with others to form the tension-creating part of Hamlet's famous soliloquy which does not reach a larger crisis until the phrase "ay, there's the rub." In fact, the whole soliloquy is a single larger rhythm beginning with the conflict between suicide and living and ending with the resolution to live because suicide might bring worse conditions than living. This larger rhythm might be called a *sequential rhythm* or a rhythmic sequence. It is usually composed of one or more constituent rhythms that can be found in all parts of its cycle: tension, crisis, or release. Hence even in the release phase of a rhythmic sequence, the tensions and crises of the constituent rhythms add the texture of minor dramatic actions and keep some excitement going even in the most subdued moments of the production.

Rhythmic sequences of various lengths combine to make *scenic rhythms.* A scenic rhythm is the division of a script into large cycles of tension–crisis–release. Most literary editors divide play scripts into scenes according to the story line, and for purposes of reading, story line division is an excellent approach. However, an audience comes to the theatre to experience a work of living art, not to read a story. Thus the director will most probably want to bypass narrative scenic division and analyze his script for rhythmic scenic division. In this regard, consider the first scene in *Hamlet.* Shakespeare himself wrote without scene and act divisions. His editors have generally followed a story line approach in dividing his plays into scenes and acts. Thus Scene 1 ends with the exit of the group from the battlement; Scene 2 commences with the entrance of the royal court. However, rhythmically speaking, Scene 1 is not complete until the entrance of the royal court, for only through the spectacle, pomp and circumstance, flourish and frolic of the court entrance is the tension and crisis of the first scene fully released. The rhythmic joining of the two scenes can be understood even more easily if we recall that Shakespeare's stage had no curtain, and that the exit of the group from the battlement was followed immediately by the entrance of the court into exactly the same space without any change of lighting or scenery. In this same regard, the use of the chorus as a tension-building or tension-releasing agent might well be studied in relation to the rhythm structure of *Oedipus Rex.* The episodes of Greek dramas are rarely self-contained scenic rhythms;

rather, they are that part of the rhythm which immediately surrounds the crisis. In most cases the choral odes provide the remainder of the tension and release aspects of the rhythmic cycle.

Two or more scenic rhythms compose a *major rhythm*. One or more major rhythms are found in every play. In one-act plays, there is usually only one major rhythm. Most directors would feel that there is only one major rhythm in *Oedipus. Hamlet* seems to have more than one, perhaps as many as three or four. Plays are usually divided into acts, and acts usually roughly correspond to a major rhythm. But the director must be careful, for acts are often a narrative or story line division and as such may not contain any major rhythms or may contain more than one.

The several ascending types of dramatic rhythms—constituent, sequential, scenic, and major—are not quantitative but qualitative concepts. There is no way of determining when a constituent rhythm is to be considered sequential, when a scenic rhythm is truly major. And, indeed, because playwrights are human they are capable of creating imperfect rhythms. Sometimes, a playwright may be so concerned with story or language that he loses all rhythm for part of his play. In such a case the director might want to seek contributions from the auditory, visual, or kinetic theatre in order to adjust the rhythmic fault. That is, the director uses music, additional sound, pauses, visual motifs, movements, or combinations of all to create rhythm where none existed or to aid in the structure of inadequate rhythms.

With most skilled playwrights, the problem is not the salvaging of poorly built rhythms but the realizing of the total potential of the rhythm in the auditory, visual, and kinetic theatres. In fact, with playwrights who know the theatre well, the director will find that the dramatic rhythm is so structured that opportunities are provided for its extension into the auditory, visual, and kinetic theatres. This means that most lines depend upon a special vocal, kinetic, and visual treatment in order to be rhythmically realized. On an obvious level this dependence can be seen in such stage directions as: "the lines are said simultaneously," "he starts to speak but is interrupted by a sign from his friend," "he sits upon the throne as he says this line." But in plays such as *Hamlet* and *Salesman*, the extensions of rhythm from script to sound, vision, and motion can be found in almost every scene, whether deliberately cited in the stage directions or not.

Rhythm is not limited to language alone. It is a structural feature of all dramaturgic elements. Character, for example, has a rhythmic factor. Compare Hamlet and Claudius. Hamlet's mood is quiet, cynical, and disengaged at the beginning of the play. Claudius is elated; his character tension is greater than Hamlet's. As Hamlet's involvement grows toward a climax, so does Claudius'. However, having more tension at the outset, Claudius reaches his rhythmic peak first—in his flight from the performance by the players. Hamlet is not in total crisis until the scene with Gertrude. It might be interesting to note that by this time Ophelia has long since passed her rhythmic peak—in her scene in which Hamlet ordered her to a nunnery.

Exposition, while it seems not to be related to rhythm, is in truth often tightly woven with rhythm. After all, suspense plays are made suspenseful by a prolongation of the tension phase of rhythm, and this prolongation is often achieved by holding back key items of exposition. This is a technique perfected by Ibsen, and it can be observed at its best in *Death of a Salesman*. In that play the tension between Biff and Willy is prolonged by an unacknowledged secret between the father and son, a secret not revealed until the crisis of the play; in fact, a secret which forms the major crisis of the play—Biff's surprising Willy with another woman. In this way, exposition becomes the crisis of the action and the peak of the major rhythm.

Exposition can also be a tension-building device in the dramatic rhythm, as, for example, when Tiresias tells Oedipus that he himself is the guilty party. Again, exposition may be tension-releasing as in the case of the first scene in *Hamlet*. After the Ghost makes its first appearance, Shakespeare eases the tension by having Horatio tell the soldiers all the exposition leading up to the current situation.

Story and point of view also have a rhythmic dimension. Note, for example, the rhythm of place in *From Morn to Midnight*. First there is the place of work, then a crisis in a snow field, next the Cashier's home, followed by a series of rapid changes of locale leading to a major crisis in the Salvation Army Hall. A simpler use of rhythm of place is found in *Waltz of the Toreadors*. Here the crisis of the action is identical with a crisis of place—St. Pé leaves the brightness of his study to encounter his wife in the dark recesses of her sick room.

Death of a Salesman offers an excellent example of both time and incident in a rhythmic cycle. Throughout the play we shift from past time to present time, from past incident to present incident. Each shift is usually the result of tension and crisis in either past or present. Thus a crisis in the present time and incident—Willy's eldest son returning home, for example—produces a rhythmic flow to past time and incident—the happy days when Willy would return from a selling trip to Linda and the adoring boys. This example of time and incident in *Salesman* is also an example of point of view in its rhythmic development. The conflict between the objective viewpoint of the present and Willy's subjective remembrances of things past develops in an increasingly tense pattern, until the two viewpoints meet in final conflict in the scene in which Willy, collapsing on the floor of a public washroom, remembers the day Biff came unexpectedly to his hotel room.

In summary, a director will want to keep in mind that dramatic rhythm may be divided into four aspects: constituent rhythms, sequential rhythms, scenic rhythms, and major rhythms. They may be realized in or through one or more of the auditory elements, or in a combination of auditory, kinetic, and visual elements. They are most directly and most importantly observed in their close affinity to dramatic action—conflict, crisis, release; and to kinetic energy—conserved, released. All the varied aspects of theatre combine at the point of dramatic rhythm.

While in their ascending order there is no clear distinction between the various levels of dramatic rhythm, it is important to the final sense of production harmony that each rhythmic level be given its appropriate treatment. To this end, the remaining goals of dramaturgy must be considered.

DRAMATIC UNITY AND AUDITORY THEATRE

Auditory unity must be identical to or compatible with dramaturgic unity. Hence if a play is complex in structure, the auditory theatre should also seek a complex statement. Specifically, the unity of *Hamlet* is gained through the character of Hamlet; but it is also dependent on the contrasts between Hamlet and the many different characters of the court. Thus while the speeches of Hamlet will have to be the single most important melodic line, the vocal quality and type of the various other characters will all contribute to the rich unity of the play. In short, the director may want to present *Hamlet* as a play unified by the very variety of its vocal differences.

On the other hand, it is possible that a director might want to stress the importance of the Cashier's point of view in *Morn to Midnight* by having all the characters have a vocal quality or approach very similar to that of the central character. Another director might wish to gain the same auditory unity for the play simply by having all characters speak at a faster than usual speed, while using all other vocal elements freely.

In making choices such as the two outlined above, much will depend on the need for emphasis, proportion, and variety.

DRAMATIC PROPORTION, EMPHASIS, AND VARIETY AND THE AUDITORY THEATRE

Proportion means that each element receives its just attention; auditory harmony requires that each sound be in its appropriate relation to other sounds. To obtain both ends, the director must not cast an Oedipus with such a thrilling voice and a Jocasta with such an uninteresting voice that he will find it impossible to design a scene in which Jocasta might have temporary vocal dominance.

In the same vein, the director will want to give emphasis to the character who needs emphasis at a given moment. For only through appropriate emphasis will proportion and unity be obtained. For example, in the first scene of the third act, Hamlet and Ophelia play a touching love duet. While Hamlet probably dominates the scene, it is a more significant moment for Ophelia, who actually reaches her rhythmic peak in this scene. Thus while the director will wish to show Hamlet as both stronger and dominant, he will not want to neglect this important moment for Ophelia. In fact, several times in the scene the young girl actually rises to a dominant status. Note in this regard the line: "Could beauty, my lord, have better commerce than with honesty?" Depending upon the rhythmic development of the entire scene, a given director might wish this line to gain a primary emphasis for Ophelia. If so, she might say the line after a long pause, or she might read the line with a reduction in speed. If the scene had been one of a rising give-and-take for the several short speeches before, Ophelia might gain emphasis by reading the line as a quiet but intense understatement.

As the examples cited above suggest, auditory variety is good in itself; nevertheless, it should also seek to increase the quality of dramatic variety. Thus even if a particular reading is selected because it would provide variety, the director should bear in mind that any vocal change alters the aesthetic and design values of a production. Thus a varied reading of a line that gave strength to a weak character or dominance to a subordinate might be good variety but poor design.

THE AUDITORY THEATRE: A SUMMARY

Auditory art begins with the translation of the literature of the play script into sound that will be heard in a theatre. The elements of auditory art are sound, rate, pitch, volume, stress, and phrasing. The goals of auditory art are unity, harmony, emphasis, rhythm, and variety. These elements and goals are used by the director to realize in sound the dramaturgic elements and goals of the play script. As the director moves from sound to script, he creates both an auditory composition and an auditory design. This work of auditory art he relates to the kinetic and visual theatre through the synthesis of all three arts in the visible, moving, speaking presence of the actor.

In the joining of sound and written script and in the uniting of sound to vision and motion, the director's understanding of dramatic rhythm is crucial. Based upon kinetic energy and dramatic action, dramatic rhythm is composed of a series of movements involving a growing tension, a time of crisis, and a period of relaxation. The basic unit of dramatic rhythm is the constituent rhythm. Constituent rhythms combine to make rhythmic sequences. Sequences make scenic rhythms, and a major rhythm is composed of two or more scenic rhythms. A full-length play may have one or more major rhythms. In the construction of dramatic rhythms, the director will want to consider the uses of auditory theatre in the creation of dramatic unity, proportion, emphasis, and variety.

CHAPTER 10

presenting the play to the actors

In the foregoing chapters attention was given to the visual, auditory, and kinetic principles which govern the director in the creation of the theatrical metaphor. Throughout, a single guiding concept was stressed time and again: The director can never expect to follow a fixed pattern in his approach to artistic problems. Each play—each cast of each play—is so unique that the director must be prepared to take up problems as they arise, and they may arise at any time from the first rehearsal to the final performance. Thus when the director comes to present his play script to his actors, he must be prepared to call upon any principle of his art at any moment. There is no typical pattern in which his problems will tend to appear.

A few difficulties will usually become apparent when the scene designer presents his floor plan, but most theatrical problems only become crystallized after the director has assembled his acting company and commenced rehearsing. Consequently, although a certain amount of preplanning is necessary, the director will do well to remain as flexible as possible. More often than not, blocking all the movements of a play before becoming thoroughly acquainted with actors' capabilities may cause the director to choose between forcing the actors into patterns they cannot execute or else completely redoing all that he has so painstakingly put together. Either choice is likely to be wasteful and frustrating.

On the other hand, after making his initial decisions about the play script, the theatre building, the costumes, and the set, the director must begin somewhere to create his production. Usually he begins with assembling a prompt book or collecting an acting company.

THE PROMPT BOOK

Whether a director begins to put together a prompt book before or after he assembles his acting company depends upon the time he has for initial preparations. In any event, the prompt book is a progressive work that grows with each rehearsal. It is a special edition of the play script containing sufficient marginal space in which to write all the necessary records of the production. The exact organization of the prompt book differs greatly from director to director. The important thing is that it be legible and that it contain a record detailed enough to provide working continuity in rehearsal and dependable guidance in production.

Among the many methods of organizing a prompt book, one that has worked well for many directors is the use of two margins for notes. On one margin are placed all notes dealing with blocking, visual composition, and line reading; on the opposite margin are written all notes containing lighting, scenery, sound, and property information. (See Plate Nineteen.) All notes are written in pencil at first, since they are subject to change as rehearsals develop. When matters of sound, lights, and props are finally fixed, they are recorded in colored inks. Lighting, sound, and props are each assigned a different color so that they may be readily distinguished one from another. Lighting and sound cues may be numbered separately, or the numbering system may be combined; that is, under the separate system the first light cue may be "lights one," the second "lights two," etc. The first sound cue would thus be "sound one."

Under the combined system, cues are numbered as they happen regardless of type. Thus cue number one might refer to lights, cue two to sound, and cue three might be a simultaneous cue for both lights and sound. For most purposes, a combined cueing system prevents confusion, especially if the stage manager is calling all cues.

ASSEMBLING THE ACTING COMPANY

With or without a prompt book, the director must have actors before he can create his production. Casting is perhaps the single most crucial phase of the art of directing. Certainly it is the most difficult, and while the actors and the director may find tryouts exciting, the more experienced a director becomes, the more he dreads the problems of casting. The experienced director knows that a single serious casting error may force him to change significantly his concept of the play. Sometimes an error in casting is grave enough to create a weak production even before the first rehearsal.

How may a director protect himself against such errors? There seems to be no sure method. Each director has his own private casting techniques; some of the more common of these have been discussed in Chapter 6. As the director gains experience, he begins to learn his particular casting weaknesses. Against such shortcomings he will want to take future safeguards. Whatever the exact casting process followed, the director should keep in mind two guiding principles. First, he must maintain flexibility; second, he should avoid "listener fatigue."

Some few directors are extremely fortunate and work with a fixed company. In such circumstances, the decision to do a certain play automatically carries with it the overall casting of that play. Whatever the disadvantages, a fixed company does reduce casting problems.

Most directors, however, must audition modest to large groups of aspiring actors. The larger the group, the more the casting director must guard against listener fatigue. By whatever method he can devise, the director must remain alert to every auditioner, and, above all, he must be able to recognize when he is no longer responding to readers. He must know when to stop auditioning and take a rest.

The director who is blessed with an abundance of good talent at his tryouts may find to his dismay that he has some fine actors but none that fit his initial conception of certain roles. Such a director must be ready to revise his thinking in terms of one or two roles, or perhaps in terms of the entire cast. Too often a director comes to tryouts looking for certain "types," and, not finding what he wants, he casts the actors who come closest. Such an inflexible policy may work, but more often than not the director lives to learn that a "near miss is as good as a mile." Normally, the director in such circumstances is frustrated by a performance that "wasn't quite right," or else the director and the actor waste all their creative energies attempting to realize the impossible rather than perfecting the possible.

Not infrequently the flexibility demanded at tryouts must also be exercised during rehearsals. Many a director has cast an actor only to discover that his reading at tryouts was entirely misleading. When such a discovery is made, the director has no choice but to readjust his approach to the role. There is no point in blaming the actor; the mistake is the fault of the director.

INITIAL REHEARSALS

After casting, the director is ready for rehearsals. Rehearsal is the time when the director and the actors do their real creative work; performance is the demonstration of the creative activity of rehearsal. Contrary to certain popular conceptions, rehearsals are not the time when the director puts on a show for the actors. Flamboyance, eloquence, or sudden shifts of temper may be characteristic of some directors; but, however interesting, personality traits should not be confused with art.

Gaining the confidence and cooperation of the actor, both as an artist in his own right and as an element of the director's art, is absolutely necessary. As in all human social situations, such cooperation is most often gained through courtesy and mutual respect. The director will normally wish to be polite and concise in his communication with his actors, so that social harmony can be maintained on the one hand and ambiguity avoided on the other.

The actor will necessarily want to know as soon as possible the director's concept of the character he is playing. In order to satisfy this curiosity, some directors begin their rehearsals by "reading-through" the play. At this initial read-through, the director stops and comments on the characters and their situations. The practice of reading-through the play has both advantages and disadvantages. The most significant accomplishment of a read-through is the assurance that everyone has read the play at least once. Along with hearing directorial comments on the play, the actors are introduced to one another at this time. A major disadvantage is that the read-through encourages the actors to think of the spoken line as separate from the deed and tends to support an approach to character based entirely upon the spoken word. Furthermore, the director who is tempted at the read-through to comment at length upon character may later regret his decision. Prolonged comment often runs the risk of creating more misunderstanding than it resolves. Even if the actor and director communicate perfectly, the director might establish a vision of the character which he will later wish to change. Since the actor is also capable of imaginative analysis, the director might do well to withhold detailed comment on character until he sees what the actor brings to future rehearsal. The director might do well to remember that if the author wished extensive additional verbal comment on the characters, he could well have done so himself.

Another disadvantage of the read-through is the director's tendency to adjust the readings of individual lines. The readings heard from a group of actors sitting about with script in hand are not likely to be entirely satisfactory. Hence the temptation on the part of the director to tamper with oral interpretation. The director should remember that no matter how versatile an actor's vocal instrument, a line read by a Hamlet who is sitting in a relaxed position is not the same as a line read by a Hamlet who is towering over a prostrate Gertrude.

Many directors begin rehearsals immediately with movement as well as line reading. Whatever the approach, lengthy discussions between the director and the actor ought to be avoided, especially at first when neither has a clear concept of all possible production issues. This does not mean that the director can never supply a motive or comment on a reading, but he would do well to do so only when all other means have been exhausted. After all, motives and readings are prerogatives of the art of acting as well as directing. If the actor is providing the director with a good performance, what does it matter if the actor's thinking is not totally in agreement with the director's? Results—and not the means of obtaining them—are important.

THE DIRECTOR AS ACTING COACH

Despite every wish not to interfere in the art of the actor, the director often finds that he must function as acting coach. Such activity is the lot of every director no matter how skilled his actors. Unfortunately, there are times in the noncommercial theatre when the director must spend almost all his time as an acting coach. He may even have to teach an actor in the proscenium the difference between stage-left and stage-right, or the names of the standard body positions. He may have to give an actor a running course in oral interpretation.

Because the director may have to be a part-time acting coach, he should be thoroughly trained as an actor; and, in order to maintain his acting skill, the director would be wise to continue to act from time to time. The man who has no training or experience as an actor can hardly hope to help others act. On the other hand, the director must not confuse acting coaching with play direction. The goal of directing is not to achieve a good performance from an actor; rather, the art of directing begins with assuming a good acting performance and continues by integrating that performance into the total concept of the production.

THE BLOCKING REHEARSALS

Blocking rehearsals are used to set up basic visual and kinetic patterns. At a blocking rehearsal the director gets the actors on their feet and begins to talk them through their movement patterns. The director's initial movement problem is one of traffic control. *Traffic*, or the smooth and uninhibited flow of actors about the stage, is vital because actors cannot be communicating subtle vocal, visual, and kinetic meanings to the audience if they are wandering aimlessly about the stage, bumping into furniture and other actors. Some traffic patterns require considerable preplanning; others can be conceived on the spot as the need arises. Traffic patterns begin with entrances and exits and continue with onstage activity.

ENTRANCES AND EXITS

It goes without saying that the director should have done sufficient preplanning to know when most entrances and exits occur. Not every entrance or exit can be identified; some may not appear necessary until quite late in rehearsal. Identifying entrances and exits is not simply reading the script to discover when characters go on and off stage. The director must distinguish between essential entrances and exits and those of convenience. Essential entrances and exits must be accomplished in order for the narrative to progress. Convenient entrances and exits are those inserted by the editor, a previous director, or the present director and are inserted for various technical, personal, or aesthetic reasons. Essential entrances and exits must be retained in some form or other. That is, although an essential entrance or exit must take place, it need not be accomplished exactly as indicated in the script. Entrances and exits of convenience may be retained, altered, or dispensed with as the director wishes. Let us take an example.

The entrance of Bernardo in the first scene in *Hamlet* is an essential entrance. Bernardo must enter, and he must enter no later than his cue, although he may enter earlier. Bernardo may be alone, or he may be accompanied by four or five soldiers. If additional soldiers enter, they are making an entrance of convenience, and the director has probably introduced them for visual or aesthetic reasons. If the director wishes, the soldiers may be dropped from the scene at any time. Naturally, entrances and exits of convenience must be logical in terms of the story line and the entire style of the play. The director can introduce a squad of soldiers to accompany Bernardo; but unless he is working surrealistically, he probably should not have Ophelia present also. Of course, once a production is designed, all entrances and exits are essential ones.

If they have read the script, the actors are usually aware of essential entrances and exits, but they must be informed of additional ones. Moreover, even the essential entrances and exits must be explained to the actor in great detail. The most crucial times in every actor's performance are when he comes on and when he leaves the stage. He must know his exact point of origin, when he is to begin, where he is to go, and the path he is to follow in going to his destination.

Actors already on stage are greatly affected by the entering or exiting actor. Consequently, they also must be instructed concerning their exact reactions to the incoming or outgoing dramatic agent. It is not enough for the director to say, "Joe, you enter here." He must tell Joe exactly which word or onstage movement cues his entrance, where Joe looks when he enters, and where he goes when he moves. By the same token, the director cannot say to the other actors, "react to Joe's entrance." They must have their reaction patterns indicated in some detail.

The necessity of being extremely precise in outlining entrances and exits seems to run contrary to the advice never to preplan movements that have not been tested on the actors. The contradiction is more apparent than real. The director should plan extremely precise entrances and exits, but he should be ready to change them whenever necessary. As with every other aspect of directing, the director must be ready to be flexible in terms of entrances and exits. On the other hand, entrances and exits are so basic—actually the keystone of the entire kinetic composition—that they need to be approached with the greatest possible precision. A carefully planned entrance or exit, even though it is subject to complete revision, gives both actor and director a strong sense of confidence and provides a solid base for future change. Neither the actor in question nor the remaining actors know what to do when a director says, "now come on in," or "now you exit." Instead of providing the actor with creative freedom, such loose directions are likely to produce visual and kinetic anarchy.

THE BASIC ISSUES OF ENTRANCES AND EXITS

Every entrance or exit involves certain basic issues. The two most significant issues are the problems of strong and weak and of dominance and subordinance. Every exit and entrance is either strong, weak, or somewhere in between. The director cannot hedge on an entrance or an exit; he must decide where the movement belongs on the strong–weak scale. While strengths and weaknesses are naturally the result of the entire theatrical situation, we can say in general that entrances and exits that begin strongly and end weakly are weak entrances and exits, while those that begin weakly and end strongly are strong entrances and exits. Others fall somewhere in between. In terms of visual theatre only, the strongest entrances and exits begin in visually weak areas—those lower in height or farther upstage in the proscenium and those lower in height and on the periphera of the stage in the arena—and terminate in visually strong areas. Body position will, of course, greatly influence entrances and exits. Any entrance that terminates in a full-front position, or any exit that can terminate in full-front or full-back, is stronger than entrances that end in other positions, if all else is equal. This is one reason that actors often save a line or so to be delivered full-front at the end of a long exit path.

Kinetic factors also color the relative strength or weakness of an entrance or exit. In general, the shorter the temporal or spatial length of an entrance or exit, the stronger is the movement. The more rapid an entrance or exit, the stronger the movement; the more energy the entrance or exit conserves, the stronger the movement. On the other hand, visual or kinetic contrast will provide strength. If all exits have been short and rapid, then a long, slow entrance might seem strong; if all entrances have been originating at a point of visual strength, then an entrance from a visually weaker area might seem strong. It might be observed at this point that since entrances and exits are merely a special kind of theatrical movement, the principles of vision and movement that create weakness and strength in entrances and exits will also create similar qualities in any movement on stage.

Just as visual and kinetic factors will affect an entrance's strength or weakness, so also will the literary theatre. If the story line locates the hiding place of the murderer upstage-left, then that normally weak position will take on psychological strength. Consequently, an entrance or exit through that point will mean an entrance originating in strength and an exit terminating in strength. Sound in the auditory theatre will also have an effect. When all actors are speaking or have been speaking, the properly emphasized silent entrance will have considerable strength. Usually, however, the normal entrance or exit will gain strength from being accompanied by speech or other sound, while exits and entrances that are silent will seem weaker.

The issue of strength and weakness in entering and exiting is naturally related to the issue of dominance and subordination. The director must decide whether the entering and exiting actor is to be dominant or subordinate. Dominance and subordination must be handled separately from strength and weakness. However, the director must keep in mind that if he does not employ mitigating techniques, strong entrances will be dominant while weak entrances will be subordinate. If the director wishes an entrance to be both strong and subordinate, he will probably have to gain strength from one aspect of theatre while obtaining subordination from another. For instance, an entrance could be strong visually but subordinated, or weakened, kinetically. That is, an actor may have his entrance strengthened by having all visual lines focused on him, but because the actors already on stage are moving and speaking, *they* retain the major burden of dominance.

The third entrance-exit issue is tied directly to the first two—the director must determine the exact amount of audience attention or emphasis to be given to each entrance and exit. Not all entrances and exits should make equal demands on the audience's attention. Indeed, many important entrances and exits should be executed so that the audience has little or no awareness of the presence or absence of one or more dramatic agents. For example, after the first scene in *Death of a Salesman*, Biff and Happy might exit without the audience's being aware that they have left their bedroom. Frequently, the decision as to how much attention should be devoted to an entrance or exit is not easily assessed. Shakespeare does not tell us how attentive the audience should be to the scene two entrance of Hamlet. Should the Prince merely enter as another member of the court, only to be identified much later in the scene, or should Hamlet's entrance be given special attention from the beginning of the scene? If the director elects the latter approach, he must deal in divided emphasis between the speaking Claudius and the listening Prince; if he decides to withhold attention from Hamlet, he can concentrate all emphasis on Claudius. Neither approach is absolutely preferable, but the director cannot be ambiguous. For the sake of the two actors performing in the roles, he must make a decision so that an ensemble can be created.

Usually the issue of attention is a matter of degree, for in almost all cases it is virtually impossible to introduce or eliminate a dramatic agent without attracting the attention of the audience to some degree. Careful control, however, can provide an almost "invisible" entrance or exit. The actor's cooperation in such cases is mandatory, for the slightest deviation from the planned pattern will destroy entirely the hoped-for amount of attention or inattention.

The fourth major entrance–exit issue is the problem of multiple entrances, exits, or a combination of both. On its simplest level, a multiple entrance or exit means the bringing-on or the taking-off of more than one person at a time. Such entrance–exit patterns are naturally more complicated than those involving a single actor. First of all, there is a simple problem of grace and coordination. If they are to follow a single path, the actors must know who is to go first, who is to follow, and at what intervals. Of course, single-path entrances have a parade quality; and when such artificiality is not desired, the director should see that his scene designer has provided more than one major entrance or exit. The more people to be brought on or exited at one time, the greater is the need for multiple entranceways.

Multiple entranceways should probably be provided in most cases for several important reasons. First, multiple entranceways offer needed variety in coming on and going off stage. More important, however, multiple entranceways allow the director to disperse large entering or exiting masses. Such masses often endanger visual and kinetic composition. For example, any large mass suddenly introduced into a visual field from a single point will probably destroy all balance, take unto itself all emphasis, and entirely reshape the prevailing unity. When a large mass is removed at a single point from a given visual field, the same phenomena will usually take place in reverse. Even greater problems are created in kinetic composition. A large moving mass entering a kinetic composition will tend to attract to it all other masses. The resulting attraction will further tend to destroy all possible dynamic tensions. If a large mass exits, it is likely to draw in its trailing vacuum all bodies remaining on stage. If, because of the demands of the story line, certain actors remain on stage despite the attraction of the exiting mass, a destruction of integrity of motion follows. Consequently, although there are times when, for purposes of stylization or because of the demands of a play script or the design of a set, the director finds he must bring on or take off a large mass of actors through a single entranceway, he should carefully construct such enterings and exitings so that the requirements of visual and kinetic composition are satisfied.

Frequently, a director will employ multiple entrances or exits for convenience rather than through necessity. Normally such multiple movements provide him with desirable visual or kinetic counterpoints. For instance, he may "create" some customers for the restaurant scene in *Death of a Salesman*. Just before Willy enters the restaurant, the director causes the customers to exit. This exit might be designed to help create the narrative illusion of a restaurant; but it might also be used so that the vacuum created by the exit of the customers can be filled by Willy, thereby gaining for the actor a dominant and kinetically emphasized entrance.

The example of an exit of convenience in *Salesman* serves to remind us that the fifth major entrance–exit issue is the problem of maintaining the total kinetic and visual design. Visual and kinetic design and composition do not begin *after* the entrance or end just *before* the exit. All entrances and exits must be visually and kinetically logical in themselves and also in terms of the total visual and kinetic patterns of the play. One or more characters should not come on stage or go off stage because the script says so, but because it is visually and kinetically necessary that a new agent be introduced or eliminated at one precise point in the production. In terms of kinetic and visual composition, then, entrances and exits should add to sequence and not appear as breaks in the kinetic and visual patterns. Consequently, when the Secretary enters a few lines after the opening of *Waltz of the Toreadors,* he should come in because of compelling visual and kinetic reasons. Such reasons are easy enough to manufacture in plays such as *Hamlet* or *Oedipus Rex,* where there are usually enough actors on stage to create innumerable visual and kinetic patterns; but in *Waltz* at this particular point, only St. Pé is present. If enough actors were available, the director might create a triangle with one of its points vacant. The entering actor would then move to the vacant point. But with only one actor, the director will probably have to seek kinetic rather than video-kinetic justification. Perhaps he can move St. Pé near the anticipated point of entrance, keep him there long enough to fix the locality firmly in the minds of the audience, then move him suddenly just before the entrance of the Secretary. The resulting vacuum will demand filling and the appearance of the Secretary in the vacuum will seem both logical and aesthetically pleasing. A simple visual solution to the same problem would be to have St. Pé focus on the entrance; but this solution, while obtaining visual logic, might tip the hand of the playwright by "telegraphing" the upcoming entrance.

The final issue in entering and exiting is concerned with unity and dramatic rhythm. Every entrance and exit tests the continuity of the total dramatic rhythm, and each time a director brings on or takes off a dramatic agent he must decide how such activity is to be incorporated into the total rhythm of the production. Some entrances and exits signal new movements in the rhythm, while others merely add to the pattern already established. Therefore, the director must determine whether a given entrance or exit marks the tension, the crisis, or the release of a constituent rhythm, or of a scenic or major rhythm. For instance, Bernardo's first entrance in *Hamlet* is actually the crisis of the first constituent rhythm of that play. Therefore, great care must be taken to maintain rhythmic continuity up to and through the entrance of Bernardo. On the other hand, some directors might view the first entrance of the Secretary in *Waltz* as the beginning point of a new rhythmic sequence, and thus would feel justified in bringing the rhythmic flow to a pause just before the entrance of the Secretary.

A complete halt in the rhythm of *Waltz* at this point, or of any play so early in its development, is probably not advisable. The rhythmic sequence beginning with the entrance of the Secretary is neither a scenic nor a major rhythm and should not be emphatically isolated from other constituent rhythms. Consequently, to let the preceding rhythmic sequence run through complete relaxation before bringing on the Secretary would seriously injure the rhythmic continuity of the play. Thus it would be preferable that the Secretary not enter on verbal cue but already be a part of the scene when his verbal cue is given.

The dovetailing of rhythmic sequences through the entering and exiting process is difficult, but it is a lesson that should be learned as

253

quickly as possible. Constituent rhythms are not usually discrete units juxtaposed one next to the other, but are rather a continuous rhythmic fibre in which the diminishing tension of one sequence usually forms the beginning of the tension of the following sequence.

Naturally, in the matter of the continuity of sequences, the problem of entrances and exits is basic. Far too many plays have "poor pace," seem overly long or are "jerky" because actors enter or leave on vocal cue, which is usually the very end or beginning of a constituent rhythm. When rhythms are not interwoven, the play seems to progress by fits and starts. The entering or exiting actor should always anticipate the end or the commencement of a rhythmic sequence, and he should normally have gotten on stage or have exited before the old rhythm has ended or the new rhythm begun. There are exceptions to this rule of thumb, but in general the director will want to design his entrances or exits so that the actor can come on or leave without breaking the rhythmic continuity of the production.

A natural break in continuity will come when the entrance or exit signals the beginning or end of a scenic or major rhythm. Just as the director must not make every entrance or exit a rhythmic pause, he should provide for those that must be pauses. Unfortunately, these entrances or exits are often the most difficult, because they frequently involve more than one actor coming on or leaving, or a combination of entrances and exits. Moreover, each particular rhythmic break must be adjusted to its proper value in the theatrical metaphor. Some breaks involve a brief stop or even merely a glide, while others must be understood by the audinece as being total and complete.

As this discussion indicates, the problem of entrances and exits is both crucial and difficult. It is not simply a matter of telling the actors when to enter and when to leave. The director must face six major issues in every entrance or exit: the issue of strong and weak, of dominance and subordination, of audience attention, of multiple entrances and exits, of overall kinetic and visual design, and of the unity of the dramatic rhythm. Naturally, the director will want to help the actor over the difficult period of getting on and getting off stage by being as precise as possible. To this end, a carefully worked-out scheme of entering and exiting will be helpful. The scheme can, of course, be altered at will, but an imprecise initial pattern of entrance or exit jeopardizes the actor's confidence in himself and in his director.

Being specific and detailed about entrances and exits does not mean that the director should discuss each entrance–exit issue with the actor. With most of these issues the actor has little or no concern. Rather, the director should describe for the actor exactly how to enter or exit. The actor may ask for a motive for such behavior, and, if necessary, the director should be prepared to supply one. In all likelihood, however, if the visual, kinetic, and auditory composition is adequately handled by the director, the actor should feel an innate logic in what he is doing and should neither need nor want a motive.

FOLLOWING UP THE ENTRANCE OR THE EXIT

What happens immediately after an exit or an entrance is almost as important as the entrance or exit itself. The firm control established on the entrance or exit patterns must continue to be maintained. Left to his own devices, the entering actor will immediately head for center-stage, or the first empty chair, or the largest item of furniture or architecture. On the other hand, actors remaining on stage after an exit are apt to begin talking too quickly or to continue looking or moving in the direction of the exited actor. While in certain specific cases each of these activities might be exactly what the director wishes, often they are not only undesirable but frequently detrimental to the quality of the scene at hand.

The entering actor must be reminded that he should never willingly move to the strongest possible position or to any location that severely limits his potential for additional change or movement. If the actor has a tendency to take full-front-center or to sit immediately, the director should anticipate such a tendency by providing the entering actor with a movement direction, a terminal location, and a body position allowing for several alternatives in terms of future development.

Entrances also signal that the actors already on stage must be adjusted to accommodate the entering actor. The director should have clearly in mind the means by which onstage actors react to an entering actor. When entrances take place, the director should give reaction blocking to each of the actors already in the scene. In many ways, onstage actors are more affected by exiting actors than by those entering. After all, actors remaining on stage must react to an exit, give it the proper attention, and yet retain enough attention for themselves so that the whole play does not "go offstage" with the exiting actor. Consequently, the director must be quite specific in giving post-exit blocking to those who remain on stage. He should remember that each exit creates a virtual line leading from the initial starting point of the exit to the spot where the exit occurred. The director must plan to break the force of such a virtual line by creating other lines of force which turn the attention of the audience back to the actors remaining on stage. Thus for every strong or dominant exit, the director must create a visual counterpoint strong enough to be interesting to the audience after the exit has taken place. Kinetically speaking, every exit is concerned with a moving mass that creates a trailing vacuum. The director must discover some means of countering the pull of such a vacuum. The simplest method is the traditional one of "breaking" the exit. Just before the actor exits, he turns and delivers his last words. This technique has the advantage of giving the actor a visually strong exit, and at the same time weakening the pull of the vacuum to his rear. Since the strength of such a following vacuum is directly related to the speed and path of the moving body, the actor who needs only a few feet to move for his exit will have neither a very pronounced path nor a very high speed. Other, more complex methods will often be necessary to handle the kinetic problems of retaining attention after an exit. Most of these methods will usually employ a second moving mass working in dynamic tension with the exiting actor or actors.

Let us take from *Hamlet* an example of the solution of post-exit visual and kinetic problems. Consider the problem of the explosive exit of Claudius after the "play-within-the-play." As Claudius moves off stage he creates a virtual line in the direction of his movement, and he further creates a strong vacuum to his rear. Since the story line calls for Claudius to rush off, the vacuum he creates is probably an extremely compelling one, especially if he is followed by his servants. If Hamlet and the court are watching and moving after Claudius, it will be difficult for them to regain attention for themselves after Claudius and his retinue leave the stage. If the court does not watch or follow Claudius, the reactions will seem unnatural. The problem is a thorny one, and among the many possible solutions, a director might employ the following. As Claudius recognizes himself in the play, he leaps up, and, in his desperate desire to flee, moves directly toward Hamlet, who has been placed between Claudius and the major entranceway. Recognizing Hamlet, Claudius stops short. The Prince gives his uncle a look of distatste and disdain and turns from him. Claudius backs off a step or so, and then turns and hurries out through a secondary entranceway. Hamlet, in the meantime, is moving in the opposite direction. For a certain length of time and place the two actors will be in a dynamic tension. At this moment the director can cause Horatio to watch his friend Hamlet, while the Queen and the court watch the King. Just as Claudius exits, Horatio moves within the line of vision of the Queen. As the members of the court follow Claudius off, the Queen turns to look at what Horatio is watching so intently. She sees Hamlet.

Through such a process, the exit of Claudius has been given proper attention, while the attention the audience must now pay to Hamlet has been secured and reinforced even before the exit of Claudius is totally accomplished. In short, visual and kinetic counterpoints have been established allowing for the passing of interest from the original point, or exit, to the counterpoint, or the actor remaining on stage.

It goes without saying that the director will not normally want to talk to the actors in terms of point and counterpoint. If talk is necessary at all, the director will find that he can supply perfectly appropriate motives and manners for the activities described above. Certainly there is good reason for Horatio to watch his friend Hamlet rather than the King, and there is even better reason for Hamlet to turn from the stricken and frightened king. Finally, Gertrude, caught up in the confusion of the exit, might well turn to see what draws Horatio so intently.

However, the director who finds that his actors are constantly badgering him for motives might do well to reconsider his visual and kinetic composition. Perhaps his use of vision and motion is not as well related to the play script as he might have thought. Any exit or entrance pattern can be changed; but changed or not, the director must have a rather clear-cut traffic pattern from which to work.

TRAFFIC PATTERNS

Between entrances and exits, actors engage in onstage activity not necessarily related to an entrance or exit. Onstage activity is the traffic pattern. Like automobiles on a complicated expressway, actors move about a complex set according to a few simple traffic guides. While these guides do not in any way accomplish a beautiful kinetic composition, they do help the actors to avoid accidents while a kinetic composition is being constructed. And just as automobiles have a basic rule of "keep right," actors should be reminded of the basic rule: always move by the shortest or most obvious route. Briefly stated, this rule means that unless told otherwise, an actor should "always follow his nose." A second basic guide of stage traffic patterns is that the actor should always position himself for the greatest possible potential for future movement. Briefly stated, the second guide means that unless otherwise directed, the actor should always avoid sitting or standing as if he is finally and forever planted. In short, whenever possible the actor should "break a level" and avoid full-front in both sitting and standing.

A popular cliché of acting is always to seek the firmest and strongest body position. While the director certainly doesn't want the actor jerking about aimlessly, he will not always want the actor to sit or stand so that no new movement is easily possible. The actor who plants himself firmly on both feet or who settles back in a chair will often find that he must spend great energies, both actual and apparent, getting into new motion. Such energy loss will tend to weaken his character. Consequently, unless the director expressly indicates immobility, the actor should always avoid postures of complete stability.

Often the most obvious route of movement is neither the smoothest nor the straightest. If the actor does not know how to move in a graceful, curved cross so that he arrives at his destination in the proper body position, or if he is clumsy moving up and down levels, the director should be prepared to coach him in horizontal and vertical movement patterns. The director should, of course, realize that the first time any such movements are attempted on a new set, even by the best of actors, they might look awkward.

Along with the principles of "follow your nose" and "break a level," the actor might have to be taught the third rule of stage traffic: "Counter when necessary." Known on the proscenium stage as "dressing the stage," countering is even more important in the arena because it is one of the chief means by which movement is given direction in the arena. Quite simply, countering is the movement by which one actor adjusts to the motion of a second actor. For example, if actor A moves from down-right to down-center, actor B, who has been up-center, automatically moves slightly stage-right, or counter to the movement of A. This counter-movement gives emphasis to the direction of A's movement and at the same time allows actor B to continue to be seen by the audience (see Diagram 1, below). In the arena, if actor A moves toward center stage, actor B will move slightly away from center (see Diagram 2, below). While such a counter does not normally affect the audience's vision of actor B, the movement gives point and direction to actor A's motion.

Actors should be taught that unless the director specifies otherwise, or unless there is no possibility of countering, a countering movement is always necessary whenever one actor approaches and crosses the

Diagram 1

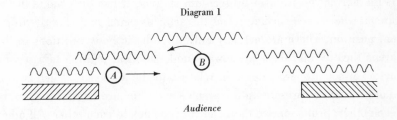

Audience

Diagram 2
Audience

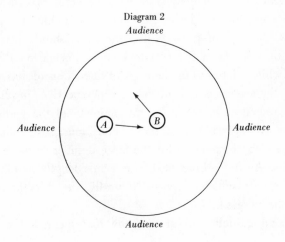

Audience   *Audience*

Audience

position held by another. Such countering clears traffic lanes, maintains adequate audience vision in the proscenium, and gives emphasis to the direction of the primary movement in both the arena and the proscenium.

In addition to the automatic response of countering, actors may also have to be instructed in standard body positions. They might have to be reminded that one-quarter and profile are the standard body positions in the proscenium because they allow an actor to share a scene with other actors, while at the same time providing the actor with potential for all types of future movement. Actors might also have to be reminded that the extremely weak proscenium position of three-quarters and the extremely strong proscenium positions of full-front and full-back should be avoided unless the director specifically requests the actor to assume such positions.

The director might have to caution the actor that while one-quarter is the normal position in proscenium staging, it has little value in the arena, where each spectator sees the actor as being in a slightly different position. There are actually only three basic body positions in the arena theatre, and these are always understood in relation to a second actor, or set property, never in relation to the audience. When two or more actors are present on the arena stage, they are either full-front to each other, profile one to the other, or full-back to each other. All other things being equal, full-front and full-back are stronger positions than profile.

Along with the arena body positions, the actor may have to learn that there are two very basic and important guides to arena body placement. The first of these is that the actor should play about an arm's length away from fellow actors under normal conditions. This guideline, while related to the concept of attraction of masses, is more pointed in the arena because of the multiperspectives produced by an encircling audience. In order for the majority of the audience to be able to perceive discrete bodies, those bodies must have sufficient space between them to compensate for the large number of varied audience perspectives. As a working basis, an arm's length in all directions seems to provide sufficient space. Naturally, the director may adjust such space as he sees fit.

The second guideline of arena body placement is that the actor should "play the shoulder" of the actor with whom he is sharing a scene. This guide is based again upon the problem of multiple perspectives. In the true arena, half the audience cannot, at any given time, see the face of any selected actor. However, unskilled actors compound this problem by being forever masked behind other actors. The result is that sometimes no significant portion of the audience ever sees a given actor. To avoid this problem, the arena actor normally plays at a slight angle to the other actors on stage. That is, under normal conditions the arena actor does not squarely face another actor, but actually stands so that his inside shoulder is facing his partner's outside shoulder, or vice-versa. When two actors are so positioned, their respective faces are visible to the largest possible proportion of the audience. There will be times, of course, when the director will want to forego this practice, but the actor should treat "shoulders" as the basic arena position.

The director might find that before he gets too deeply involved in his blocking, he should take the time to demonstrate how certain clichés of acting are sometimes in contradiction to the two basic guides of stage traffic. One of these clichés is the convention of the "open turn," a movement by which the actor always turns so that his face is to the audience. Such turns may sometimes have value in the proscenium where the audience is clearly located only on one side of the actor, but the open turn has little or no value in the thrust or arena theatres. However, even in the proscenium there is reason to discard the open turn as standard. Consider that at times the open turn might require the actor to make a major change in the direction of his movement. Such a change with its expense of energy might weaken a strong or dominant character. Again, since the open turn is always strong visually, it might well work against the presentation of a weak character. Without doubt the open turn has its uses in the proscenium, but to employ it without discretion is not wise.

To sum up the problem of the basic traffic pattern, we can say that although every play and every set has its own peculiar traffic lanes, certain basic traffic guidelines will permit the director to introduce his special traffic network with a minimal amount of stumbling among the actors. Often actors must be reminded of the three basic traffic "laws" of "follow your nose," "break a level," and "keep the stage dressed." In addition, the actor may have to be asked to remember the value of the five proscenium body positions or to realize that only three such positions exist in the arena. Along with the three body positions, the arena actor must remember to "keep an arm's distance" and "play the shoulder" of his fellow actors.

TRAFFIC PATTERNS AND NARRATIVE BUSINESS

A certain amount of business is necessary to maintain the narrative illusion of any play. The business may be an integral part of the story line, such as the comparison of waist lines between the general and the doctor in *Waltz* or the tape recorder scene in *Salesman;* or the business might be inserted by the director for greater metaphorical illusion. Jocasta, for instance, might have a ritual to perform as she prays before the altar, or Argan and his younger daughter might go through a stylized dance as he attempts to spank her for not telling on her older sister. Ultimately these bits of business must fulfill the demands of visual and kinetic composition, but the initial problem is to mold them into the general traffic pattern.

Whether the director invents the business or whether it is required by the playwright, the traffic patterns must be so controlled that the required activity can be accomplished without awkward shifts of position; abnormally long, short, or involved crosses; and without forcing the actors to rush about knocking each other down. Of course, unless the director preblocks the entire play, he cannot anticipate every item of business. In fact, some items will only be added later in rehearsal, as they are thought of or as the need for new business arises. But major and essential pieces of business must be anticipated before blocking begins. As his traffic pattern develops, the director must constantly keep in mind that in the middle of a certain scene actor A must be near the desk if he is to discover the note left for him, and that actress B must be near enough to the window to see someone spying on her. Experienced directors keep many such items in mind at once and are usually able to channel their actors into the appropriate locale in a logical manner. Apprentice directors may have to spend more time preplanning the total traffic pattern so that the actors are able to accomplish their business expeditiously.

A final word must be said before leaving the matter of narrative business. Often an item of business required by the play script is but the culmination of a series of implied activities. The director should be aware that all business must be built and that the building of business is his responsibility. Before the actor rushes across stage to get a glass of water, he must demonstrate, through a logical line of activities, that he is thirsty. Some directors, wishing to move a character from stage-left to stage-right, send that character across stage to get a cigarette, or a book, or a piece of candy, when the character has never indicated that he is a smoker, a reader, or the victim of a sweet tooth. Such directors usually argue that the cigarette, book, or candy gave the actor a motive for movement. Business, no matter how necessary to the narrative illusion, is not normally a motive for movement. It would be wiser to depend upon the principles of kinetic composition as motives for movement. The function of most business is to "hide the art," to make kinetic and visual composition seem to be lifelike. Depending heavily on narrative business as a motive for movement—not taking care to build business from base activity to goal—may well cause all characters to seem to be hopeless compulsives.

THE TRAFFIC PATTERN AND VISUAL
AND KINETIC COMPOSITION

Concurrent with the development of a basic traffic pattern, the director is also organizing his kinetic and visual composition. We have already touched upon this problem in warning that kinetic composition is the soundest motive for movement and that all entrances and exits must be visually and kinetically logical. Everything an actor does or does not do makes a visual and kinetic statement. Therefore, the basic traffic pattern must, from the start, be shaped by the aesthetic needs of the theatre-visual and theatre-kinetic.

It is not enough that the Cashier in *From Morn to Midnight* comes onto the scene at the bicycle races without bumping into the judges. There must first be a visual and kinetic reason for his entering. Perhaps this reason can be as simple as the creation on stage of considerable negative space demanding to be filled or as complex as the creation of a large, onstage vacuum. After the Cashier is drawn on stage, other visual and kinetic problems present themselves. If the

Antigone by Sophocles. University of Virginia.

Director: David W. Weiss   Designer: David W. Weiss

Note how the formal balance of the composition is relieved by the balancing of the mass of the chorus on stage-left by the single horizontal body on stage-right. Note also how this provides divided emphasis between center and right. Finally, observe that the space on stage-right provides a possible vacuum into which some or all of the mass on stage-left might move.

production is in the proscenium, the Cashier and the judges will probably form some sort of triangle. Since the play is Expressionistic, the triangle might well be irregular. Who is to be at the point of emphasis in the triangle—the Cashier or one or more of the judges? If the Cashier takes major emphasis, will he appear too strong? How long is the original holder of emphasis to stay in his position? Who will move first? In what direction? With what speed and energy? Essentially, while the Cashier might use such narrative business as moving across stage to pick up a megaphone to shout at the crowds, the real meaning in his movement will be read in the direction, speed, energy, and control of his motion, not in the narrative illusion. If the Cashier is to be emphatic but weaker than the judges, perhaps he can be moved more frequently but at a higher speed and with numerous changes of direction. If the Cashier is to be stronger than the judges, the kinetic shape of the scene might be designed so that all the Cashier's movements seem to conserve rather than expend energy.

While the specific application of the principles of kinetic and visual composition and design must wait upon the set and the actors, the director should keep in mind that the basic traffic pattern of his play is not something separate from the final visual and kinetic design. As the traffic pattern develops, a concurrent development should take place in the visual and kinetic shape of the production.

PACING THE REHEARSALS

Each new rehearsal introduces new spatial and motion problems. The director who attempts to present all his blocking to his actors in the first few rehearsals may be in for disappointments and frustrations. Very few directors are able to analyze the needs of the playwright, the needs of the actors, and their own needs before they have worked a considerable time with the play and a particular cast. Moreover, most actors are simply not able to assimilate a total blocking pattern in a few rehearsals. In short, plays and actors are best understood on stage, and every play script has to be adjusted in some degree to the talents and skills of the performers. Usually such talents and skills are not fully revealed until late in the rehearsal period. Moreover, actors are not born with a knowledge of a particular play and a particular set. They require time to learn both their lines and the traffic lanes of the set, not with their eyes but with their whole body. The director himself also requires some time working with the set before he understands its strengths and weaknesses. Certain activities in a play cannot be done well with book in hand, whereas the best way to learn lines is through rehearsal—learning the word with the deed, the deed with the word. Therefore, the wise director does not attempt to introduce blocking any faster than the average actor's memory rate.

Most directors set a basic traffic pattern for a few lines at a time and rehearse that pattern until the actor has acquired some start on physical as well as oral memory. Blocking whole acts at a time may well lose time for both actor and director. Most actors can no more learn blocking for an entire act in one night than they can learn lines for that act in a single evening. It is better to block small units of the play and rehearse these several times before going on to other units. Hopefully these units will be a rhythmic sequence in the play, with the ideal being the blocking of the constituent rhythms, then the scenic rhythms, then the major rhythms. Unfortunately, rhythmic sequences are not always easily identifiable early in the rehearsal period. Thus until they have isolated the rhythmic sequences, directors frequently work from entrance to exit or from entrance to entrance in their initial blocking.

In a six-week rehearsal period, the director under normal circumstances should not be unduly concerned if he has not entirely completed his blocking by the end of the fourth week. Blocking can, of course, continue until performance time, although blocking inserted too late will often make even the most experienced actor ill at ease. Whatever the case, the director should never rush blocking. He should take all the time necessary to set his primary traffic patterns, for without these as a base no visual or kinetic statement can be attempted.

About midway through a normal rehearsal period, the director will find that he has completed his fundamental traffic patterns and can now get down to more subtle visual and kinetic composition. He will further discover that if he has taken enough time in his early rehearsals to set firm patterns, he can now begin to move more rapidly and his actors will be both more flexible and more responsive. A sequence which two weeks ago took him a whole evening to compose may now be rehearsed in five or ten minutes. This phase is a particularly dangerous period for a director. Having worked so hard to establish a basic pattern, he might be too willing to accept the fact that his greatest task is behind him. In truth, his major work is usually just beginning.

It is normally at mid-rehearsal that rhythmic sequences, as they apply to the director's particular company and production, begin to become apparent. Now the director's task is to adjust his theatrical design to the emerging rhythms. Rhythms, of course, vary from one acting company to another. The actor playing Willy, for instance, may bring the scene in the hotel room to a crisis before it is returned to the restaurant washroom. The director must decide whether he can live with this particular rhythmic structure or whether he would like to attempt to get the actor to build the scene so that it peaks a bit later.

At midpoint in rehearsals most actors are still "on book." This slowness to put down the book frightens many directors into thinking that their main task is now to see to it that the actor memorizes his lines. It goes without saying that the actor *must* know his lines and must know them *early* enough to polish his character and contribute to the ensemble as a whole. On the other hand, the director—unless he knows he is dealing with a chronically "slow study"—should not press actors to get "off book." Lines learned before the bulk of the blocking has been established and rehearsed are likely to slow up the blocking, separate word from movement, and make the actors subconsciously reluctant to try new blocking since they learned their lines in terms of the old patterns. As the blocking becomes more intricate, and as the director becomes more and more demanding in terms of kinetic and visual finesse, the serious actor is apt to want to "get off the book" simply because the book is now getting in his way.

Once a scene's blocking has been sufficiently established so that the director feels he can begin polishing sequences, he should begin to remark on sloppiness or mistakes. Run-throughs at this point may be dangerous, for they may encourage the actor to think that he is doing satisfactory work. Worse yet, too-early run-throughs reinforce mistakes. When the actor has conquered the basic traffic pattern, he tends to relax and become artistically untidy. Cleanliness and clarity of outline in the actor's visual and kinetic patterns should now be stressed by the director. Anytime a mistake occurs, the director ought not to hesitate about stopping a sequence. A useful technique under such conditions is for the director to call a halt at the point of the mistake, back up to the beginning of the rhythmic sequence, and start again.

This process, time permitting, should be repeated for every mistake. Presently the actor will begin concentrating on his performance, in order not only to do well, but also to avoid having to repeat the same sequence so often.

The middle of the rehearsal period is also the time to begin to establish stern discipline about entrances and exits. The actor must be asked to remember to make his entrances on time and to follow through on his exits. The latter process means that the actor should make his exit exactly as he will do in performance, following the prescribed path both on stage and off stage. As the pace tightens and performance draws near, untimely entrances and sloppy exits will become more and more detrimental to the establishment of a total dramatic rhythm.

Before the rehearsal period is two-thirds completed, the actors should be "off book." When the actor does go off book, disastrous things are likely to happen to a production. Scenes that were tightly knit before will now seem to fall to pieces. Rhythms often return to the anarchy of first rehearsals. Entrances and exits are a shambles. At this point the director must employ infinite patience. He should remember that a well-designed show will survive this period if he does not try to force things. The director cannot afford to become nervous; his actors are nervous enough as it is.

Every actor reacts differently to going off book. Some "quick studies" make the transition with hardly a hitch. Less-fortunate ones may not remember a single cue; some become weeping wrecks; some that are seemingly quite cool might take to giggling at a moment's notice. Though the director must remain calm, he must, without forcing the situation, keep constant pressure on the actors. In particular, he must constantly remind the actor that it is not a sin to forget a line but that it is unforgivable to "break character." Again and again the actors should be told that they must stay in character and blocking, that they should simply call for "line" when a cue is dropped, and not take their lapse of memory as an excuse to relax the discipline of the rehearsal. A director who lets his actors drop out of character or develop nervous ticks as they search for a line is likely to find that habits learned in rehearsal will return in performance, and that an unconscious tick in rehearsal will almost invariably show up as an unwanted tick in performance.

Of course, prompting cannot go on forever. After a reasonable period, the director will want to set a deadline for learning lines. The matter of deadlines should be approached with caution, because establishing deadlines that cannot be met will destroy the discipline and cooperation of any company. On the other hand, lines must be thoroughly learned before the actor can polish his character or the director can polish the production. In fact, many essential items of business— love scenes, fights, etc.—cannot be truly blocked until lines are conquered. The whole literary orchestration of the play must wait upon the memory of the actors. Therefore, the director must allow himself time for at least five or six rehearsals to work with the fully memorized play in all its sequences.

Once a deadline has been established, the director should refuse to prompt any actor from that point on. After all, the actor who cannot memorize the words of the playwright must have some words, even if these are words of his own composition. Moreover, the actor who is too lazy to memorize will never do so as long as he has the prompter to depend on. With those actors who through lack of discipline or fault of nature seem never to learn lines, the director might want to have some private line rehearsals.

When lines are learned, it is time for final polishing rehearsals. Polishing rehearsals are a time when considerable reworking of lines and blocking is usually necessary. With the problem of memory—both kinetic and auditory—now solved, the actors and the director can concentrate on refining patterns and developing details that give the production texture and brilliance. In this regard whole scenes might be reworked. Visual images are now given final construction and outline. Kinetic design is refined, the play is given verbal orchestration, and rhythms are fixed.

While run-throughs of the entire production might be necessary in some cases, the practice is not mandatory. There are times when run-throughs might be dangerous. Some actors are encouraged by the run-through to think that the work of the rehearsal is finished. This attitude might cause the actor to bring his character to a peak before production. Directors usually turn to the run-through rehearsal because they hesitate to put a show into production that has not run from start to finish at least once, and it does help the actor's confidence to have had a run-through. However, if time is short, a complete run-through is not absolutely necessary. Cinema dramas are not put together in sequence.

Often the final scene of a movie is photographed first. The important element of a production is the design of the rhythmic units and the kinetic patterns that tie such units together. If these rhythmic units are well designed, a play may go into production without a single run-through. The real need for these run-throughs is to establish the tie-ins between rhythmic sequences. Consequently, the director should concentrate in the run-through rehearsals on establishing appropriate entrances, exits, and tie-ins between rhythmic units.

THE ACTOR AND TECHNICAL REHEARSALS

The technical rehearsal is primarily devoted to blending the work of the nonacting artists into the production as a whole. During technical rehearsal the director has little time to give to the actors per se. He must pay attention to lights, properties, scenery, music, and costumes, as well as to actors. During the first technical rehearsal, the production is likely to disintegrate once more into the kind of condition prevailing when the actors first went off book. The director should insist that the actors continue to maintain character and make every effort to move the play in the pattern in which it was rehearsed.

The director would do well to spend sufficient time planning the technical rehearsal so that his actors are not kept standing about for unnecessarily long periods while technical problems which should have been foreseen are discussed and solved. Above all, the director must not lose patience when an actor in a new costume forgets a detail of blocking or stumbles in the verbal rhythms. At such times the director should remind himself that a well-designed and well-disciplined show will recover from the shock of technical rehearsal. On the other hand, technical rehearsal is the time to reblock a scene if a costume or a property forces reblocking.

THE DIRECTOR, THE ACTOR, AND
CHARACTER ANALYSIS

Every actor ought to play his role according to the director's vision of that role; every director ought to do his utmost to adjust every role to the talent, skills, potential, and understanding of the individual actor.

In short, character analysis is a mutual task of both director and actor. The director analyzes the manner and motives of a character in terms of the interaction of the dramatic agents as a group, and also in terms of a realistic appraisal of his actor. This analysis is presented in general outline to the actor, who in turn analyzes the character within the outline offered by the director.

The process of mutual analysis is not as simple as its description may imply. First, it does not happen in a neat package but is truly a process. Character analysis begins for the director on his first reading of the play. It is adjusted after casting, and then readjusted several times during the rehearsals as the director gains more insight into the character or as the actor reveals more of his skills and talents. Usually the adjustments are a give-and-take process between actor and director. The director suggests, the actor responds, and on the basis of that response, the director adds further suggestions.

Often the process is varied. The actor takes the initiative in suggesting and the director responds. Sometimes the director or the actor will offer counter-suggestions. The director should give thoughtful consideration to each response or suggestion made by the actor. The better and more experienced the actor, the more thought should be given to his responses. However, the director should always bear in mind that the ultimate responsibility in character analysis is his. He ought further to remember that his duty is not to the single actor but to the entire acting company and the other artists of the theatre, from the playwright to the lighting designer. Consequently, the wishes of the single actor may have to be overruled in favor of the entire body of the cooperative theatre.

The give-and-take between actor and director in terms of character analysis is not always a verbal one. While the director is free to use any method of communication that works, the normal process of character analysis between director and actor is communicated through blocking. The director makes a few general statements about character if he feels they are necessary, and then he begins blocking. Through seeing what his character does, the actor is usually able to discover what the character is or might be. In short, the director supplies the manners patterns and the actor translates them into motive patterns. A second way in which the director demonstrates character to an actor is through the reaction pattern of the other characters. If the Secretary reacts to St. Pé as a large and frightening man, then the actor playing St. Pé should realize something about the image of the general.

From time to time, the actor might have a specific question concerning motive, justification, attitude, or even line reading. The director should be prepared to answer as quickly and as directly as possible. As a general rule, most directors avoid long discussions of character with the actor. After all, the author has already supplied enough words. Further discussion always runs the danger of ambiguity. Even when not colored with abstract words, discussions of a character may serve only to set up a screen of verbiage between the actor and the character. The director's and actor's task is not to construct lectures on characters but to contribute vision and deed to the playwright's words.

In terms of character analysis, the best actor–director relationship is one of mutual respect for each other's art. Although the director must depend on the actor for his own art, he should remember that the analysis of character for a system of motives belongs to the art of acting. In the long run what does it matter if the director and the actor are operating from a different set of character motives, provided the actor is delivering an appropriate performance? But when the actor turns to the director for help in character analysis, the director should be ready to provide such help. Usually a word or two is enough to get the actor working again. A suggestion of mood such as "Hamlet is really angry at Laertes here," or a direct statement of a need such as, "Willy would like Biff to touch him now," is enough to set the imaginative actor on the right track. Unfortunately, some actors must be told each step and each motive. In such cases, the director regretfully must assume more than his rightful share of character analysis.

The best type of analysis does not rest upon the single character but rather upon the reaction patterns of all characters. In this manner, the actor understands his character as an interacting dramatic agent involved in a situation. Thus Willy is not a man with a wrong ideal, but a man who expects Biff to live up to his dreams and who is frustrated by Biff's determination not to act according to Willy's ideal.

The use of analysis through reaction avoids the error of attempting to analyze the character in terms of nonorganic events. The director should encourage the actor always to think of his character in terms of what happens to him in the play. Since we do not know what the character might do in other circumstances, we may be creating more harm than good by attempting to guess what Oedipus usually does around the palace in normal times. The point of the play is that times are *not* normal. We must try to understand Oedipus as a man under extreme pressures, surrounded by unusual circumstances, and therefore not himself a normal man. It is extremely difficult to judge how he would act normally from the evidence of his particularly *extraordinary* circumstances.

To sum up, when the director comes to character analysis, he adapts his own vision of the character to the needs of the actor. While he is the final arbiter in matters of manners and motives, he should always be ready to listen to the opinions of his actors. He should be prepared and willing to change his attitudes toward characters when he discovers that his actors have come up with insights he had not suspected. The director, however, should be cautious about inviting long analytical discussions of character with his actors; rather, the director will want to communicate through kinetic and visual suggestion. On the other hand, if analytical discussion is the only manner by which the director can help a particular actor, then the director should not shrink from such discussion. In the long run, anything that will aid an actor is acceptable directing practice.

THE ACTOR, THE DIRECTOR, AND GIVING DIRECTIONS

If the director communicates to the actor through direct instruction rather than through discussion, then the individual direction or suggestions must be approached with great care. Each director has a different style of giving directions. Some prefer to proceed through gentle hints; others are more explicit. Whatever the method, the actors and director must understand that the director is actually giving instructions, no matter how those instructions might be presented. A good director is humble in the face of his responsibility to give directions. But give them he must, and the sooner he recognizes his duty to give direction to the actors, the more efficient he will become in his art and the greater the aid he will be able to offer to the actors in their art.

While it is not necessarily true that the director who directs least is the director who directs best, the director should always strive to make his instructions as brief, concise, and explicit as possible. Normally, the more a director has worked with an actor, the less he will have to say to him. When dealing with a highly skilled actor, the director may have to do little more than see to it that the kinetic and visual design is well controlled. The actor will usually provide all else that is necessary. When an actor is doing a good job, the director might be wise to limit his remarks to a few words of encouragement or a compliment or two.

On the other hand, in certain situations the director will need to provide detailed directions for even the most skilled and experienced actor, while the inexperienced actor in such circumstances will require almost constant supervision. For example, an inexperienced actor playing Laertes may need almost as great a proportion of direction as the actor playing Hamlet. Yet even the best of actors will demand precise instructions concerning when to enter, when to speak on entrances, when to exit, where to go after entering, how to stand, and sometimes how to read a line. For instance, the actor playing Oedipus must know exactly when to make his first entrance, how to move among the chorus, and whether his initial attitude toward the chorus is one of concern, annoyance, dismay, or disdain.

While the director should know when to keep silent, he should never shrink from giving directions. Directors often begin by phrasing directions in terms of what the actor is or should be doing. For example, instead of saying that Oedipus is angry with Creon, the director might tell the actor playing Oedipus to turn his back on Creon. Sometimes the actor cannot coordinate Oedipus's motives with the suggested activity. The director's next step might then be to construct some sort of visual or kinetic analogue. For instance, he might say that the sight of Creon is to Oedipus like putrid flesh. If both explicit directions and suggestions fail, the director may have to show the actor what to do. The demonstration of what to do might well be an exaggerated pattern accompanied by some advice such as, "don't imitate exactly what I do, but the movement might be something like this." If all else fails, the director may have no choice but to say "do it exactly as I am doing." With beginning actors, direct imitation is sometimes the only successful method.

The Trial by Franz Kafka. University Theatre, Louisiana State University, Baton Rouge.

Adapted, directed, and designed:
Don F. Blakely

Note the extreme dominance and contrast gained by increasing greatly the vertical line of a single, slender figure. Note also the dependence on sharp angles and diagonal lines in both scenery and characters to create a mood of grotesque terror. Consider in this regard the diagonal patterns in the arms of each of the actors.

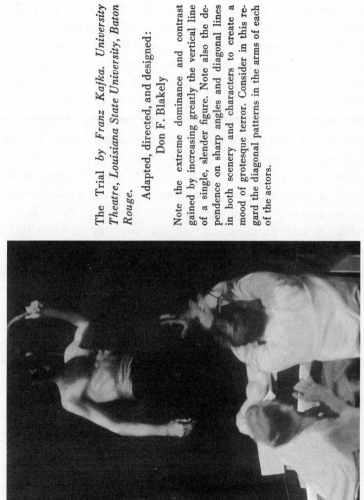

Usually the director will not be forced into giving a line reading to an actor. If the director has been sufficiently inventive in devising the necessary kinetic framework, and if the actor is at all skilled and talented, the appropriate reading will follow. From time to time, however, the director may be forced to read a line for an actor. When the director has exhausted his kinetic and visual possibilities, and when all talk about the character's particular motives and manners has failed to produce the appropriate reading, the director may have to ask the actor to imitate his reading. Naturally, direct imitation of any type is not desirable, but whether it is in terms of deed or word the director should realize that there are times when he must require the actor to imitate him. Consequently, the director should himself be an able actor if he is going to ask an actor to imitate his reading and movement.

The most difficult part of the play for the individual actor and his director is the long set speech. For example, Oedipus must give a long explanatory narrative of his past life; the Cashier in *From Morn to Midnight* has a long and difficult soliloquy early in the play; Hamlet has several major soliloquies. The long set speech is the one time when the actor is most isolated from the other members of the cast, when the play depends almost entirely on the art of the actor, and yet the one time when the actor is most likely to need the greatest help from the director. The natural tendency in the long speech situation is to let the actor "have his head." With the skilled actor this approach is sometimes satisfactory; but the less technique an actor possesses, the more necessary it is for the director to keep a tight rein. Even with the skilled actor, the director cannot entirely abdicate his responsibility.

In terms of the long speech, the director can give the actor help in all three phases of theatre. In terms of auditory theatre, the director must work with the actor in setting the rhythmic patterns of the speech. Through mutual cooperation, the director and actor must decide the overall rhythm of the speech, the number and quality of constituent rhythms, and the organization of these rhythms. Isolating vocal rhythms is not the only task of the director. He must aid in the establishment of these rhythms by structuring the actor's visual patterns and his movements.

On an elemental level the actor's sight and motion patterns must have variety in order to be interesting to the audience and to stimulate the actor's own interest in his speech. Often simple visual and kinetic emphasis is not sufficient to support the actor in his long speeches. Pity the poor actor whose director sets him up with good visual emphasis, freezes all other actors so that the principal speaker can move about at will, and then abandons the speaker to work his own way. The director should remember that the actor cannot see himself. He does not know when he appears interesting and when he does not. Therefore, if only to provide interest and variety, the director should have a distinct kinetic and visual design for the long speech. Variety alone is not enough. The director should also see that the actor's movements and positions give him continuously good kinetic and visual composition and design. What he does and where he is positioned should make a comment on what he says.

Frequently the director will find that the actor and the speech are insufficient, perhaps because of a shortcoming in the speech or the actor, or perhaps because the director wishes to use the speech to make a broader statement. Whatever the reason, the director might wish to aid or reinforce the actor in delivering the speech by using other aspects of theatre. For instance, the director may broaden the visual impact of the speech by changing scenery or costumes. Such changes are usually effected through lighting, although a literal change of scenery or costume might also be accomplished. The director may make use of music or sound effects to enlarge the audible impact of the speech. Finally, the director may employ other actors as subordinate elements in the composition or as major counterpoints to widen the visual and kinetic aspect of the speech. For example, in *Morn to Midnight* searchers and police could be used as counterpoint to the Cashier's soliloquy in the snow field. More obviously, the chorus is already present in *Oedipus;* they may well be used in both visual and kinetic shapes to heighten the long speeches of the leading figure.

A word needs to be said at this point about those highly specialized forms of the single speech—the solo song, the long pantomime, and the solo dance. In general each of these can be treated exactly as the long set speech, but each also has peculiar problems. The solo song is based first in music, and until the music is learned, the director can do little with kinetic, verbal, and visual patterns. However, in musicals and in modern operas, the music is not the end-all. The singer will want to have movement and visual character. The long pantomime requires that the director and actor work much harder on visual and kinetic elements and on dramatic rhythm. The pantomime must be exciting as well as narrative. The solo dance is really a lyric form of pantomime just as the song is a lyric form of speech. In dealing with the dance, the director may seek the aid of a choreographer just as he may use a musical director with singers. A dancer must pay special attention to achieving visual and kinetic variety and to building a good dramatic rhythm.

To summarize, the director should recognize his responsibility of giving directions to the actor. He need not talk incessantly, but he should be ready to give all required instructions. If necessary, he might have to act arbitrarily and demand that the actor imitate what he says and does. In all of his directions, he should strive to be as cogent and as economical as possible. His most difficult task in terms of the individual actor comes when the actor must deliver a long speech. In cooperation with the actor, the director should analyze the speech in terms of auditory rhythms. Providing the actor with a pleasing visual and kinetic composition and a meaningful design is also the responsibility of the director. Directors approach such a task in various ways. Usually, when working with a skilled actor the director will let the actor develop the basic pattern, while the director himself contributes development and refinement. On the other hand, the actor has the right to expect the director to invent both the basic pattern and the development of the long speech, and often even the most experienced actor will wait upon the director before commencing a long speech.

DIRECTING THE ENSEMBLE

To the problem of directing the single actor are added the problems of directing the whole company. Directing the entire company means more than a simple multiplication of the demands of the single actor, for the director must create the reaction pattern of the entire group—in short, he must build and direct an ensemble. To construct the ensemble, directors often begin by making each actor aware of what he owes to the whole group. Because they concentrate so hard on their individual role, actors have a way of seeing the play as an extension of their own character. They should, therefore, be advised that no matter how large their role, it is a piece of a larger fabric. Analyzing each character in terms of interaction of all characters helps to establish in the actor's mind an attitude of the whole ensemble.

Another important aspect of creating the ensemble is the arranging of strong–neutral–weak, dominant–equal–subordinate, and contrast relationships throughout each scene. Either through the visual and kinetic pattern or through direct discourse, the director indicates to each actor when his character is strong, when it is sharing a scene, and when it is weak; when it is dominant, when it is sharing, and when it is subordinate; when it is in high contrast with another agent. Finally, the director must orchestrate all characters into a single visual, kinetic, and auditory whole. When two or more actors speak, stand, or move, the director should decide when the characters speak or move together, when one or more has visual emphasis, which actor "tops" which other actor in speaking dialogue, and which character stands still when others move.

Two specialized forms of the ensemble are the dance chorus and the musical chorus. These choruses share with every member of the company the needs and problems of the ensemble. In addition they must develop skills in music, dance, or both. In handling singers and dancers, the director often seeks the aid of a musical director and choreographer; but the ultimate responsibility rests with the director for execution, quality, and relation of the singers and dancers to the production as a whole.

The matter of creating an ensemble necessarily involves securing the cooperation of the acting company and maintaining discipline within that company. Discipline is largely a matter of respect; when the actors respect the director as a man of the theatre, they are likely to give him their willing cooperation. When cooperation is freely given, discipline usually follows as a matter of course. Therefore, the director must demonstrate that he is skilled, confident, and efficient in his craft, and that he is also knowledgeable in all the other crafts of the theatre.

Furthermore, the director will want to demonstrate to the actor that he respects him as an artist. A good way to show respect for an actor is for the director to give him a willing ear and a firm answer. Whether the answer be agreement or disagreement, it should be logical and clear. Moreover, the director should bear in mind that acting is not an instantaneous art. The process of creating a character that suits the playwright, the director, the actor himself, and his fellow actors is a slow and often painful one. Consequently, the director needs to exercise infinite patience. Although a little judicious complaining or well-justified anger might be necessary from time to time, the director will want to strive at all times to control his attitudes and his temper. The average actor is trying very hard to please his director, and harsh words will probably do little more than increase the actor's nervousness. Patience and control may have little to do with a director's talent and skill in his art, but absence of these two qualities may well do damage to the final theatrical product.

Being patient and understanding does not mean being permissive. Whatever his rehearsal schedule and procedure, the director has the responsibility of seeing that his production plan is followed. In this regard, he will require that actors be at rehearsal on time, that they work during rehearsal, that they meet such deadlines as going off book when these deadlines are set, and that they show the proper respect and cooperation for the other artists and technicians of the theatre. In order to protect himself against problems, the director will do well to set realistic deadlines. Actors cannot go off book before they have gotten "settled" in their parts. Some actors are quicker studies than others; some have larger line loads. Therefore, the needs of all the ensemble should be considered when setting off book deadlines. Rehearsals ought to be called at times and intervals when the actors can be present without undue hardship. To set rehearsals at impossible times or to call rehearsals too frequently or for too long a period are all decisions which are likely to promote disciplinary difficulties.

The director ought to be sufficiently organized to set a rehearsal schedule that provides for a minimum of sitting and waiting by the individual actor. To call for all the characters of an act of *Salesman* at 8:00, for example, and then not to use Stanley the waiter until 9:30, is straining cast morale and discipline. Naturally there will be times, particularly during the final phases of rehearsal, when the whole cast must be present and waiting; but as much as possible such situations should be avoided. If the actor must be on hand and idle for long periods, the director might plan to make use of this time by having the actor run lines, work with other actors on problem sequences, or schedule a costume fitting.

When the actors are rehearsing, the director should expect them to give full attention to their work. Anything that is not going to be done in performance should not be done in rehearsal. Ideally, actors ought never to be better in performance than they are in their best rehearsal. If an actor improves greatly on the night of performance, the director must acknowledge that he has somehow failed because the improvement demonstrated in performance should have been achieved in rehearsal. From an actor's viewpoint, improvement in performance means that he may well have been even better if only he had worked up to his performance level during rehearsal.

Actors rehearsing a scene should chew gum, smoke, look at their watches, break character, or whisper to each other *only* if they intend to engage in those activities during performance. Whenever actors are not working as they ought to, the director has reason to stop rehearsal to remedy the situation on the spot. Waiting until the scene has been completed to give notes may be less effective than stopping, because normally the actor who knows that he is to be stopped whenever he is not working in an acceptable manner will soon become more precise in his rehearsal habits.

Sometimes actors rehearse poorly because they are tired, distracted, or bored. The director should be alive to such conditions. If actors are too tired to get anything out of a rehearsal, the director might do better to send them home. If they are distracted by visitors, working conditions, or personal matters, the director should make every effort to remove the distraction before attempting to continue with the rehearsal. Often, however, the actors are bored. A scene is overrehearsed at its particular attainment level. In such circumstances the director might want to retire the scene for a while from the rehearsal schedule or to introduce additional problems into the scene.

The creating of an ensemble out of a group of actors involves more than patience and fatherly discipline. Unless they have been working together for some time, actors will need to get used to each other. They need to become aware of the different manners in which they move, stand, and read lines. They need to learn to listen to each other and to adjust to physical rhythms. During this period, the director can be of great help in pointing out the vocal or physical attack of actor A to actor B or vice versa, so that actor A may be prepared to make the proper adjustment. Actors should be encouraged to work out their mutual problems in the presence of the director so that backstage misunderstanding may be avoided. The director should try to be alive to personal or professional problems of the actors or to any kind of jealousy that might develop. He should attempt to catch such problems early and solve them right away. As for himself, the director should make every effort to give each actor his just share of attention and help. While he may have his special friends among the actors, such friendship should be reserved for extraprofessional times. In rehearsal, there should be no favorites. Each actor should be treated equally as an important member of the company.

On rare occasions in every director's career, stern disciplinary action becomes necessary. While the director should make every effort to understand his actors' personal and professional problems, he will be wise to deal as early and as swiftly as possible with major breaches of discipline. No director should make idle threats, but the actors should be informed as tactfully as possible that they cannot remain in the company if they do not do their work, if they cause trouble, or if they constantly miss or are tardy for scheduled rehearsals. The director ought to attempt to spot potential disciplinary problems early, and he should be strong enough to accept the fact that undisciplined actors may have to be dropped from the cast. If the director puts off such a decision or does not recognize the danger until nearly performance time, he is in real difficulty. The closer the play approaches production, the more difficult it is to replace an unwanted actor. Consequently, if dismissal is called for in handling a troublemaker, action should be timely.

A final observation might be in order concerning dropping actors from the company. The director will have to learn to distinguish between a disciplinary problem and a casting error. More often than they wish, directors miscast actors. However hard the miscast actor tries, he simply cannot perform as the director wishes. No matter how the director is tempted, he ought not to drop such an actor from the cast. His shortcomings are traceable to the director's casting. Since the error was initially that of the director's, he should live with it. Moreover, while the practice of replacing actors who are miscast may improve a particular role, it is likely to injure the morale of the entire ensemble. Casting is a declaration of faith and the first step in a social contract between the director and his actors. The director who breaks faith with his actors in rehearsal might find that they are not overly scrupulous about breaking faith with him in performance.

When dealing with the company as a whole, the director will find that there is a point beyond which the company will not progress. Individual actors might get better, but the ensemble may not. On the other hand, the general level of the ensemble might be far above that of any single performer. The latter condition is the one to be preferred. Whether dealing with the single actor or the company as a whole, the director should try to recognize when the limit has been reached. Attempting to pass the maximum level may be both pointless and frustrating, and may even result in a poorer rather than a better performance. When the single actor has reached his peak, the director might then turn to the ensemble as a whole for an extension of character statement. When the ensemble has reached its peak, the director might enlist the musician, the costumer, or the lighting or set designer for a more extended statement, but he normally should not attempt to strain the capabilities of the ensemble. Rather, he will want to spend his time in rehearsals perfecting, cleaning, and clarifying the level the company has achieved. A production that is clean, smooth, and evenly and competently acted is usually a better work of art than one having flashes of individual brilliance but, in straining after that brilliance, is generally cluttered, uneven, and disunified.

To sum up, the director who deals with a company of actors is not simply directing more than one actor; he is attempting to create a whole greater than its parts—the ensemble. To create the ensemble, he needs to orchestrate all the efforts of the acting company in the visual, literary, and kinetic theatre. He needs to teach each actor the value of working for the whole ensemble. To do this, he will want to secure the cooperation of the entire company, so that each actor realizes that his character is understood by the audience in terms of all other characters.

The director also seeks to create an atmosphere of firm but flexible discipline. He demands work at rehearsals; he expects high achievement, but he is patient in aiding the actor to reach his expected performance. He tries not to make unrealistic demands, but he should be willing to take disciplinary action if necessary. Above all, he should refrain from playing favorites. When the director realizes that the actors and the ensemble have reached their highest possible level, he will usually want to make use of his remaining time in polishing and perfecting what is possible. In all likelihood, if the director has paced the rehearsals properly, the company will not reach its peak until just before the first technical rehearsals.

PRESENTING THE PLAY TO THE ACTORS: A SUMMARY

In presenting the play to the actors, the director begins by constructing a prompt book and assembling a cast. In casting, the director attempts to remain alert and flexible. When the play enters rehearsal, the director's first task is to establish a basic traffic pattern. As the traffic pattern is being constructed, the director commences his auditory, visual, and kinetic design.

Ideally, the director leaves the art of acting to the actor, but every director sooner or later faces the problem of serving as acting coach. Even with the most experienced of actors, the director might find that there are times when he must "teach" line readings or movement patterns.

The director not only deals with the individual actor but also strives to create an ensemble. To this end the director attempts to get each actor to understand his role in terms of the interactions of the entire company. A theatrical metaphor based on a sound ensemble is usually more effective than one characterized by individual flashes of brilliance but lacking cohesion.

CHAPTER 11

creating the theatrical metaphor

As rehearsals progress from the early blocking of a basic traffic pattern to the final polishing of dress rehearsals, the director creates his theatrical metaphor. To accomplish this end, he uses all the means of his own art, joining to these the arts of the playwright, the actors, the choreographer, the musicians, and the various designers of the theatre. His basic problem is to orchestrate all these diverse elements into a single theatrical metaphor. To this end the director employs a process through which he gives his attention simultaneously to all the myriad aspects of the auditory, kinetic, and visual theatres. When writing of this process it is often necessary to deal in categories; but in practice the working director operates in seeming disorder, dealing first with one category, then with another, or with several categories at once.

CREATING THE THEATRICAL METAPHOR IN THE VISUAL THEATRE

Perhaps the simplest task of the director is the creation of a good visual metaphor. The task is simple because so much of it is done by other artists, albeit under the director's guidance, but usually with little of the director's labor. However, once the director begins working with the actors on the set, the remaining visual problems are his. The first task is to analyze and understand the set. This task is solved only after considerable work with the scenery. Unhappily, many directors are forced to hold rehearsals away from the actual setting. Such directors must operate on guesswork; at times the guessing is faulty. Rather than make too many wild guesses, some of the directors keep their visual metaphor deliberately simple, far too simple for the play script.

Ideally the director begins working almost immediately with a significant portion of the final set. What is initially necessary is a close approximation of the final arrangement of floor levels and furniture sizes. Even with a good approximation of these important items, visual gaucheries are unavoidable, so that the director who argues that he can do just as good a job in a rehearsal room as on his set may be making a mistake. Unless he is an exceptional man, the director can hardly analyze an imaginary setting. Often the difference of a few inches in the height of an actor will change entirely both the visual design and composition. Such differences are not easily seen away from the actual playing set.

As rehearsals progress, the director becomes more and more aware of the effect the actors have in relation to the fixed setting and to the costumes they will be wearing on that set. When he fully understands an individual effect, the director can begin to fix limited aspects of his final visual metaphor. For instance, before rehearsals began, the director might have hoped to place Oedipus next to a large column on his first entrance. In theory, such a position would have emphasized

Oedipus' height by adding to it the height of the column. However, once the director positions Oedipus near the column, he discovers that because of actual spatial proportions the column dwarfs the actor, makes him seem small because it is so tall. The director must now rethink his approach to the set in this particular aspect. He may well place Oedipus next to the column, but in a different context. Now Oedipus is placed near the column, not to make him seem tall but to make him seem small. Where the director originally planned to use the column in scenes where Oedipus is strong, he now uses the same visual factor in scenes where Oedipus is weak.

As in the example above, certain compositions and designs are obvious from the nature of the scenery; others must be created on the spot. If the director has a formal setting for *Hamlet,* he might logically use that formality as the basis for the visual organization of the first court scene. However, if only for the sake of variety, he will not want to repeat the same visual image for all subsequent court scenes. Therefore, as each new court scene comes up, the director will need to analyze the set in order to discover how to use its formality in new ways, or how to work deliberately counter to the formal balance of the setting.

Additional visual issues are raised by *Hamlet* or by a play such as *From Morn to Midnight.* In both plays there are scenes ranging from two people to a large crowd. If the director has only a single arrangement of platforms with which to work, he must investigate ways of making the large scenes fit the setting even as he devises means of making the smaller scenes seem appropriate to the same setting. To this end, he must search out spots of prominence in the set where his intimate scenes will be logical and discover places of retreat in the set where he may locate members of the crowd scenes who are necessary for sheer numbers but who would be disunifying if watched too closely.

Entrances and exits raise further issues. As we know, the entrances and exits of every set have particular problems that are not apparent until they have been used. No matter how thoroughly the floor plan is studied, the exact visual quality of each entranceway is not clear until all vertical elements, including the actors, are present on the set. For example, an up-left flight of stairs may seem an excellent entrance on the floor plan, but in practice the stairs, because of audience sightlines, may seem so narrow that they actually weaken actors standing on them. Thus every entrance begins weakly and every exit ends weakly. The director must now compensate for this tendency. Unhappily, unless he is in possession of the final setting in sufficient time to understand the problem, the director may find his attempts at compensation not completely satisfying.

The director will encounter numerous specific difficulties in the use of his particular set, difficulties ranging from the drape and color of a window curtain to the height and exact location of a footstool. As soon as he becomes aware of the nature of these problems, he begins to work toward their solution. At the same time he also commences composing the overall visual metaphor of the production. For the sake of unity as well as design, the general visual statement is normally organized around recurring motifs. For example, oblique lines are a common visual motif of such plays as *From Morn to Midnight*. When such a play is staged in the proscenium, irregular triangles might be used to continue the visual motif established by the oblique line. In the arena, deliberate breaking of the basic circular shape of the stage would provide a similar result. To continue the motif, actors could be massed in large geometric groups, the sort of groups not normally found in crowds of people. The use of space might be highly regular or highly irregular; texture might be overly simplified. Finally, color harmonies might be deliberately ignored and color clashes actively sought after.

As opposed to *From Morn to Midnight*, the more traditionally romantic *Hamlet* might seek its visual motifs through curved lines, less-geometric masses. Both color and texture might be muted. *The Imaginary Invalid*, on the other hand, might call for highly serpentine, Baroque curves, while containing such curves in rather formally stated masses and forms. In fact, the use of large masses might actually be avoided in Molière's plays, while color and texture might be bright, varied, and yet closely harmonized. For the sake of unity and balance, visual motifs should be limited; but in the interest of rhythm, emphasis, and variety, visual motifs should have both change and pattern.

While the director addresses himself to the problem of visual metaphor, he simultaneously addresses himself to the issue of coordination of all areas of theatre. In the interests of coordination with the theatre-auditory, the visual metaphor must reflect in its composition the

Antigone by Jean Anouilh. University of South Dakota Theatre.
Director: Miklos Szakats   Designer: Richard F. Wilcox

Note the variation on traditional triangular composition. Note also the use of heavy vertical masses treated with hard, smooth surface. The effect is cold and austere.

composition of the play script. Consequently, visual balance should mirror literary proportion and visual emphasis reflect literary emphasis. What is true in composition follows in design. Thus the visual image of a play should create a visual analogue to the play script's handling of dramatic agents, point of view, story line, dramatic rhythm, etc. Both the theatre-auditory and the theatre-kinetic take place in time as well as space. Therefore, the director has the special problem of providing sequence for his visual metaphor. While the painter or the sculptor might not concern himself with future visual images, the director must provide for a meaningful development of one visual image out of another. In short, even as he composes the first visual image of a play, the director must be arranging the next in such a way that it grows out of the first.

The problem of sequence recalls that the visual theatre is wedded to the theatre of motion. Whatever the director might devise in the visual theatre, he must see that all visual composition is related to the kinetic composition. In this regard, the director should guard against creating a series of still-life images as the major visual statement. Rather, he will want to compose his visual images so that they are an inseparable part of his kinetic shapes. A basic problem for many directors is to reorient themselves from a visual or auditory approach to a kinetic one. The director who tells the actor to move about but only in a certain restricted locale probably has not yet made this reorientation and is letting the overall visual design control his kinetic composition. There are exceptions to this rule, of course. If by story line requirements the actor is restricted to a certain space, then he can occupy only that space.

Some of the most important decisions in the theatre-visual must be postponed until the technical and dress rehearsals. In particular these decisions are centered about the contributions of the prop man, the costumer, the makeup specialist, and the lighting designer. As much as possible, problems in costumes, properties, makeup, and lighting should be anticipated by the director. He should visit the costume shop frequently in order to study the color and shape of each costume as it is put together. He should visit the scene shop to check on construction of properties and determine actual shapes, sizes, and paint colors. If possible, he should examine costumes and paint mixtures under the proposed light filters. Difficult or unusual properties should be introduced into rehearsals as soon as they are available. When not available, working substitutes might be used. While costumes are usually not ready until late rehearsals, the director can often secure a muslin rehearsal dress for actresses or a working cloak for an actor. Such substitutes are as useful in the kinetic as in the visual theatre.

To sum up, in creating his visual image from the first rehearsal to the first technical rehearsal, the director begins by attempting to understand the special problems of his specific set. Having analyzed these problems, the director begins visually to compose his actors in terms of the fixed stage set. In his overall visual pattern the director will normally make use of certain visual motifs that give unity and rhythm to the composition and form the basis of visual design. As he creates his visual patterns, the director must coordinate these with the patterns of the auditory and kinetic theatres. A special problem in visual theatre, not met in other visual arts, is the matter of sequence. By appropriately combining his visual pattern with his kinetic composition, the director should be able to solve most of the problems of visual sequence. Some of the most important visual issues will have to be postponed until the technical rehearsals, but the director should anticipate these as much as possible and be ready for all eventualities.

CREATING THE AUDITORY METAPHOR

As much of the visual metaphor is provided by other artists, so also is the auditory metaphor created in great part by the playwright, and, in some plays, by the musician. However, the director has two important functions in the theatre-auditory. The first of these is to complete the auditory contributions of the playwright or musician; the second is to coordinate the theatre-auditory with the visual and kinetic theatres.

Turning to the first problem, the director should be aware that his obligations to the play script do not cease with analysis. To begin with, analysis is a continuing process commencing with the first reading and ceasing only after the last dress rehearsal. Secondly, the play script is not a work of literature sufficient unto itself. It will need to be adjusted to the actors, the costumes, the setting, the lighting, and the anticipated audience of each individual production. If the play is too long, it may have to be cut. If the story line is confused, the director should take steps toward clarity. If several themes are equally possible, the director must make his choice. If the play as written cannot be played by the actors or produced by the director's theatre, then the play may have to be adapted. If internal references in the play are outdated, then updating may be in order; and if viewpoint is unclear, it will have to be made more pointed.

All of the above are obvious matters. Caution, however, should be the touchstone in handling all such issues. It is easier to talk about cutting than to make good cuts. Aside from the ethics involved, a well-written play does not cut easily. The same is true of rewriting to suit individual actor's abilities. On the other hand, all such problems are really secondary to the major problems of dramatic rhythms and vocal orchestration.

Completing and refining the implied dramatic rhythm of the play script and composing the vocal orchestration are the two major means by which the director contributes to the theatre-auditory. The latter—vocal orchestration—is a function of the former—completion of the dramatic rhythms. The rhythms of a play script are not as tightly outlined as those of an orchestral composition. As pointed out in previous chapters, the director himself will have to decide on the details of the majority of rhythmic sequences. He makes this decision on the basis of the overall rhythms of the play script, the style of his production, his own analysis, and the rhythmic tendencies of his actors. In plays such as *Hamlet, Invalid, Morn to Midnight, Waltz, Oedipus,* and *Salesman,* the problem of exact rhythms is a joy rather than a burden to work out. Naturally *Hamlet* and *Salesman,* being written in the director's own language, will be the easiest of the group. Depending on the translator, specific speeches and scenes in the other plays will be more or less well-developed rhythmically. On the whole, however, sequential, scenic, and major rhythms are fairly well formed in all our sample plays. Such is not the case with many popular hit plays, some of which are little more than narrative dialogue. And while the literary critic rails against such plays for being philosophically shallow or for weakness in character outline, the director may be more unhappy about the shortcomings in rhythmic patterns.

When working with a script that is rhythmically weak, the director must be prepared to create a good portion of the total rhythmic pattern from constituent rhythms to major rhythms. As tedious as this might be, it is often not as difficult as the remedying of one or more scenic rhythms in an otherwise well-constructed play. Perhaps this is so because in the case of the rhythmically weak play the director has control of the rhythm from the outset, while in the well-built play the director should seek his rhythmic solutions in terms of the patterns already established by the playwright. Whatever might be the case, the responsibility for a rhythmic pattern of the final production falls on the director. If necessary in order to gain the proper rhythmic metaphor, the director should be prepared to rewrite lines, reconceive characters, or revise the story line of a script. Of course, if the script requires too extensive revision, the director might consider abandoning production plans entirely.

A major means by which the director obtains dramatic rhythm for his production, and perhaps the director's most important auditory contribution, is the orchestration of the voices of the play. Even the most precise adjectives cannot indicate exactly how a speech is to be read or how one or more speeches are to be related in a vocal pattern. Consequently, the playwright must depend in great measure upon the director for the auditory details of his script. Auditory details also include music, song, and sound effects in general.

The director begins his orchestration with the accenting and pronunciation of the single word. Although much line reading is left up to the actor, the director still has the responsibility of indicating line readings if necessary. While the single speech can sometimes be handled by the actor without vocal direction, the scenes calling for duets, trios, and larger groups of speakers require careful orchestration by the director. Using the factors of rate, volume, pitch, stress, phrasing, and language, the director must decide, among other matters, when and how the vocal tension is to be increased and decreased, when and how cues are to be picked up, when and how a line is to "top" or "come under" another, and when and how speeches are to be counterpointed, dovetailed, or overlapped.

Adjusting the audible tension or relaxation of a scene actually means adjusting the scene to the total dramatic rhythm. This adjustment is paramount and is the decisive factor in all other vocal issues. Any change in the rate, volume, pitch, stress, phrasing, or language in the audible theatre will result in a change in the vocal tension or relaxation of a scene. The important thing for the director to bear in mind is that there are many ways in which the elements of sound in the theatre—pitch, rate, volume, stress, phrasing, and language—can be used to adjust the tension of a scene. Especially among beginning actors, there is a tendency to assume that increasing rate, raising pitch, increasing volume, or overstressing important words will increase the tension of a speech or a scene; whereas slowing rate, lowering pitch, quieting volume, or reducing the degree of word stress or close attention to phrasing will relax the tension of a scene. However, the reverse often holds true. In many cases, increased rate may serve as a tension-releasing device, while slower rates may be tension-creating. Certainly slower rates tend to conserve energy, and all other things being equal, conserved energy is more tension-creating than is released energy. The same is true of higher pitch and increased volume. That is, lowering pitch or volume may often increase tension.

Pausing, or negative sound, should be given very careful attention by the director. The dramatic pause is mentioned so often that some tend to assume that any pause is dramatic. Pausing is sometimes dramatic and sometimes not. One must remember that pausing is related to sound as negative space is related to the visual theatre and rest is related to the kinetic theatre. Thus most pauses set off sound or aid in comprehension of sound. Such pauses are certainly functional but can hardly be called "dramatic." Often pauses are inserted in the production as tension-gaining, crisis-stating, or tension-releasing elements.

The director should be aware that pauses have a "life of their own." When the director recognizes this life, he can better determine the exact quality of his pauses. Think for a moment of a room of people in lively conversation. Suddenly all talk ceases. If the silence remains for a little space of time, tension will build. At the moment of crisis, someone giggles or makes a comment on the silence, and the tension is broken. Everyone has had such an experience. It is a demonstration that a pause can go through an entire dramatic rhythm from tension to crisis to release. Because pauses are capable of maintaining a full rhythmic sequence, they are as complicated as speech or song and must be handled in the same manner.

The director must bear in mind that the pause will be conditioned by the speeches preceding and following it. The following rules of thumb might be helpful. All things being equal, a pause beginning in relaxation will, if held long enough, rise to a tension. If speech resumes at the moment of tension, that pause may be considered tension-creating. On the other hand, a pause that begins in tension will, if held long enough, relax from that tension. If speech begins after relaxation has started, the pause may be termed a release pause. No matter how colored by surrounding audible circumstances, any pause if held long enough will go through recurring cycles of tension and relaxation. After a point, the audience may take matters into their own hands and release, through giggles or coughs, a pause held too long.

The matter of pausing naturally introduces the problem of the orchestration of cues. Not all cues should be "picked up" immediately. Obviously, some cues should be introduced by pauses intended to increase or release tension. On the other hand, some directors and actors, quick to learn the value of a pause before some cues, forget that not all cues demand pausing. Most cues should be picked up. The problem is exactly when the cue should be picked up. Obviously, in ordinary conversation we do not wait politely until the last word of a sentence before we begin responding. Certain words, perhaps quite early in a statement, trigger a response. The same holds true in theatrical dialogue. The responding character does not react to the last word of a speech but to the key words of the speaker. Such key words might be the result of the story-line pattern, the character patterns, or the rhythmic patterns of a play. In well-written plays, these patterns are usually coincidental; in the well-directed play, they are always coincidental. On the key word, the responding character begins to respond. Such response may or may not be at the very end of the first character's speech. While the director may hear complaints that overlapping cues or dovetailing speeches prevent the audience from hearing each word, he must bear in mind that his problem is to present the audience with an exciting vocal work in which important words are properly emphasized while the total dramatic rhythm is retained. Waiting until the end of every speech for a response will let the audience *hear* everything, but it may prevent them from *experiencing* dramatic rhythms. If each word is so important, the audience might do better to read the play at home. However, every play is filled with texture words, sounds that add bulk and life to a script without necessarily being intended for a separate hearing. Consider in this regard the scene in *Hamlet* in which Horatio questions the Ghost. As Horatio shouts at the Ghost, his comrades call out, "Speak to him, Horatio; Question him, Horatio." Such lines need not be heard independently. Shakespeare could easily have written the following stage direction: "As Horatio talks, the others shout in fear and encouragement."

The problem of when to respond to a cue involves the larger problem of all counterpointed speeches. Many plays have such directions as: "They all speak at once," or "they enter in conversation." Even if the playwright has given no indication, the director will need to decide the specific "attack" for each cue. Cues may be handled in normal rotation or in two other ways: through dovetailing or overlapping. In dovetailing the second speaker begins talking just before the first speaker has finished. Overlapping means that one or more lines are said simultaneously. Overlapping may be of two types: counterpoint or unison. Counterpointed speeches are speeches in which one speaker takes dominance over the other. Unison means that all speakers are given equal importance. Sometimes simultaneous speakers say the same lines; sometimes they say very different lines. For example, in the final scene in *From Morn to Midnight,* the onstage audience or the Cashier might deliver some lines in direct counterpoint to the lines being delivered by the confessing sinners. As General St. Pé and his wife argue, their lines might be said simultaneously. On the other hand, the chorus in *Oedipus* need not always speak in unison. Single lines or several lines might be assigned to one or another chorus member. Sometimes one chorus member might be stating a new idea even as another echoes, in an undertone, the previous line. All such orchestrations require that the acting company perform as a very tight and cooperative ensemble, each member working closely with the others to achieve the desired choral result. Overlapped lines and cues, simultaneous speeches, lines in chorus, and counterpoint are not easy for the actor to adjust to. He must be able to listen for his cue, pick it out of a number of conflicting sounds, and carry on his part of the orchestration without being distracted by the speeches of others. At first the actor may have considerable difficulty. The director must be patient; overlapped and simultaneous speeches should be introduced slowly.

The actor may have a tendency to speed up his speeches or try to outshout the competition, and the director may have to warn the actor against such tendencies. He should encourage the actor to complete all overlapped speeches. In the early rehearsals, the director might want to instruct the actor to approach the problem slowly and with precision. Once precision is acquired, the appropriate rate and volume may be easily introduced.

Many of the problems of rhythms, cues, and coincidental lines are best understood by the actor in terms of whether he "tops" or "goes under" his fellow actors. The two terms are often used rather loosely and are not easy to define. In general, however, to "top" another actor is to respond on an increased level of volume, pitch, or rate. To "go under" another actor is to respond more slowly with less volume, pitch, or rate. Neither is preferable and neither is absolutely indicative of strength or dominance. Much depends on the dramatic situation. All other things being equal, the actor who tops another is stronger and more dominant; but if two actors have several times exchanged topping lines in a sequence, then the actor who suddenly goes under may gain strength and dominance. At any time when the audience expects a topping line and the actor goes under, a change in the dominant–subordinate and strong–weak relationships is likely to occur. Much the same is true of tension and release. While some topping may be tension-building, continual topping will expend so much energy that tension will be lost. Conversely, continual going under, while it might be energy-conserving, will reach a point at which further conservation will seem foolish. Either the actors must then release tension or the audience will do so for them by coughing or laughing.

We should bear in mind that all that has been said of speech alone is also applicable to any audible device used in the theatre-auditory. We are all familiar with the use of background music as a mood device; but we must remember that such music is also part of the overall auditory pattern, and that a language pause with background music is not the same as a pause with no sound whatsoever.

In discussing vocal orchestration, nothing has been said of the quality of a particular line, that is, the amount of pathos, fear, laughter, or irony in the way a line is read. While they will certainly affect the final quality of the audible orchestration, these matters are properly the concern of character analysis. However, in the final auditory metaphor, they will greatly affect such matters as counterpointed speeches, overlapped and dovetailed cues, topped lines, and the general tension of the dramatic metaphor. Consequently, before coming to definite conclusions about the audible design of a play, the director will want to have a clear idea of how his actors are likely to read each line. Therefore the final orchestration of the play might have to be postponed until the latter third of the rehearsal period.

To sum up, in creating the audible shape of the play, the director begins by designing the vocal rhythms into dramatic rhythms. If the play is well written, the task should be easy enough; but if the play is poorly written, the director may be forced to provide every rhythmic sequence for the script. Such a case might mean that the director will need to rewrite lines or portions of the story line, or redesign characters.

In addition to creating the vocal rhythms of the play, the director must orchestrate every audible element of the final production. In orchestration, the director's chief problems are using the sound factors of rate, volume, pitch, stress, phrasing, and language to create the proper increase or decrease of tension, the exact manner in which cues are to be picked up, the necessary patterns of overlapping and simultaneous speeches, and the appropriate relationship of topping and going under in dialogue structure.

CREATING THE KINETIC METAPHOR

The primary task in the creation of a kinetic metaphor is the synthesizing of the auditory and visual metaphors in and through the kinetic metaphor. Of course, this synthesis has been taking place since the initial decision to produce a particular play script. In every decision concerning his production, the director will have always kept in mind the needs of the kinetic theatre. If the actor cannot move properly and also say a given line, the director will realize that the line needs adjusting; if the actor cannot move on the set or work easily in a given costume, then the set and the costume might have to be adjusted. On the other hand, before major revisions are made, the actor should be encouraged to make every reasonable effort to read the speech as written, move on the set as designed, or wear the costume as given. When an adjustment is necessary it should be as minor as possible. Neither the director nor the actor should expect a perfect synthesis of the visual, auditory, and kinetic theatres. Friction between the major elements of theatre can never be totally eliminated, but the director should work for a minimization of that friction.

As the director creates his kinetic metaphor in rehearsal, his first task is identical to the first problem in visual theatre—he must understand his particular set. The scene designer has given him a specific spatial universe in which to operate; he must now comprehend the motion limits and potentials of that universe. Some settings are by their very nature more conducive to movement than are others. For instance, a proscenium set consisting solely of a broad flight of stairs from upstage to downstage would invite a considerable amount of vertical movement. The narrower the treads of such stairs, the more invitation to movement. On the other hand, such a formalized setting may provide for movement but may not allow for sufficient variety in motion patterns. Loss of variety means loss of potential complexity in kinetic statement.

On the other end of the spectrum from the stairway setting would be the set that actually defeats attempts at motion. Motion-negating sets are usually lacking in differences of floor heights, have large and massive architectural pieces occupying great areas of the stage, and have only one or two traffic lanes through which actors might move. Unfortunately, many highly effective visual settings are at the same time motion-restricting. This shortcoming is particularly apparent in "realistic" plays. There are times when so much effort is put into creating a vivid narrative illusion that little thought is given to kinetic possibilities. Most people have seen in the theatre, the movies, or on television the dining room scene which is dominated by a huge table downstage-center. The table looks exactly as such a dining table would look. Surrounding it are several chairs. The table is dressed with the appropriate realistic properties. The remaining floor space is occupied by a china cabinet, a large sideboard, and a serving tray for wines. Everything is exactly as it should be for a large supper, and all the actors have to do is to enter and sit, and sit, and sit, and sit! In most circumstances, the director should avoid such settings. Narrative illusion is important, but it should always add to, never detract from, the necessary kinetic statements.

Every set has its own particular and special motion advantages and disadvantages. Although preplanning will help to see these factors in a general way, only actual movement on the set will enable the director fully to understand his problems. For example, a large easy chair on a set may be planned by the director as a strong motive for movement; that is, the chair would provide two good reasons for movement. As a large mass, it would tend to draw other masses; and as an incompleted familiar form, it would tend to draw an actor into its seat. However, once the director began using the chair, he might find it was more motion-restricting than motion-inducing. That is, once an actor sat in the chair, he was immobilized practically by its soft envelopment and aesthetically by its mass. Consequently, although the director originally planned to use the chair to create motion and make statements of strength, he might afterwards adjust by using the chair to impede motion and make statements of weakness.

As in the visual metaphor, so in the kinetic metaphor certain compositions or designs are obvious from the nature of the setting, while others must be created on the spot. Some settings have obvious vacuums which help to promote motion, especially at the beginning of the play. A set that contains several large masses and balances those masses with negative space has its own native vacuums in those areas of negative space. At the same time, the masses that oppose the negative space act as attracting agents to draw actors out of the areas of vacuum.

Every setting has its indigenous highways and byways. There are certain paths that support primary movements and certain lanes best suited for secondary movement. For instance, on a completely bare proscenium stage, movements upstage and downstage are primary, while movements left and right are secondary; that is, the latter will be less emphatic. In the arena, movements toward and away from center are primary, and movements around the edges of the stage are secondary. But, of course, these rules of thumb are affected by every change, however slight, introduced by the setting, the costumes, the lights, or the actors. Any shift in visual, literary, or kinetic emphasis will call for a shift in the primary and secondary paths of motion.

Blackgum Birthday *by James M. Ragland. Department of Drama and Communications, Louisiana State University, New Orleans.*

Director: August W. Staub
Designer: D. Taylor Brooks

A sudden release of energy is always exciting and creates its own emphasis. Note the differences in potential energy between the actor in the foreground and the actor in the background.

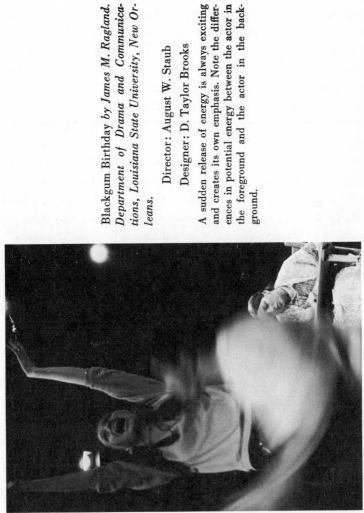

As in the visual metaphor, the director is likely to build his kinetic metaphor about recurring motion shapes or motifs. In visual design these motifs are best understood as unifying devices, but in kinetic design they are best understood as rhythmic and sequential devices. A kinetic motif is a recognizable process by which energy is conserved and expanded, while at the same time integrity of movement is maintained. While it is both difficult and dangerous to describe kinetic motifs with popular adjectives, we often read that certain productions were "action-packed," "fast-paced," "powerful," "quietly stated," or "told with suppressed tension." As often as not, each of these terms refers to certain kinetic motifs selected by the director. "Action-packed" and "fast-paced" productions usually feature numerous short cycles of conservation and release of energy. The "action-packed," as opposed to the more simple "fast-paced," production will usually employ a greater variety of rhythmic methods, that is, more varied use of direction, rate, energy, and control, as well as many different approaches to sequence, emphasis, and dynamic tension. "Powerful" and "explosive" productions, on the other hand, may not seek as much variety in kinetic motif, but are likely to use fewer and more impressive motifs. For example, the director of an "explosive" production might use as a basic kinetic shape the sudden integration and the just-as-sudden disintegration of masses. The enormous energy and great attractive power of a suddenly integrated mass and the immensely compelling force of a suddenly disintegrated mass would give the impression of a series of implosions and explosions. Thus such a production would be kinetically powerful or "explosive." "Quietly stated" productions and those "told with suppressed tension" would likely seek less-spectacular and less-varied kinetic motifs. Such productions are normally characterized by a smaller kinetic field. Large masses are either avoided, or never suddenly integrated or disintegrated. In more "quietly stated" productions, energy is never allowed to be conserved to a high degree and is rarely released suddenly. In "suppressed-tension" shows, energy is never fully released, and when released it is usually under tight and even control.

These "types" of kinetic motif are, of course, neither the most typical, the most common, nor the most inclusive. They are merely cited as examples of possible kinetic motifs that might provoke certain common critical adjectives. Nor are these types suitable for all play scripts. The director must decide what he wishes to say with the kinetic metaphor in terms of the total theatrical metaphor. Let us take *Oedipus Rex* as an example. Visually, the director may establish balanced and very formal movement patterns. Kinetically, he may seek motifs described as "quietly stated"; that is, he may have only six chorus members. Three might be assigned to either half of the set; they may never combine in a larger mass than a trio. Most of the movement may be done by each choral member acting as a small and discrete mass. At no time would the chorus move with strength toward a point of emphasis. They would never move great distances or at more than moderate rates. In short, the chorus would never be allowed to develop great stores of energy, and thus they would have no opportunity for major conversions of conserved to actual energy. On the other hand, another director using the same formal visual motifs may counterpoint those motifs with "fast-paced" kinetic motifs. The chorus may dart about, moving in many directions and covering long distances at high speeds. Yet another director may double the number of chorus members and may combine them suddenly into formal masses which might just as suddenly disperse. His motifs may be described as more "explosive." If this same director altered the visual motifs to more asymmetrical forms, then the combination of visual and literary motifs would be informal and romantic in style, as opposed to the more symmetrical and quietly stated classicism of the first director.

The question of combining visual and kinetic motifs into a single metaphor or style reminds us that the kinetic metaphor is the catalyst for all the metaphors of the theatre. Consequently, while the director may sometimes consider certain aspects of the auditory and visual metaphors in isolation, the creation of the kinetic metaphor means not only a movement metaphor but also the assimilation of auditory and visual statements in and through the theatre of movement. The kinetic metaphor is always built in terms of the statements that will or must be made in the other areas of theatre. If the visual theatre has created a mass, then the kinetic theatre must move that mass; if the play script has generated a certain reserve of energy, then the kinetic theatre must spend that energy. For example, in the final scene in *From Morn to Midnight*, the visual and auditory theatres have combined to establish a unified mass of auditors on stage. The metaphors of the kinetic theatre will have to be made in and through this particular mass. In another case, when the old shepherd reveals to Oedipus his true identity, new energy or excitement is introduced into the theatrical metaphor, and it is the burden of the kinetic theatre to share in spending the newly acquired energy.

On the other hand, the contributions of the kinetic theatre must now be amalgamated with those of the other areas. Thus if the kinetic theatre is moving the massive audience in *From Morn to Midnight,* the visual theatre must provide appropriate color for such a mass, appropriate space in which the mass can move, and appropriate light in order for the audience to see the mass as a body. The play script must provide a story line with appropriate logic for mass movement, a dramatic rhythm to serve as support for the movement, and a pattern of motives and manners that permits the director to move so large a group of actors as a single mass.

In the case of *Oedipus,* what the kinetic theatre does after the awful revelation of the old shepherd must be finely attuned with the auditory and visual theatres. If, before his fall, Oedipus had been costumed in a highly saturated, highly textured costume in order to give him additional mass and contrast, something must now be done to detract from the strength of that costume. Kinetically, the director may cause Oedipus to move from a high platform to a low one; but unless the visual effect of his costume is muted, he will still retain considerable strength. Perhaps lighting can be employed. A special spotlight held in reserve can now be brought up on the fallen Oedipus. If the spotlight is filtered in a color designed to fade or gray-down his costume, then the visual and kinetic theatres have successfully combined. The next contribution belongs to the auditory theatre. If the director inserts a long, low moan immediately following the revelation, a moan serving as an energy-releasing device, then the total theatrical metaphor has combined to thrust Oedipus from a position of strength to one of weakness. Now careful thought will be needed to continue Oedipus as a weakened agent. After the fall, the director will want to see that the actor reads the pathetic laments of Oedipus as speeches of weakness. He might call upon the visual theatre to provide both a change of costume and an alteration in lighting. He might decide to take movements of strength from Oedipus and assign such movements to Creon and the chorus.

The final problem in the kinetic metaphor is the creation of sequence for the total production. Since movement itself is pure sequence, the director should have little or no problems in handling the kinetic shape alone. Complications arise from the fact that the visual theatre depends almost entirely upon the kinetic theatre for sequence. Added to that problem is the habit of playwrights of breaking the line of sequence, particularly in terms of space. Since literature, as a purely temporal art, has no spatial restrictions, the playwright may sometimes overlook the spatial and kinetic limitations of the theatre. The first act takes place in 1920; the next act is in 1940. While the auditory theatre may be little affected by the changed time, the spatial theatre must reflect appropriate material changes, and the kinetic theatre must realize that the hero, now twenty years older, cannot possibly possess the same rhythm of motion or the same relationship of potential to realized energy. On a more technical level, the end of every act means the end of a visual and kinetic sequence. Unless the next act is designed to begin immediately where the former left off, the director must reestablish, at the beginning of the act, the spatial and kinetic limits and potentials of his stage. This is an especially important need when the new act also calls for a new setting.

In summary, the creation of the kinetic metaphor begins when the director attempts to understand the special motion problems of his scenery. Once these problems are understood, the director begins to compose and design the motion of his actors in terms of his specific setting. As in the visual metaphor, the director is likely to build his kinetic metaphor around certain kinetic shapes or motifs that provide the kinetic rhythm and integrity of his metaphor. Perhaps his most important kinetic task is to unify the visual and auditory metaphors in and through the kinetic metaphor. In general, the final unification of all three theatrical metaphors must wait until the technical and dress rehearsals.

THE TECHNICAL REHEARSALS

In the technical rehearsals, the director has an opportunity to see where his guesses have been good and where they have gone astray. When the director accepted the costume designs, selected the music and sound effects, called for certain properties, and accepted the light plot and the color schemes of the set, he was making educated guesses. He hoped that he and the various artists and technicians were communicating and that what they thought might work would actually operate. From time to time in the rehearsal period, the director has had an opportunity, or should have taken the opportunity, to check on the building of costumes, properties, special effects, and the organization of the music and lights. If things have progressed smoothly in the scene shop, the director has had an opportunity to work directly on the final set before technical rehearsals. However, despite all the checks and counterchecks, despite all the thinking and rethinking, the technical rehearsal is the first time when the director may begin to realize the complete theatrical metaphor and understand how well or how poorly he guessed and what must now be amended or discarded.

Since the technical rehearsal is a time of disorder in the face of final organization, most directors feel that it is best approached in stages. Instead of introducing the lights, music, sound effects, properties, set dressing, costumes, and makeup all at the same time, the director may do better to take up such matters by degrees. Two technical rehearsals are usually better than one; three are usually better than two. However, rehearsal time and space are often factors over which the director has little control. He may have to have only a single technical rehearsal, followed by a dress rehearsal. The fewer the technical rehearsals, the more careful should be the prior planning. Some sort of working organization should be established with a clear chain of command. The average commercial theatre usually makes use of a stage manager who acts as a go-between from director to other artists. There is nothing in particular to recommend this arrangement over any other the director finds workable. Each director should seek the organization and chain of command that best suits his staff and their process of communication.

Most directors feel that as much technical material as possible should be rehearsed without insisting that the actors always be present. In particular, the director should be able to have a preliminary light and sound cue rehearsal before calling together his actors. Actors should be encouraged to use props as they become available or to substitute some similar object throughout rehearsals. This practice is particularly useful in terms of such hand props as purses, fans, canes, knives, pipes, and the like. Also, when unusual costumes are to be worn, the costumer is often able to provide "rehearsal" coats, vests, shawls, and skirts.

During the running of a technical rehearsal, the director will not always want to strive for a continuous run-through. Rather, he may want to approach the lights, the sound, the set, and the costumes exactly as he has treated the actors in earlier rehearsals, correcting mistakes as they happen. Thus the door will be repaired when it breaks, or at the next intermission. The lights that came in late may be halted and, after appropriate notes are taken on the light cue sheet, the light cue rerun. Minor adjustments to costumes and properties might be made on the spot. In short, the director will find that careful technical rehearsals will usually save him and his fellow artists both time and frustration in the dress rehearsals and performances.

Particular attention should be paid to the beginning and ending of every act or scene and to the transitions between such acts or scenes. After all, the beginning and end of every act or scene is really the entrance and exit of the lights and sound, sometimes of the entire setting. These entrances and exits of the set, lights, and sound are just as crucial to the play as are the entrances and exists of the actors. The beginning and ending of acts and scenes not only are important but also are likely to be far more complicated than are the interior parts of the production. Consequently, the technical cues should be run and rerun until the beginnings and endings of scenes are a smooth and automatic process.

Because so many people are involved in technical rehearsals, and because stopping to correct the mistake of one person may mean wasting the time of many people, discipline is a specially difficult job in the technical rehearsals. Yet the technical rehearsals, by straining the discipline of the entire production organization, are the very time when the director has the best opportunity to instill the basic "discipline of the theatre." By stressing the fact that everyone is too busy to cater to the whims and minor needs of the individual actor or technician, by taking advantage of each breach of discipline to point out how such thoughtlessness robs the entire organization of countless man-hours and destroys the sense of group cooperation, and finally by expecting the highest level of social cooperation, the director may use the disorder of the technical rehearsal as the primary time for teaching the need for order and cooperation throughout performance.

This is not to say that the director should prance about as a martinet shouting, damning, and commanding. The immense pressures of the technical rehearsal make it more imperative than ever that the director maintain an attitude of firm courtesy. The director should remember that he sets the tone and manners of the entire company. A firm and courteous director will probably find that members of his company cooperate and communicate with each other with a minimum of misunderstanding and tension. Directors who have constant fits of temper may find that they often have temperamental actors, costumers, scene designers, and even stage hands. Directors who are officious and dictatorial may find that their actors are officious with the technical people and that the reigning attitude of the entire company is one of mutual distaste and distrust.

Technical rehearsals extend beyond the limits of the playing area. In cooperation with the scene designer, the lighting director, the costumer, and the technical director, the director will have to oversee the activities of the entire company from the stage door, to the main entrance, to the lobby. Actors and technicians must know where to go, how to place themselves, and what activities are essential at what times. Traffic patterns in the lobby, in the light booth, in the wings, in the entranceways, in the dressing rooms, and in the green room or waiting room must be established and rehearsed as part of the entire production. Hopefully through tight organization mistakes can be avoided during performance. Thus although the makeup may be so simple that the director hardly feels it is worth the effort, he should include in at least one technical rehearsal the putting-on and taking-off of makeup so that traffic patterns can be established in the dressing rooms. The same is true with the shifting of scenery and the placing of properties. It is amazing what hidden difficulties may lurk in the simple task of exchanging one set of window drapes for another.

The technical rehearsals are a time of great pleasure for the director. He is afforded frequent opportunities privately to compliment himself on his good judgment and publicly to compliment his cooperating artists for their many fine and beautiful contributions. Paradoxically, it is also a time of major disappointments. No production staff is perfect; not every decision has been a good one. The director will want to impose a stern aesthetic discipline on himself. He must objectively judge the contributions of himself and others. Anything that injures the theatrical metaphor should be cut, reworked, or played down. The costumer, for example, may have contributed some beautiful jewels for the neck of the leading lady, but the jewels flash so brightly in a certain scene that they destroy the visual composition. The jewels may be the costumer's favorite touch, but they must be eliminated. The lighting director, for example, may have worked long hours establishing a system of tonal lights, but they make for poor lighting in the acting areas. The tonal lights must be rehung or "re-geled." Lighting is especially touchy, for the lighting designer often wonders why the actor cannot move a foot or so to the left or right, why he "cannot find the light." What seems to be a simple matter of "finding the light" may turn out to be the weakening of a carefully created visual or kinetic statement. While there are times when the actor can find a light, the practice should not be encouraged. The kinetic statement normally comes first. The actor moves because of the kinetic composition, not because of the needs of the lighting designer. Under normal circumstances, the light should find the actor. What is true of lights and costume is also true of scenery, music, and makeup. Doors might have to be rehung; false noses or special eye shadow redesigned; music or dances added to or dropped from the show.

Naturally, major items such as the platforming of a set or the costume for the central character cannot be easily changed. Usually some alterations are possible, but in the end the director may have to accept certain shortcomings as an inevitable part of his production. What is unworkable and can be eliminated should be eliminated. What must be accepted should be accepted, and without grumbling. In the end, the director must remember that all decisions are ultimately his; that every part of the theatrical metaphor was inserted, at one time or another, with his consent. Therefore, any element that falls short of perfection does so because of the decisions he made.

THE DRESS REHEARSALS

Technical rehearsals over, the director usually calls a full dress rehearsal. The dress rehearsal is the least understood and most often misused part of the rehearsal period. Far too many theatres treat the dress rehearsal as a performance, forgetting that it is still a rehearsal. The director who invites a full audience to his dress rehearsal may not be rehearsing the play at all, but simply going into production one day early.

While there is a certain advantage in running the dress rehearsal as close to performance conditions as possible, the director should remember that it is a rehearsal. It is a time when both he and the other artists of the theatre take a final look at the completed theatrical metaphor. Mistakes and shortcomings not spotted before should now be marked and corrected if possible. If necessary the rehearsal may have to be stopped and corrections, additions, and alterations made on the spot. Sequences, scenes, or entrances and exits might have to be run and rerun. Final polish might have to be given to dramatic rhythms, and in order to acquire such polish the rhythmic sequence might have to be rerun several times. In short, the dress rehearsal should be treated as a rehearsal, and any activity appropriate to a normal rehearsal should be undertaken if necessary.

Some directors hope to avoid breaking the continuity of the dress rehearsal by taking notes and repeating these notes to the actors between scenes or after rehearsal. Although the practice of note-taking and giving is widespread, there is no evidence that the continuity of rehearsal gained by note-taking is to be preferred to the stopping of rehearsal to make the appropriate changes on the spot. After all, repeating an error tends to reinforce the tendency toward that error. While the director should strive for reasonable continuity in dress rehearsal, he should not permit an unwanted activity to become part of that continuity.

Notes have the further shortcoming of being verbal rather than theatrical. The actor is *told* that he did or did not do something, or he is *told* to add a new activity. He nods and agrees. He understands, but with his mind, not with his body and voice. By the following night he may have forgotten the note entirely, or he may concentrate so hard on remembering his new instructions that he slights other equally important aspects of his performance. However, stopping a dress rehearsal constantly for minor matters does destroy all rhythmic patterns. Hence the director will want to use notes to avoid incessant breaking-in. Giving notes, then, is a matter of balancing between too many and none at all.

While some directors sacrifice too much to the continuity of the dress rehearsal, others take the edge off their final theatrical product by having too many dress rehearsals. If the rehearsal periods have been well used and if the technical rehearsals have been satisfactory, one or two dress rehearsals should be sufficient. If technical rehearsals have been demoralizing to the cast, perhaps the director might wish to have three dress rehearsals simply to establish for the entire company that they are indeed in possession of a sound theatrical metaphor. However, each additional dress rehearsal wears out the costumes, wearies the technicians, increases the cost of the production, and often gives the actors the impression that their performance is a bit empty and hollow. The latter effect is especially true in productions in which audience reactions, such as laughter, are a part of the total theatrical metaphor. It is in order to give the actors the feeling of audience reaction that the director invites an audience to dress rehearsal, thereby turning his rehearsal into a performance.

Some directors save the day before performance for an "undress" rehearsal. That is, the final rehearsal is with sets, props, and lights, but without costumes and makeup. Such a final rehearsal serves to relax the company and to reassemble and recover the sense of ensemble that has been disrupted by the technical rehearsals. Too often the distractions of the technical and dress rehearsals have encouraged the actors to isolate themselves from each other, and in their desperate effort to conquer the problems of a full skirt, an overly tall hat, or a cup of tea, they sometimes forget that the ensemble lies at the heart of the theatrical metaphor. Thus in the "undress" rehearsal the members of the chorus are reminded that no matter how strangely grotesque Oedipus appeared at the end of the dress rehearsal, he is still the same actor in the same scene they have rehearsed so often. By the same token, no matter how silly Argan looks in his costume, he is still the same actor working at the same movement patterns, be he in seventeenth-century French attire or the rehearsal clothing of today. In the relaxed and intimate atmosphere of a final "undress" rehearsal, the director and his actors can secure a final polish for opening night; while at the same time the costumer and the other technicians have an opportunity to make last-minute repairs on and alterations to the scenery, lights, and clothing.

THE PRODUCTION OF THE THEATRICAL METAPHOR

A hard lesson for directors to learn is to give up their own productions; but in the end, that is what the director should be prepared to do. The better the director, the more perfectly he has organized his production staff and created his acting ensemble, and the less need there is for him at production time. The perfect theatrical metaphor *does not need* the services of the director in production. Sometime before the curtain goes up on the first performance, the director should turn the show over to his actors and the production staff. It is now their show; they have earned the right to enjoy it and to own it. Each director has a different method of turning the show over to the company. Some do so with great ceremony; others have little rituals and signs of mystique; others simply say nothing at all. Inspirational speeches may be dangerous. However inspiring it may sound, telling a group of actors to go out and be better than ever is actually giving them permission to introduce new items into the theatrical metaphor. Many find that all that is necessary is to remind the cast of how hard they have worked to acquire a structured metaphor and how important it now is to maintain the show as rehearsed.

Naturally, the director will want to remain on the scene in case his services are needed, but he will want to avoid rushing backstage to give little bits of advice or admonishment. He should try not to be tempted to redesign the show for the following night. What is done is done. Of course, if an actor must be replaced because of illness or if an entrance must be changed because of mechanical difficulty, then the director will have to rework a part of the show.

After the production has opened, the director has three remaining problems: the reviews, the call-back rehearsal, and the strike. Every director dreads reviews—not because they might be negative, but because they might mislead the actors. Most reviewers are well-meaning people, many are quite intelligent; but sometimes they know little or nothing about the art of theatre. They know what they like, but they may not know why they like it. Worse yet, they know what they don't like, but not just *why* a production has failed to please. They may blame the playwright when the director was at fault, the actor when the music cue was late, the costumer when the actor was awkward, and everything that seems weak may be attributed to poor pace and lack of timing. Unfortunately for the director, the actor often does not respond logically to a review, be that review favorable or unfavorable. The actor who has won praise, often undeservedly, may become cocky and over-state his next performance. The actor who has been slighted, sometimes for no real cause, may become morose and lifeless in the following performance, or tend to push too hard. In short, the danger of the review lies in its threat not only to the individual actor but to the entire ensemble. Therefore after the reviews are out, the director might like to assemble his actors and remind them that, favorable or unfavorable, the review is merely one man's opinion; that it is nice to have the opinion of one of the members of the audience; but that no matter what the opinion, the goal of the company is to maintain the play as they have rehearsed it.

The director's second production problem is the call-back rehearsal. During longer runs or when the production must "lay over" for a number of days, a call-back rehearsal may be necessary. Like any other product, a theatrical production tends to get rusty, to loosen up, to become sloppy. The call-back rehearsal, normally without costumes or props, serves to return the play to a more polished and well-oiled condition. In some theatres call-backs are handled by the stage man-ager; in others by the director. No matter who directs the rehearsal, the number and kind of call-backs are the responsibility of the director.

The director's final responsibility to the production, although this is far too often unfortunately shirked, is the organization of the strike. If possible the director and his actors should participate in the strike. The strike reminds the initiated that theatre is a finite and mortal art, and that from beginning to end it is a community project requiring the cooperation of large numbers of people not only to put together a theatrical metaphor but also to dismantle it. To the new actor, strike teaches once again the lesson of the cooperative ensemble. For the director, strike is an opportunity to offer final help to his cooperating artists, a sort of seal and signature to the social contract of theatre. It is also a time to give thanks and congratulations to all the participants in the social contract, to soothe over any wounds or in-juries, and to begin planning for the next production. It is at strike that the managing director of a theatre can review with his staff the problems encountered and the possible solutions that might be employed in the future.

CREATING THE THEATRICAL METAPHOR:
A SUMMARY

The theatrical metaphor actually begins with the selection of a play script. As rehearsals progress, the director begins to create his visual motifs, his vocal orchestration, and his synthesis of visual and vocal metaphors in and through his kinetic metaphor. Technical rehearsal is that time when the final fusion of visual, vocal, and kinetic metaphor takes place. Dress rehearsal gives the director and the other artists an opportunity to experience the entire theatrical metaphor and to make necessary adjustments. A final "undress" rehearsal often aids in recreating the ensemble weakened by the sudden addition of much new visual and vocal material during the technical and dress rehearsals. When the theatrical metaphor is complete, the director gives over the production to his actors and production staff. He himself has only the final duties of call-back rehearsals and strike. The director will want to keep free of what belongs to the actors and the production staff—the completed theatrical metaphor. He should remember that the test of his ability as a director is how much the running show depends upon him. The better the production is put together, the less it needs the presence of the director.

CHAPTER 12

the new media

*The Director Works in Cinema
and Television*

The new media of cinema and television have increasingly occupied
the attention of theatrical artists. Some would see film and television as
distinct art forms requiring a set of principles peculiar to themselves.
However, the principles of theatrical art remain constant whether the
medium be stage or screen. This is why so many theatre artists move
freely from stage to film to television. Among directors who have
worked in both stage and film or television are Elia Kazan, Josh Logan,
Arthur Penn, and Mike Nichols.

Just as specific adjustments must be made for the differences between the proscenium, the thrust, and the arena stages, so too must adjustments be made between the stage production and the film or television production. The major differences between the stage and the new types of dramatic media is that the new media do not combine the audience and the artists. In television and cinema, the production is performed for a camera which records and stores the event on film, tape, or simply on electronic impulses. In a place away from the production, the primary audience is shown the stored event on either a television or motion picture screen. The separation of the primary audience and the performer creates two new problems for the director: (1) the understanding of the construction and uses of the camera, and (2) the understanding of the motion picture screen and the television screen. Out of these two major problems grow all the great and small differences between stage production and drama in the new media.

THE CAMERA

The motion picture camera and the television camera have dissimilarities in structure, since one is based on a mechanical process and the other upon electronics. However, the basic similarities of "seeing" are shared by all cameras, and these similarities the director must understand immediately. First, and most importantly, all present cameras have only one eye; that is, they do not see in three dimensions. Among other things, this means that while the human eye—at least in the average playhouse—has unlimited depth of field, the problem of depth of field is a constant one with the single-eye camera. The depth of field is the area between the lens of the camera and the farthest point from the camera in which focus is sharpest. The depth of field is governed by an interaction of the f-stop or iris, which allows light into the camera, the distance between the camera and the performer, and the focal length of the lens. Other things being equal, the larger the f-stop, the smaller the depth of field; the farther the camera is from the performer, the greater the depth of field; and the shorter the focal length, the greater the depth of field. For example, if the camera is set at $f/2.8$, using a one-inch lens in a long shot, there will be considerable depth of field. However, with the lens and iris opening in a medium shot, the depth of field, or the area in which the performer is in focus, will be greatly decreased.

Having gotten the performer in focus, the camera must now create the illusion of tridimensionality. This is done by assuming that the performance is a cross between the proscenium stage and the arena. Because it has only one eye, the camera, if not manipulated, would present the illusion of a very shallow proscenium stage. But by assuming first that the camera is watching an arena production, and second that the camera is constantly changing its seat, the director can produce the illusion of depth by frequent shifts of the physical point of view. Thus the camera is continuously moved to provide changing angles of vision. The various standard camera angles are based on: (1) shots taken with a stationary camera but with changing lens, (2) shots taken with a moving camera, (3) shots taken with a moving performer, and (4) combinations of the first three. Shots taken with changing lens on a stationary camera are the long shot, the medium, and the closeup. We may also speak of medium-long or medium-closeup. The various shots may be gained through changing lenses or through the use of a zoom lens. If individual lenses are used they are described as wide angle (for long shots), medium, and closeup.

Moving the camera involves the pan, the tilt, the pedestal, the dolly, the truck, and the arc. Panning means to turn the camera right or left on its pedestal or tripod. Tilting means to tilt the camera up or down on its tripod or pedestal. Pedestaling refers to raising or lowering the camera on its tripod or pedestal. To dolly is to move the camera toward or away from the performer. Dollying does not have the same effect as zooming. In zooming, because the camera remains stationary, no new information can be introduced into the picture. A dollying camera may move to a performer for a closeup and then past that performer toward another object. To truck is to move the camera to the right or left. Combinations of tilting, pedestaling, trucking, dollying, or panning are possible. Thus a camera may tilt up and truck left. When a camera turns while it is trucking or dollying, the turn is called an arc—usually a quarter of a circle. When the performer moves, the camera is sometimes instructed to follow the action. Following does not mean that the camera is lagging behind the action. A following camera may often have to anticipate or "lead" the action.

As already mentioned, there are certain fundamental differences between movie and television cameras. Because of its mechanical nature, the movie camera is comparatively lightweight and rugged and can be carried to almost any location. This is particularly true of 16mm equipment. Most expensive commercial films are made with heavy 35mm cameras. Excellent commercial quality work can also be done with a good 16mm camera, and such a camera is within the budgetary reach of most producing theatres. However, with careful planning and editing, work of high artistic quality can be achieved with Super 8mm equipment, which is clearly within the limits of the most modest budget.

While motion picture photography equipment is reasonably inexpensive and highly portable, film stock and processing can become quite expensive. Moreover, once wasted, film is not recoverable. Hence the film producer can save on the expense of scenery by going directly to location. However, he must plan his shots carefully to eliminate waste. Out-takes, or the amount of film discarded as unsatisfactory, should be not more than a ratio of seven feet lost to each foot used. Going above this ratio indicates waste, inefficiency, and poor planning.

Another problem of the motion picture camera is the recording of sound. There is no perfect system. Some highly portable cameras have a sound-on-film characteristic. These are used in journalistic work, but because there is not adequate lip-movement synchronization, sound-on-film cameras are usually avoided in filmed drama. Instead, the director may create an entirely visual and kinetic statement without sound, or he may film silently and record sound on machines designed for film and sound synchronization. Two types of machines are available. Some tape recorders, such as the Nagra Recorders, are outfitted with a device that records along the edge of the tape the running speed of a camera set at exactly 24. frames per second. Another device is to connect the camera and the tape recorder electrically so that the running speed of the camera is recorded along the edge of the tape. Both of the machines presuppose a location in which microphones can be hidden from the camera and in which the weather permits their use. Where special recording devices are not available or where conditions do not permit recording on location, sound may be placed on the film in two ways. The scene can be rerun in a sound studio and the actors then match their words to the silent lip-movements in the film, or sound can be added to the film regardless of what is seen or said visually. The latter process is called sound-over or voice-over and is frequently used to add narration or sound effects to a film.

As contrasted to the film camera, the television camera has fewer sound problems because sound is electronically recorded simultaneously with vision. However, it is far less portable and is not easily used in all types of weather. Moreover, television cameras are more delicate and more expensive than movie cameras. Television cameras can transmit their image directly to a television screen or to a watching audience, whereas movie film must be processed prior to presentation. It is true that most contemporary television drama is stored on videotapes. However, videotape is not the television version of film. Film is capable of being cut and edited independently of the camera that shot the film. In fact, editing is a recommended process in film making. Videotape does not edit easily, and there is little reason for it to be edited. When a picture is filmed, no one is sure until the film is developed just exactly what image has been captured. However, the television camera shows immediately on its monitor the image being recorded. Instant image selection is therefore possible. Moreover, unlike film, videotape is reusable. If a sequence is not acceptable, the tape can be erased and the sequence reshot. Because television tapes are not edited, or are edited only slightly, television makes use of more than one camera so that multiple angles can be acquired immediately. In motion picture filming, the film is stopped and the camera moved for each new angle. Finally, television can absorb and mix other media electronically. Thus although the television camera may not go easily on location, it may incorporate film that has been shot on location and mixed into the television production at the appropriate moment.

In summary, although television and movie cameras do differ, they are similar in such basic problems as depth of field, and they both share the techniques of basic camera angles—the medium, long, and closeup shot; the tilt and pan; the truck, dolly, follow, and arc.

THE SCREEN

Even if movie and television cameras took identical shots (and movie cameras are often used to create television shows), the normal television screen differs greatly in size from the traditional movie screen.

The average television screen is less than two feet square. The smallest movie screen is at least twice that size. The importance of this difference in size has been brought home to every person who has watched the late movie on television. Among other problems of watching movies not designed for television is the difficulty in reading words which on the movie screen would have been clearly legible.

Because of the large size of the movie screen, long shots and scenes involving many people are more frequent in the motion picture. Long shots in television lose detail and make people seem as tiny as ants. Television is, therefore, currently a medium of the tight, close shot. Often television has been compared to the kind of visual images one sees in the comic strips. While it makes frequent use of the closeup, the motion picture just as commonly employs the medium and long shots. In fact, too much reliance by the motion picture on the closeup makes the audience feel as if it is being overwhelmed by giants.

Both screens will allow going from the minute detail to the large overview with a single motion of the camera. Thus in both cinema and television the screen and the camera provide the director with easy means of directing focus and emphasis, particularly in terms of small detail. Stories that hinge upon a tiny visual detail can be told directly in these media, while they could only be narrated on the stage.

The screen and the camera allow the director great freedom in the selection of locale, but they cannot provide him with the impact of the living actor nor the vitality of the interplay between actor and audience. He must substitute for this crucial loss employment of the various and dazzling special visual effects at his disposal. Such effects are gained chiefly through editing film or calling for special camera treatment during the taping of a television show.

EDITING AND TAPING

The editing of film or the taping or shooting of a live television show is the time when the final kinetic and visual composition and design is given to the media productions. As with stage productions, kinetic sequence and dramatic rhythm are the chief problems in editing and taping. Sequence begins with the issue of entering and exiting. In terms of the camera, entering and exiting are matters of what the camera sees and what the camera elects not to see. In regard to the problem of entrances and exits, it might be well to review Chapter 8's discussion of kinetic sequence and Chapter 10's discussion of entrances and exits.

Entrances and exits begin in the new media with focus. That which is in focus has entered; that which is completely out of focus has exited. To be in focus, the subject must have entered frame. To be "in frame" is to be in the line of vision of the camera. In addition to focus and framing, entrances are normally achieved by cutting from a view of one performer to a view of another locale or performer. The cut is the basic means of achieving entrance and exit of people or places. Entrances or exits are also gained through use of the various wipes or fades. Fades may be from white to black for exits and from black to white for entrances, or from subject to subject. Fades may be accomplished in the movie cameras through shutting off the light or through double exposure, but they are most often done in processing or editing. Fades and wipes can be and usually are accomplished electronically in television.

In addition to creating an entrance and exit pattern, the special techniques of focusing, framing, wiping, or fading can be used within the ongoing rhythmic unit to change angle to gain variety or to increase tension, crisis, or release. Additional techniques such as slow motion, high speed, the freeze frame, the montage or superimposed image, the trick shot (such as bodies appearing or dissappearing), the hand-held camera, and the distorted focus can all be used as devices to increase the impact of one or more of the elements of visual, auditory, and kinetic theatre. Also, such special effects as sound-over image, musical accompaniment, and animation may add to the auditory image of the motion picture and television production.

In motion picture editing, it is up to the editor or the director-editor to select from the various "takes" those which will create the best sequence and dramatic rhythm. In this choice he is guided by the principles of the visual, kinetic, and auditory theatre. Certain technical problems face the motion picture editor, including selecting the process by which film clips are joined and matching of film clips in quality, speed, and sound synchronization. A special problem is that of being certain that subjects are consistently oriented to frame-left or frame-right during a given rhythmic sequence. If a subject is first presented as facing frame-right in a given sequence, that subject should be continued in orientation to frame-right throughout the sequence. This problem is exactly the same as the problem of establishing offstage locales on the stage. If the kitchen is established as offstage-right in a given scene, then all entrances from the kitchen must be made stage-right.

A special editing problem is that related to story. Because the camera changes angle often and frequent use is made of medium and closeup shots, the audience must be reminded from time to time of the period and locale of the scene. This information is passed on in what are called establishing shots. Usually establishing shots are long shots that show an overview of scenery and costumes. However, an establishing shot may be a closeup of a sign saying the name of the town or the airport. The selection of establishing shots will be made first by the director and then by the editor-director.

In television, editing is not done at leisure; it is accomplished almost entirely during the performance. The television director usually has at his disposal from one to five cameras. By watching on the monitor the images produced by each camera and by giving special-effects instructions to his engineers, the television producer-director makes immediate decisions on camera angles and effects. However, because of the pressure of instantaneous selection, many kinetic, visual, and auditory choices are made and carefully rehearsed prior to television taping.

THE CAMERA AND THE PERFORMERS

The camera makes peculiar demands on the actors, and the director must be prepared to aid actors in meeting these demands. In television and in some motion picture situations, the actor is restricted to movements and positions that make it possible to unite sound with camera. Moreover, the camera demands that the actor be in the appropriate position to be framed, focused, and shot. Therefore actors are usually given extremely precise instructions about where to stand, where to look, and where to move. In short, the actor is not told simply to cross to a chair and sit on its arm. He is told to move to the chair, sit on an exact spot on the arm, and look right at an exact angle. To move to a spot marked so exactly is sometimes referred to as "taking your mark." Thus an actor might be instructed: "Take your mark by the chair."

Actors must also become used to performing among a tangle of wires, tripods, lights, grips, gaffers, cameramen, and assorted technicians and directors. They may be asked to repeat an exact movement and inflection for a retake or to start a new sequence after a take has been completed. Finally, actors may be requested to perform scenes away from the environment of that scene, the scenery being added later in editing. More disconcertingly, actors may have to play love or fight scenes to the camera only.

In motion pictures, it is not uncommon to film the story out of story-line sequence. Thus the last scene of the story might be shot first, and the actor must produce the final emotional state without any previous "build." This practice of filming out of story-line sequence is followed because takes are made in the most convenient and economical manner, not in terms of the story line.

In contrast to cinema, television productions are most often taped in story-line sequence because of the difficulty of editing videotape. Thus it is more usual to rehearse a television production much like a stage production, making special adjustments for the size of the television studio and the general tightness of the camera shots. If a major shortcoming occurs during the taping of a sequence, the whole sequence is retaped. Two special problems face the television actor. The first is the matter of identifying the live cameras. Because not all cameras are in use at all times, and because the actor may often be asked to perform a scene alone while his colleagues make appropriate changes, he might have to be able to identify the live cameras. This is done by finding those cameras on which the red light is glowing. If the performer cannot read the light, he should be reminded to look toward the floor manager, who will point out the live cameras. Many productions are planned so that the performer need not concern himself with finding live cameras. However, all television performers must learn the signals having to do with beginning, ending, and timing the program. These signals will usually be given by the floor manager.

The signal to "stand by" is an arm raised from the elbow, fingers extended, and palm toward the performer. The signal to start is given by pointing at the performer. The signal to stop within five seconds is the drawing of the index finger across the neck in a cutting motion. Timing within the program is generally concerned with speeding up— the index finger turned in a circle—if the program is running long, with slowing down—both index fingers drawn away from the face in a stretching motion—if the program is running too short. As a segment nears its end, the performer should pay attention to the three closing signals—a raised index finger meaning one minute, both index fingers crossed meaning a half-minute, a closed fist with palm toward the performer meaning fifteen seconds.

Cinema productions are composed of countless very brief takes. In television production, the camera angle is changed by switching to another camera. Cinema practice more commonly calls for the action to stop and the camera to be shifted to a new position for the new angle. When this is done, the actor may have to produce the identical action in which he was engaged for the previous angle.

Because of the brevity of the takes, motion picture scenes are not usually rehearsed as long as stage and television scenes. But while the demands on the actor's memory are lessened in movies and may also be lessened in television by the use of "cue cards," a greater burden is placed on the actor to express himself more subtly both physically and vocally in these media. A style that might be considered underplaying on the stage might appear in the closeup medium of film or television to be overstated. Actually, work in the intimate arena stage is the closest to the style and techniques best suited to the new media.

THE DIRECTOR, THE NEW MEDIA, AND THE SCRIPT

When analyzing the television script or the movie scenario, the director has all the concerns of the stage production. He must further consider the special needs and abilities of the camera; that is, he considers not only what his actors do but what his camera does. In cinema, he might plan various camera angles for the same set of dialogue so that he can select the best sequence during editing. Usually the angle, the focus, the framing, and the approximate footage to be shot are planned before the filming takes place.

In television the major camera positions are indicated in the production script. Thus if four cameras are used, angles for at least two or three of the cameras are predetermined. While the television producer is not concerned about wasting videotape footage, he is very much aware of time. Seconds on the air are costly in television. Moreover, for purposes of scheduling, television runs in multiples of fifteen minutes. Within each fifteen-minute segment must be included time for commercials. Consequently, a fifteen-minute production runs only a little over twelve minutes; a half-hour production something over twenty-five minutes. To achieve exactitude in time, each television sequence is given a time allotment. A director of a twelve-minute television drama might, therefore, divide his script into three takes of two minutes and six takes of one minute. A further time log is kept in each television production script, to record accumulated time. Thus as each take is accomplished, the total time is added so that the producer can easily see both individual shot timing and the running time of the production. Along with the stage directions for the actors and the directions for the various cameras, the television director must also decide before production the specific timing of a sequence and the accumulated time for his entire script. Because of television's special relationship to time, each television performer must learn the various time signals used by the floor manager.

THE NEW MEDIA: A SUMMARY

The principles of theatrical art remain in any medium—stage, film, or television. Specific adjustments must be made for each medium. In terms of film and television, most of the adjustments center on the camera and the screen. The director must take into account the means in which the camera may be used and the screens upon which the final product is shown to an audience. Acting adjustments are also related to the cameras, and each medium has its special equipment and concerns. As in older theatre forms the director cannot hope to achieve an entirely satisfactory production unless he knows both the principles of the entire art and the technical demands of the specific medium. In film and television, he must know the technical problems of camera construction, usage, control of light, lens employment, and film and television editing.

CHAPTER 13

business and
house management

Not every director must also bear the burdens of being the business and house manager of his theatre. But because so many directorial decisions are based in part on the financial organization and public image of the theatre for which he works, every director should know and understand the economic and managerial problems of running a theatre. The general practice of the New York commercial theatre is to separate the director from the business and house manager, the latter assuming the title of producer. Outside of New York, the usage in professional, community, and educational theatre is for one member of the directing staff to assume the title of managing director, combining the responsibilities of both the director and the producer. No matter what the arrangement, the problems of business and house management remain fairly constant. Money must be provided to support one or more productions, and means must be discovered for informing the public about the production and for getting them in and out of the theatre at the appropriate times. Specifically, these problems begin with securing one or more scripts and end with disposing of the remains—costumes, properties, etc.—of each production.

SECURING THE PLAY SCRIPT

Whether a given theatre is organized about a repertory, a fixed season, or a single production, a constant problem of theatre management is the securing of desired play scripts. Plays are of two kinds: those protected by copyright and those which are not. Plays protected by copyright have been registered under the laws governing international copyrights. In most cases these laws forbid the reproduction of the play script in any form, for any audience, without the express permission of the author or his representative. Usually such permission is granted upon the payment of a stipulated amount of royalty.

Plays not protected by copyright are either originals that have yet to be registered or those in public domain. When dealing with an original play, the director may purchase the copyright to the script, or he may simply arrange for the production of the play for some or no royalty. When dealing with an uncopyrighted play script of unknown origin, the director may plan production without paying royalty, though he would be under a moral obligation to discover any person rightfully entitled to royalty. However, in the case of a newly discovered Elizabethan play script, the director should feel free to produce if he wishes.

Plays in public domain are those on which copyright has expired or those written before copyright laws existed. In theory copyright extends twenty-eight years with the right to renew for an additional twenty-eight years. This would mean that all plays written before the middle of the nineteenth-century are now in public domain. Care must be exercised, however, in terms of translations, which can be copyrighted no matter what the date of the original, and in terms of certain nineteenth-century plays that were not copyrighted until many years after their first publication or production. In general, whenever there is any doubt concerning plays less than ninety years old, the wisest course is to write to the publisher of the book in which the play is found. Most modern plays are found in the catalogues of the major agents for dramatic authors along with the normal royalties for production.

THE PRODUCTION BUDGET

After a play script has been legally secured, a production budget must be provided. In repertory theatres, whether professional, community, or educational, a budget is usually provided for a series or season of plays. In the Broadway theatre and in some other types of commercial theatre, budgeting is on a single-show basis. Whether a budget is provided for a season or for a show, each show will have a specific cost which must be anticipated and provided for.

The first step in budgeting is to inventory resources on hand. If the theatre has done a production of a classic Greek play, then some of those costumes might be available to use in a production of *Oedipus*. On the other hand, the materials for set construction might be depleted at the moment. The resources are high in one department, low in another. The second step in budgeting is to analyze the needs of a given production. *The Imaginary Invalid* is a very large costume show; *Death of a Salesman* could be done in modern dress if necessary. On the other hand, while people may have heard of *Death of a Salesman,* considerable funds might have to be devoted to informing the public that *Invalid* is an enjoyable and funny play.

The third step in budgeting is to provide for the fixed expenses of the production. These expenses might include everything from the cost of the electricity or rent of the theatre to the salary of the box office help and the building custodian. The fourth step is to estimate the anticipated income from the production. In theatres that operate by subscription or subsidy only, this is a relatively simple step. In others, especially those planning to continue beyond a single production, it is both a difficult and crucial step.

The last step is to estimate the salvage possibilities of the anticipated production. In some theatres salvage is a simple matter. Anything of value remaining from the production is simply sold to the highest paying outlet. In other theatres, particularly those planning to continue over a period of years, salvage is a matter of adding to the stock of future necessities, thereby reducing the cost of future productions. Plays such as *The Imaginary Invalid* may call for a high expense in costumes, but those costumes can be reused, thus reducing the costs of future Molière productions. On the other hand, while it may be cheaper for the theatre to rent rather than build costumes for *Invalid,* the rented costume has no salvage value.

When all five budgeting steps have been carefully weighed one against the other, the decision may be taken not to produce. If, however, there is a positive reaction to the cost of the play, a budget should be distributed according to the available resources, including the amount of capital on hand, the special needs of the production in terms of each area of theatre, the fixed expenses of the theatre, the anticipated income from the production, and the salvage possibilities of the production. Once the budget has been fixed, the managing director should insist that his staff work within its limits. While occasional estimates may be too low, the director who consistently allows his staff to go beyond their budget is inviting the ruination of his theatre, with the resulting loss of work for those very staff members who were so casual about controlling their budget.

Some managing directors are fortunate enough to have a business manager; others must maintain their own accounts. If the director has to anticipate an audit each year, he should hire a part-time bookkeeper or be sufficiently knowledgeable about accounting himself. Whether he has a business manager or not, the director should not commit all of his funds to an operating budget. Some should be kept aside for contingencies. Among the accounts that should be watched carefully are those set aside for properties and those devoted to publicity.

Properties and publicity are often the most proportionately expensive of any of the production expenditures. A dollar here and two dollars there can amount to an amazing sum spent on properties by the end of a production. Moreover, considerable waste is often involved in props, as it is, too, in publicity. It is often difficult to determine when the supply of posters and brochures is plentiful enough to provide adequate coverage and when the supply is actually glutting. The same is true of advertisements. The rule of "better too much than too little" does not always apply to all theatres. If the director becomes aware of extra posters and brochures constantly about the theatre, he might seriously consider cutting down on his order for the next season.

As the development of the production progresses, the managing director might wish to check expenditures from time to time. He may discover that he has overallocated in some areas and underallocated in others. If there is very good reason to make adjustments, he might wish to redefine one or two budget items. This redistribution should be done with caution.

ORGANIZING PUBLICITY

A theatre, even a well-supported subscription theatre, cannot exist long without a sound publicity policy. Frequently the managing director has a staff publicist, but many publicity decisions are still his responsibility. He or his publicist should arrange and post, as soon as possible, a publicity schedule for the actors and the theatre staff. Such a schedule should include deadlines for news releases; dates for radio and television interviews; deadlines for copy for posters, programs, brochures, and flyers; dates for publicity photographs; deadlines for establishing mailing and complimentary ticket lists; and a list of any special publicity devices or programs not normally utilized by the theatre. In arranging a publicity schedule, the scene designer, the lighting designer, the costumer, the actors, and sometimes the playwright all have to have their schedules coordinated with the special needs of the publicist.

Publicity is a touchy matter with all members of the production staff. Not only actors but costumers, scene designers, playwrights, and stagehands are apt to feel that they have not been given adequate credit. Thus the managing director should stay in close touch with his publicity assistant, and he should consult with his publicist on all major publicity decisions. Every news release should be read by the managing director. In each release, such essential information as playing times and dates should be carefully proofread. All names should be checked for correct spelling.

A well-organized publicity campaign begins slowly and gains in intensity as opening night approaches. Advantage should be taken of every chance for public notice. News media should be provided with a steady supply of newsworthy copy. The production of a play is news, and the various news media are happy to publish and broadcast information about the play. But news media distinguish between news and advertisement. The publicity release that is filled with overstatements intended to serve as mere "come-ons" and as thin disguises for advertisement about ticket prices is likely to be ignored. The best publicity release gives valid information about the play; human interest material about the cast, production staff, or playwright; and factual information about production dates. Most news media will use photographs if these are interestingly composed and skillfully executed. Many radio and television stations have interview programs and may devote a portion of such programs to interviews with actors, directors, and playwrights.

The news releases should be supported by paid advertising whenever possible. The major forms of paid advertising are the newspaper ad, the television commercial, the radio spot, the brochure, the mailed notice, the flyer, and the poster. The paid advertisement should be well designed, attention-getting, and informative. However, the real purpose of advertising is saturation. Therefore, the more money the theatre can afford to invest in an advertising program, the greater the chances of success. On the other hand, the theatre will not want to waste advertising funds. If the auditorium is small and the planned run of the production is limited to a short period, there is no reason to reach more people than can be logically handled.

Of the major forms of advertising, the newspaper ad, the television commercial, and the radio spot reach the most people but are often too expensive for a small theatre. Many theatres can afford only a small investment in newspaper, radio, and television advertisement and supplement this area of advertising with a large mailing. Since the post office has special rates for bulk mailing, many people can be reached at a minimal cost through the use of a postcard. The key to advertising by mail is the assembling and maintaining of an up-to-date mailing list. To this end, many theatres provide guest books in the lobby. The guest book will increase in effectiveness if an attractive hostess is also employed to urge those interested to sign the book. In order to test the effectiveness of their mailing, many theatres use such devices as special rates on tickets if the customer will present the postcard at the box office. The brochure is also a mailing device, although it is often distributed through direct contact. The brochure is more complete and dignified than the mailed postcard and is usually employed by theatres wishing to announce a series or season of productions.

The flyer is designed to be discarded by one reader in the hopes that it will be seen by a second and even third and fourth reader. While the flyer should be attractive, it need not be expensive. It is normally distributed in public places—restaurants, hotel lobbies, transportation terminals—delivered from door to door, or placed on automobile windshields in large parking lots. The flyer is the least dignified of the available means of publicity and should be used with caution by theatres seeking to establish themselves as cultural centers. The poster, and its big brother the billboard, are placed where they will be seen by the largest number of people. Public buildings, show windows, restaurants, and lobbies are excellent places for posters and billboards. If possible the theatre itself should be provided with a large posterboard or billboard.

The first and last place, the beginning and the end, of a publicity program is in the theatre itself. In the lobby and in the play program should appear announcements of coming productions. After all, people who have come once to a play are more likely to return again. Moreover, word of mouth is the best possible advertising.

Newspaper, television, and radio reviews are also good sources of advertising, although a very bad review can destroy all hopes of continued success with the present production. The publicist should bear in mind, however, that the review is really a news story. As such, no news medium is committed to give a review if such reviewing is not considered sufficiently newsworthy. Hence the publicist should not depend on a review as an integral part of his program.

Since paid advertising is expensive, careful planning is needed to insure that each form of advertising is as attention-getting, concise, and informative as possible. In whatever form, the average advertisement should be limited to attracting attention, arousing interest, and stating absolutely essential information. If nothing else, every advertisement should state very clearly the production dates and where and how to obtain tickets.

The managing director and his publicist should make every effort to check constantly the effectiveness of each form of advertising. Whenever possible audience members should be questioned about when and how they came to know of the theatre and its production. Since many people resent it, such questioning should be done with tact and restraint.

Managing directors of continuing repertory, community, and noncommercial theatres approach advertising on a long-term basis. They feel that any news story, paid advertisement, or review for a single production, no matter how immediately effective, is good long-term advertising. In line with this philosophy, they often replace the strikingly original poster, flyer, or brochure with one bearing a standard motif or overall design. By following this practice, they feel that a fixed image of the theatre is gradually built up throughout their community.

ORGANIZING THE BOX OFFICE

Very soon after a production has been decided on, the managing director must establish box office policies and procedures. In continuing theatres, such procedures are usually planned for an entire season. Whenever or however the box office is organized, every theatre shares similar problems. First, types and special varieties of tickets must be selected; and second, the methods of distributing the tickets to the customers should be established. In both cases, the aim is to avoid confusion and save time and energy.

Some theatres are so well subsidized that their box office problems are really quite simple. All tickets are free and distributed on a first-come, first-served basis. The only box office decision in such theatres is when and for how long the box office should remain open. In some theatres, even the seats are unreserved, and the only function of the box office is to limit the number of tickets distributed for each performance to the capacity of the house. However, even in heavily subsidized theatres, the managing director often elects to charge for psychological reasons. Audiences are more prone to value that which they have paid for than that which they have received for nothing. Whenever money is involved, the question of price scales is raised. In small theatres, all seats are priced identically. In larger theatres, tickets are often scaled in price, the higher priced seats being closer to the stage. Other pricing practices are also employed. Many theatres, in order to provide a basic audience, make use of season tickets or other special reductions. Sometimes such special reductions are announced only through one or two paid advertising media in order to test the effectiveness of particular forms of advertising.

On special rate tickets the theatre will usually place certain restrictions. Group rates and special reductions are usually limited to particular performances. Season tickets normally are sold only during specified periods and are also subject to various restrictions. Typical practice for season tickets is to sell the ticket for a specified day during each performance period, or to sell a coupon that entitles the holder to a special reduction for each production provided the coupon-holder reserves a seat before a specified date. After the "cutoff" date the theatre no longer guarantees the season coupon-holder of a seat. Another popular variation of the season ticket is to sell a fixed number of admissions that may be used either throughout the season or all on one production. As in other types of season tickets, the group-of-admission ticket is usually subject to certain cutoff dates and prior reservation restrictions.

Some theatres also find that their ticket price scale is influenced by age or membership considerations. For instance, certain subscription theatres offer one price to subscribers and a higher price to nonsubscribers. Some theatres have one price for adults, another for children. Noncommercial theatres usually charge one price to students and a higher price to nonstudents.

Whatever the pricing policy of a particular theatre, the rules and practices should be made very clear to each customer. Much hard feeling, and in the long run great loss of audience, can result from selling a ticket to a customer without making plain to him the uses and restrictions placed on such a ticket. To insure that misunderstandings do not occur, the managing director should take great pains in instructing his box office personnel. The more complicated the ticket policy, the more imperative it is that the box office personnel be intelligent, patient, courteous, and well informed.

The final complication in every box office is the matter of complimentary tickets. There are two types of complimentary tickets: the service comp and the publicity comp. The service comp is a method of partially or completely repaying services provided for the theatre. In this category fall complimentary tickets allowed to actors and the production staff or given in exchange for such services as the right to display posters or brochures in restaurants or lobbies. The publicity comp is given to those people who have in the past or who might in the future provide major financial or moral support for the theatre. Into this category fall the members of news media, distinguished supporters of the theatre, and those people whose public influence is helpful in securing and maintaining the desired public image.

The problem of complimentary tickets is extremely difficult. There is a tendency for the complimentary list to grow to huge proportions. Thus the managing director must place limits on the number and kind of free tickets without injuring the feelings of those who desire complimentary tickets and without overlooking those who rightfully deserve complimentary seats. He must also see to it that his box office personnel do not take the attitude that the holder of a complimentary ticket does not deserve the same attention as a paid customer. He must instruct his box office people that holders of complimentary tickets are to be treated with great respect and courtesy.

When the types and varieties of tickets have been decided on, the managing director faces his second box office problem—distributing the tickets to the individual customer. The first step in ticket distribution is to set up dates and times when the box office will be open. Just when and for how long the box office will be open depends upon the size of the box office budget. Normally, the director will find that most customers will not call for tickets earlier than a week before opening night. Thus the box office can usually plan a light schedule and a skeleton crew up until a week before production. Thereafter the box office schedule depends on the success of the production and the length of the run. In theatres where the run is limited, the audience is consistent and loyal, and the publicity is well planned, the average production should sell out by the afternoon following opening night. Much, however, depends on the size of the theatre and the potential audience. Some very successful theatres never sell out.

In order to avoid traffic congestion in the lobby, it is desirable to place as many tickets as possible directly in the hands of the customer. The safeguarding of the ticket then becomes the responsibility of the ticket-holder. Most theatres will take some form of telephone reservation. If the theatre operates on a telephone reservation policy, the director should allow for a certain number of "no-shows." Most theatres set up a policy of not holding telephone reservations past a certain time, usually ten minutes before curtain time. If such a policy is established, the box office personnel must be instructed to tell each person reserving a seat that such reservation will not be honored after a certain hour.

Even in theatres not using the telephone reservation, most managing directors use some modification of that system for complimentary tickets. Either the theatre will print complimentary coupons explicitly stating that the holder must call for reserved seats, or it will send complimentary letters indicating that if the recipient wishes to reserve a ticket he should telephone the theatre. In special cases, such as with certain members of the news media or with special dignitaries, the managing director may simply send complimentary tickets. By insisting that the holder of complimentary tickets make reservations and by actually retaining the reserved seat ticket, the managing director protects himself against those who take free tickets and then never attend the theatre.

In every theatre, the method of dispensing tickets should be as simple and as standardized as possible. Tickets should be colored differently for each performance. Ticket numbers should be carefully checked for errors, misprints, and duplicates. If at all possible, a ticket rack should be provided so that box office personnel can tell at a glance what tickets are available, in what locations, in what groupings, and for what performances. Reserved tickets should be pulled at the moment of reservation and filed alphabetically under the appropriate performance date. Many theatres follow the practice of having the box office clerk taking the reservation initial the envelope in which the reserved tickets are placed. This way mistakes can be traced.

Even in the most efficient box office, mistakes frequently happen. Thus it is a sound practice for the managing director to hold several tickets in reserve. These "house seats" may be used to seat the customer whose tickets have become lost or misfiled. House seats may also prove useful in seating certain very important people who surprise the theatre by appearing unannounced. At curtain time, unused house seats may be sold to those who have come without tickets or reservations. Even if a few house seats go empty, this is a small loss compared to the ill will that can result from an irredeemable box office error.

BEFORE, DURING, AND AFTER THE PERFORMANCE

Theatres must be prepared for an audience, and such preparation is the responsibility of the managing director, who may or may not be aided by a house manager. First, the auditorium must be cleaned and dusted. The lobby must be made neat. If shows or displays are to be presented in the lobby, the director must make arrangements for such items to be mounted and maintained. Entrances and exits are to be opened, marked, and cleared. Drinking fountains and rest rooms are to be cleaned and put in operational order. If refreshments are to be served, then space and arrangements must be planned in advance. The lobby ought to be opened at least an hour before performance. The house itself should be opened to the audience no later than one half-hour before performance. Word must be sent backstage when the house has been opened, in order to avoid having a half-costumed actor wander into full view of the audience.

The box office should be open at least one half-hour before performance. In theatres operating entirely or almost entirely on the telephone reservations system, the box office manager and his clerks should arrive in enough time to check and carefully alphabetize all reservations. Such a check includes counting tickets inside each envelope instead of depending on the number listed on the outside. In addition, tickets should be read for date and requested price range. Many patrons become annoyed when they are given tickets out of the price range requested or when those who were told that they have complimentary tickets are asked to pay at the box office. Finally, the box office manager should check his house seats and be sure he has enough in reserve to allow for mistakes in reservations or for the last-minute appearance of dignitaries.

Another matter of importance before the box office opens is the counting of money on hand and the setting-up of change. To facilitate movement of the box office line, many theatres post a chart indicating the total cost of the more frequent combinations of tickets and the change for these combinations up to the nearest dollar. Finally, the box office manager will want to check with the house manager or the director about the methods to be used to set up a waiting list for patrons without reservations, the time for selling unpicked-up reservations, the method of handling latecomers, and the time for closing the box office.

When the box office opens, the director or his house manager must now move the audience from the lobby to their seats. To accomplish this task with a maximum of ease and a maximum of courtesy, the house manager will need the aid of one or more ushers. A signaling system such as a chime or the dimming of the lobby lights is also helpful to move the last group of audience members into the theatre before the performance begins. Ushers normally have three duties: (1) to guard the door so that nonticket-holders do not enter and so that patrons do not bring unwanted items such as soft drinks and lighted cigarettes into the theatre, (2) to give out programs, and (3) to show ticket-holders to their appropriate seats. The director or the house manager should oversee these tasks so that all is done without confusion and with cheerful good manners.

At a prearranged time, reservations not picked up can be sold to patrons who have been waiting. If the waiting list is long and the time is short, a secondary box office may have to be set up to facilitate quick sales. Normally, in selling off tickets, the reserve or house seats are sold first, then the unpicked-up complimentary tickets, and finally unpicked-up cash reservations. If possible, a special row of seats that can be approached without disturbing the audience should be saved for latecomers. At any rate, each theatre ought to have a standard procedure for seating latecomers after the performance has begun.

When the audience has been seated, the director must signal all the appropriate people to begin the show. The system for such signals should have been worked out in dress and technical rehearsals. But a final check by the director will not be out of order. He must alert the stage manager, the assistant director, the cast, the house crew, the box office personnel, the light and sound crews, and the stage crew. During performance, some member of the theatre staff should be present in the lobby at all times to help in case of emergencies. Whenever any sizable group of people are gathered together in one place, some event out of the ordinary is not unlikely. The managing director or his representative should be on hand to aid in any way possible.

Intermissions should be organized as carefully as any other aspect of the production. Lobby lights must be turned on at the appropriate moment. The intermission should be timed, and the audience should be warned when the intermission is drawing to a close. Normally several signals are necessary to get the audience back into the theatre. Consequently, the intermission should be planned with enough time to empty and refill the theatre. When the audience is reseated, a signal should be sent backstage.

When the performance is completed, plans must be made for opening the house on the following night. In some theatres, the house is cleaned after each performance; in others the cleaning is postponed to just before the next performance. Box office receipts should be tallied and cash entries made. Finally, the theatre must be closed and secured for the night.

SALVAGING THE PRODUCTION

When the run of a production is completed or interrupted for a time, the managing director must organize striking and salvaging operations. If the production is to be resumed in the future, the managing director will want to arrange for and supervise storage of all property, settle interim accounts, and pay debts that have accumulated. If the production is to be terminated, the managing director must prepare and supervise final strike and salvage.

In some commercial theatres, striking means mainly returning what has been borrowed, selling off what costumes and properties are salable, and discarding all the rest. In more permanent theatrical organizations, strike is an elaborate and difficult operation. The director must decide what materials are worth saving and what should be discarded. In reaching this decision, the managing director is guided by the space available for storage and by the cost of cleaning and dismantling. Sometimes it is cheaper to build a new costume than clean and store an old one; sometimes it is cheaper to discard a setpiece than to pay the cost of dismantling and storage.

Strike is also the time for the director to take inventory of his permanent capital equipment. Some items might be shopworn and need refurbishing; some might he so depreciated as to be worthless. Repairs and replacements must be planned for. Stocks in makeup and light filters might need to be built up. Before strike is completed, the wise managing director sees to it that the theatre, both house and stage, is cleaned. Cleaning that is postponed until after strike is often cleaning that is not done until the next production is begun.

The final step in salvaging is to balance accounts and pay bills. In any theatre where tickets are sold, money received must be balanced against number of tickets sold. A formal accounting must be entered in the appropriate business records. Before drawing his final balance, the managing director will want to check carefully to see that all bills are paid. Even if the director is positive of his bills, he should allow a certain sum for contingencies. All too frequently, a stray bill for a can of hair spray does not arrive until several weeks after strike.

BUSINESS AND HOUSE MANAGEMENT: A SUMMARY

Even though every director does not have the burdens of business and house management, he should be aware of the general problems since so much of his art is directly tied to the public and financial affairs of his theatre. The process of business and house management begins with securing the rights to a play script. Once the script is secured, a production budget must be drawn up. Almost immediately a publicity program is organized and set into motion, while the managing director turns his attention to establishing a procedure for pricing and distributing tickets. On the days of performance, the managing director is usually responsible for preparing the house for an audience and organizing the orderly filling and emptying of the playhouse. When the production has completed its run, the managing director may want to supervise striking and salvaging operations. As his final responsibility, the managing director tallies receipts, discharges debts, and balances the accounts of the theatre.

epilogue

The purposes of this book were to discuss the body of aesthetic principles upon which the play director operates and to survey the issues and problems attendant upon the specific application of those principles. Theatre was studied as a trifold art—auditory, visual, and kinetic. The director was viewed as the essential coordinating agent in theatrical art and was seen as the assembler and coordinator of a group of contributing artists. Through securing the cooperation of each of the contributing artists and in his role of final aesthetic arbitrator, the director is ultimately responsible for both the shortcomings and successes of the theatrical product. From the moment he selects a play script to the final performance, the director's task is to create a theatrical metaphor by uniting and synthesizing the auditory and visual theatres through the kinetic theatre. In creating his metaphor he is guided by a number of auditory, visual, and kinetic principles. There are, however, no rules for applying these principles. Hence the use of each principle must be judged in terms of each specific situation in each specific production.

Although it is hoped that some aid has been provided for the talented and for the unskillful, there is nothing in this book that will make directing easier for the uncommitted or less chaotic for the undisciplined. In the final analysis, no book, lecture, or demonstration can replace hard work and individual practice. Directors become directors by disciplining themselves and by actual directing. The best advice that can be given to a beginning director is to seek out every possible opportunity to direct, and when directing, to remain humble in the face of his great responsibilities.

appendix a:
a director's workshop
Projects and Exercises

PROJECT ONE: THE DIRECTOR PREPARES

Exercise One

Assume that you are limited to *Hamlet, Death of a Salesman, Waltz of the Toreadors,* or *The Imaginary Invalid.* Out of this group, select the script you most want to direct at this time. Do not assume an ideal theatre, but base your choice upon a real situation: either a theatre with which you have been connected in the past or the theatre with which you are now connected. Make a list of the reasons why you selected the script that you did and a list of the disadvantages of your selected script, indicating which ones might well become advantages if handled creatively.

Exercise Two

Make an analysis of each agent in your selected script. Report your findings by placing under each agent's name a pair of columns: one entitled "manners" and one entitled "motives." Number each motive and letter each manner as in the example below. Remember to include such nonhuman agents as the Ghost in *Hamlet.*

LAERTES

Manners	*Motives*
a. dutiful son	1. wishes to avenge his father
b. loving brother	
c. impetuous young man	

Indicate in a short paragraph the manners–motives relationships. For instance, in the example above, we might say:

Motive 1 grows out of Manners a and c; motive 1 triggers manners c.

Exercise Three

When you have completed your analysis of each agent, make a chart of agent interaction based on your outlines of manners and motives. In analyzing, you might be helped by setting up a conflict–agreement, strong–weak, dominant–subordinate chart as in the following example. In this chart concern should be with the general situation, not with scene-by-scene variations.

Hamlet	*Ophelia*	*Hamlet*	*Laertes*
Strong	Weak	Strong	Strong
Dominant	Subordinate	Dominant	Equal
Agreements:	Agreements:	Agreements:	Agreements:
Manners a, f, g. r; Motives 1, 2, 7	Manners a, b, s, t; Motives 1, 5, 9	Manners a, b; Motives 1, 2	Manners a, b; Motive 3
Conflicts:	Conflicts:	Conflicts:	Conflicts:
Manners b, h; Motives 3, 5	Manners h, i, j; Motives 3, 7	Manners c, d; Motive 3	Manners c, f; Motive 1

Exercise Four

Examine the first scene of your play for all expository items. As a result of your examination, construct and complete a chart as in the example below. Note how all elements of theatre interact for expository purposes.

SCENE 1 IN *Hamlet*

Dramaturgical	*Visual*	*Kinetic*
Language: Whispers, use of pass words. Agent: Soldiers, Ghost.	Soldiers' costumes, nighttime lighting, etc.	Soldiers' frightened movements at opening of play, etc.

Story: Night, on the
ramparts, change of
guard.

Action: Immediate
crisis on entrance of
Bernardo tells us
something is very
wrong.

Point of View: For
most part, objec-
tive; but introduc-
ing subjective when
Hamlet alone hears
final cries of Ghost.

Exercise Five

Assume that it is absolutely necessary for you to cut some material
from the first scene of your selected script. What and where would you
cut? Demonstrate in a short paragraph how your cuts make sense not
only grammatically but also in terms of each element of dramaturgy.
Remember that your cuts must remain consistent with overall linguistic
style. Therefore, if your play is in verse, you must retain the verse form
as much as possible.

Exercise Six

Outline the story as found in the first act of your selected play, using
the following scheme.

HAMLET

Scene 1:
> *Time:* Near midnight, a winter night in the Middle Ages.
> *Place:* The ramparts of the Royal Castle, Denmark.
> *Incident:* A ghost appears, first to Horatio and the guards, later to
> Prince Hamlet. The Ghost claims to be Hamlet's father, murdered
> by his brother Claudius. Hamlet has doubts but plans to investigate.

Scene 2:
> *Etc.*

Exercise Seven

With the information gained in the first five exercises, return to the first major scene of your selected script and locate the action cycles. You might be helped in this analysis by reading first only to identify moments of conflict without regard to the exact point of crisis. Remember also that it is unlikely that any two directors will agree completely on the exact number and quality of a play's action cycles. When you have isolated to your satisfaction the action cycles, construct a chart identifying each cycle and indicating on one side the elements that produced conflict and those that released or resolved conflict. See the example below.

HAMLET

How Created	*Actions*	*How Resolved*
Night, sense of fear in solitary guard, sudden appearance of an unknown agent.	First cycle— through recognition of Bernardo.	Recognition of friendly person through password, greeting: "you come most carefully upon your hour. . . ."

PROJECT TWO: ASSEMBLING THE ARTISTS

Exercise One

Assume that you are planning a production of *Oedipus Rex*. Analyze the script as in Project One. Then consider the actual playing spaces available to you. Make a list of the advantages and disadvantages of each space, then make a choice of playing space and write a paragraph defending your choice.

Exercise Two

Consider both the physical and human resources of your theatre. In light of these resources, design a form to be used at tryouts for your upcoming production of *Oedipus*. When you design your form, take into account such matters as age, experience, freedom to schedule rehearsals, minimum qualifications imposed by your theatre or parent organization, and special talents or interests. Design your form so that all necessary information is available at a glance. Save a space for your comments. Be prepared to discuss why you designed your form as you did and why you included some questions and excluded others.

Exercise Three

Analyze your script of *Oedipus* in order to isolate each action cycle up to the entrance of Tiresias. Using the chart below, characterize each action cycle by a particular line, form, mass, color, etc.

Visual

Line: Curve, tending toward
   horizontal.
Form: Organic.
Mass: High volume, loose.
Color: Blue, gray, brown,
   low saturation, cool.
Texture: Rough, simple, soft.
Space: Negative, slowly filled
   to positive.

Script Action

First Action: Entrance of chorus up to first appearance of Oedipus.

Be prepared to discuss the script with your designers in terms of your analysis. It might help to search out photographs or paintings that illustrate what you have in mind. These illustrations need not be Greek nor have anything to do with the subject matter of the scene.

Exercise Four

Repeat the work of Exercise Three in terms of kinetic characterization. Be prepared to discuss your characterization with your designers and your choreographer, if you have one. Be prepared to demonstrate your motion concepts, using the pattern below.

Kinetic

Body-in-space: See visual
   chart.
Direction: Multiple, not
   specific.
Rate: Slow, with great
   difficulty.
Energy: Little expenditure,
   low potential.
Control: External, crowd
   driven as herd, bumping
   into each other.
Motion: Very weak positive
   motion becoming negative.

Script Action

First Action: Entrance of chorus up to first appearance of Oedipus.

Exercise Five

Complete the chart below showing special problems you anticipate in your production of *Oedipus*. Explain why you consider these problems "special."

SET   COSTUMES   PROPERTIES   LIGHTS   MUSIC & SOUND

Exercise Six

Assume that you will have to design and costume as well as direct. Make a floor plan and rendering of a set for *Oedipus*. Design a set of costumes and attach swatches of material to represent each part of the costume. Finally, draft a light plot for the set you designed. Be prepared to defend your various designs in terms of Exercises Three, Four, and Five above.

PROJECT THREE: THE DIRECTOR EXPLORES

Exercise One

Using a single actor, vary his visual line to make him:

a. Strong and unhappy
b. Weak and unhappy
c. Strong and happy
d. Weak and happy

Exercise Two

Using a single actor, vary his form or body position to make him:

a. Weak but dominant
b. Strong but subordinate
c. Strong but confused
d. Weak but determined

Exercise Three

Using two actors, vary their line, body position, stage space, and focus so that:

a. They are equally strong.
b. They are equally weak.

c. The dominant actor is weak.

d. The subordinate actor is strong.

e. Both actors are dominant but one is stronger than the other.

Exercise Four

Add a third actor and repeat the same exercise as above but confine yourself to the arena stage.

Exercise Five

Compose and design the opening of Scene 2 in *Hamlet* so that the King is given primary emphasis and Hamlet is given secondary emphasis. For purposes of this exercise, use a flat stage floor with only stools and chairs for properties. Do this composition for both the arena and proscenium stages.

Exercise Six

Repeat the same exercise as above for motion picture and television. Indicate the angle and type of shot, the kind of transition between shots, and the length of time devoted to each shot. If your plan is to include special wipes or "supers," indicate these, too. Be prepared to defend your selection of each shot, angle, time, and special effect.

Exercise Seven

Select any two-person scene from *The Imaginary Invalid* and compose the scene so that all variety is obtained by varying the length and quality of visual line, while keeping all other factors equal. Repeat the same exercise using as a sole variety factor:

a. Form

b. Mass

c. Color

d. Texture

e. Space

Exercise Eight

Using the same scene as above, compose and design so that:

a. All variety is obtained by changes of kinetic direction.

b. The stronger person is always seated.

Repeat the same exercise using as a sole variety factor:

a. Changes in kinetic rate
b. Changes in energy
c. Changes in external control

Exercise Nine

Examine the first scene in *Hamlet* at the point where the Ghost makes his initial appearance. Using actors "on book," obtain variations in auditory design by using:

a. Increased vocal volume as a statement of excitement
b. Lowered vocal volume as a statement of excitement
c. High vocal pitch as a statement of excitement
d. Increased rate as a statement of excitement
e. Decreased rate as a statement of excitement
f. Overlapped lines as a statement of excitement
g. Simultaneous lines as a statement of excitement

Which of the above shows more terror? Which more confusion? Which more awe? Which shows more courage in the face of a fearsome thing? Which gives the actors more strength? Which weakens them the most?

Exercise Ten

Select a choral ode from *Oedipus*. Using four or five actors and actresses on book, read the ode in unison. Try such variations as chanting the ode or reading the ode to a simple rhythm beat upon a single drum. After the chorus has become accustomed to working together, try the following vocal variations:

a. Single voice reads the ode for meaning while others chant ode softly in background.
b. Single voice reads ode while others echo each line.
c. Chorus is divided into male and female voices; female voices read loudly, while male voices say same line softly.
d. Lines are divided between a lead reader and two pairs of duo readers.
e. Lines are distributed so that some are read separately, while others are read as duets, trios, or in full chorus unison.

Exercise Eleven

Plan to film *Oedipus* outdoors. Scout for appropriate locations, and take a still photograph of each location. Number the photographs and assign each scene in the script a photograph number. Be prepared to defend your choice of locations.

Exercise Twelve

Prepare the café scene in *From Morn to Midnight* for movie or television production. On the margins of your script indicate the shot, angle, and focus your cameraman should work for. In a second column indicate how your editor might move from shot to shot, using the form indicated below.

Script	Shot	Sequence
	Long, overhead, establishing shot	Cut to
	Closeup of Cashier Waitress	Zoom out to

Is it possible that some of the lines in the script can be replaced by such camera techniques as the closeup? Which are these lines?

Exercise Thirteen

Make a videotape of the second scene between Oedipus and Creon as if Oedipus and the camera were one. Reverse the scene by taping it entirely through Creon's eyes. How does the statement of the scene change in each taping?

PROJECT FOUR: THE DIRECTOR COMBINES THE MODES

Exercise One

Stage Scene 2 in *Hamlet* so that Claudius is kinetically stronger but visually weaker than Hamlet. Reverse the image. Is there a change in meaning as the image is reversed?

Exercise Two

Do the scene between Oedipus and Tiresias so that the chorus is used to give Tiresias visual emphasis and dominance. Next, adjust your image so that Tiresias retains visual emphasis but is subordinated by the chorus kinetically. What is said about Tiresias in each design?

Exercise Three

Limiting yourself primarily to vocal and kinetic elements, stage the closet scene between Hamlet and Gertrude so that Hamlet begins as strong but subordinate and ends as weak but dominant. Adjust the scene so that Gertrude begins visually strong and ends visually weak. What is said about the relationships between mother and son in each case?

Exercise Four

Consider how you might do the scene between General St. Pé and his wife in *Waltz of the Toreadors* in three different visual styles. Keep in mind that style has both a traditional aspect (Realism, Expressionism, etc.) and an individual aspect (the unique combination of elements made by specific artists). How would the meaning of the scene change, if at all, from style to style? Do you feel that one or more of the styles violates the intent of the author? Why?

Exercise Five

Do Scene 1 in *Hamlet* from three different points of view. First stage the scene from the soldiers' point of view, then from Hamlet's, and finally from the viewpoint of the Ghost. If you were making a film or a television tape of this exercise, how would it differ from your staged designs?

Exercise Six

Stage Scene 2 of *The Imaginary Invalid* so that all unity is gained through curved visual line, while all variety is obtained from change in kinetic direction. Repeat the same exercise so that:

a. All unity is gained through curved line and body position, while all variety is obtained vocally.
b. All unity is gained through curved line and changes in kinetic direction, while all variety is obtained through color.
c. All unity is gained through curved line and changes in vocal pitch, all emphasis is obtained kinetically, and all variety is found in body position.

Exercise Seven

Consider filming Scene 2 of *The Imaginary Invalid* so that all unity would be obtained through:

a. Consistency of camera angle
b. Consistency of sequence between shots
c. Inconsistency of sequence between shots

If you have a television video recorder, make use of it in this exercise.

Exercise Eight

Do the second scene of *The Imaginary Invalid* so that it has two sequential rhythms. Recompose the same scene so that it contains:

a. One sequential rhythm
b. Three sequential rhythms each composed of three constituent rhythms

Exercise Nine

Analyze Act 1 of *Death of a Salesman* for all entrances and exits. Make separate lists of entrances of necessity and convenience. Confining yourself only to cue lines immediately preceding and to adjustment lines immediately following each entrance or exit, stage every entrance and exit. For purposes of this exercise, confine yourself to a single floor plan.

Exercise Ten

Using the short script provided below, stage a scene so that:

a. It is a love scene in which A begins as a strong character and ends as a weak one.
b. It is a scene from a Western in which the dominant character ends as subordinate.
c. It is a comic scene in which the weak character ends as dominant.
d. It is a domestic drama in which both characters end as weak and confused.

A STORY

A. Oh.
B. Yes?
A. It—

B. Well—
A. But . . .
B. I see. Then—
A. If you—
B. There is—
A. Perhaps.
B. Perhaps . . .
A. I have never . . .
B. Perhaps.

PROJECT FIVE: THE DIRECTOR AS SELF-CRITIC

Select a one-act play or a scene of over ten minutes from a longer play. Be sure the play or scene selected can stand as an independent work. Design sets and costumes for the play, or enlist the aid of designers. Cast the play, construct a complete prompt book, and rehearse the play. Give at least one public performance of the play. The public performance is the crucial test. After the performance, list all those points in which you achieved your goal. Why were you successful? Give all credit due to others. List all those points at which you failed to achieve your goals. Be extremely honest. Can you explain your failures? Do not place the burden on others. Finally, list all points that surprised you, such as an unexpected audience reaction, a new line reading, a change in rhythm, and a change in characterization. Can you explain why these surprises took place? From your three lists, is it possible for you to draw one or more principles that will aid you in your future directing ventures?

appendix b:
a director's resources

A director will want to stay in touch with the work of his colleagues in his own field and in the theatre arts in general. He will also want some ongoing contact with the allied arts—music, especially opera, dance, fine arts, and literature. Listed below are a sampling of important periodicals in the arts.

Alpha Psi Omega Playbill (organ of Alpha Psi Omega honorary drama fraternity)
Art News
Dance Magazine
Dance Perspectives
Dramatics (International Thespian Society)
Educational Theatre Journal (American Theatre Association)
Encore (special emphasis on Black Drama; National Association of Dramatic and Speech Arts)
Musical Educators Journal (Music Educators National Conference)
Musical Quarterly
New York Drama Critics Reviews
New York Times Film Reviews
New York Times Magazine
Opera News (Metropolitan Opera Guild)
Players (National Collegiate Players, ANTA)
Plays and Players (England)

Publication of the Modern Language Association (Modern Language Association)

Quarterly Journal of Speech (Speech Communication Association)

Saturday Review

Southern Speech Communication Journal (Southern Speech Communication Association)

Southern Theatre (Southeastern Theatre Conference)

The American Cinematographer (American Society of Cinematographers)

The Drama Review (formerly *Tulane Drama Review*)

The Speech Teacher (Speech Communication Association)

Theatre Arts Monthly (no longer published)

Theatre Crafts

Theatre Design and Technology (organ of U.S. Institute of Theatre Technology)

Theatre Survey (American Society for Theatre Research)

Theatre Workshop (no longer published)

Today's Filmmaker

Topics (Southwest Theatre Conference)

Variety

World Theatre

In addition to the above periodicals, a number of other publications of a journal, catalogue, bulletin, booklet, manual, or monograph nature might prove extremely useful to a stage or media director. Probably the single most important resource catalogue is:

Simon's Directory of Theatrical Materials, Services & Information
now in its fourth edition; published by
Package Publicity Service
1564 Broadway, New York, New York 10036

Without a doubt the most informative and complete supply catalogue is to be obtained from:

Paramount Theatrical Supplies
Alcone Company Inc.
32A West 20th Street, New York, New York 10011
Paramount also publishes an informative newsletter.

Also publishing extensive catalogues with useful listings are:

Olesen Company
1535 Ivar Avenue
Los Angeles, California 90028
Oleson has excellent filmstrips on modern and historical theatre.

Theatre Production Service
59 Fourth Avenue
New York, New York 10003

Certain specialists also publish useful catalogues or free bulletins. Among these are:

Alan Godon Enterprises   (*film supplies and equipment*)
1430 North Cahuenga
Los Angeles, California 90028

American Stage Lighting Company's Catalogue
1331 North Avenue
New Rochelle, New York 10802

Dramatic Publishing Company Catalogue of Plays
86 East Randolph Street
Chicago, Illinois 60601

Dramatists Play Service Catalogue of Plays
440 Park Avenue South
New York, New York 10016

Eaves Costume Company   (*free illustrated costume charts*)
151 West 46th Street
New York, New York 10036

Samuel French, Inc.   (*catalogue of plays*)
25 West 45th Street
New York, New York 10036

Hub Electric Company   (*free bulletins and bulletins at small cost
940 Industrial Drive   based on the work of James Hull Miller
Elmhurst, Illinois 60126   with open stages*)

International Thespian Society   (*excellent series of monographs at
College Hill Station, Box E $1.00*)
Cincinnati, Ohio 45224

Rosco   (*book of color swatches of Roscolene and
Harrison, New York 10528   Roscogel*)

SOS Photo Cine Optics   (*photography and cinema supplies and
7051 Santa Monica Blvd.   equipment*)
Los Angeles, California 90038

Tams-Witmark Music Library
757 Third Avenue
New York, New York 10017

The director's basic resource is still the book devoted in whole or in part to one or more aspects of his art. The following is a selective bibliography intended to suggest rather than represent the kinds and contents of books available.

BIBLIOGRAPHY

Texts on Directing

Several contemporary textbooks have been devoted to the problems of the theatrical director. Among the more important of these are:

Canfield, Curtis. *The Craft of Play Directing.* New York: Holt, Rinehart & Winston, 1963. Stresses preparation, analysis, and craft.

Dean, Alexander. *Fundamentals of Play Directing.* New York: Holt, Rinehart & Winston, 1941. This work is, and probably will remain, the classic discussion of the director in the proscenium theatre. A revised edition that includes a brief chapter on arena staging was done in 1965 by Lawrence Carra.

Dietrich, John. *Play Direction.* Englewood Cliffs, N.J.: Prentice-Hall, 1953. A standard work best known for its analysis of action through rhetorical means (the motivated sequence).

Gallaway, Marian. *The Director in the Theatre.* New York: Macmillan, 1963. Pays considerable attention to script analysis; has a good glossary of terms, an appendix that serves as a model for a detailed production schedule, and a limited list of suppliers for theatrical scripts and materials.

Sievers, David W. *Directing for the Theatre.* Dubuque, Iowa: Brown, 1965. Especially aimed at educational theatre production; excellent suggestions for directors working in the secondary schools.

Texts on Film and
Television Production

Bobker, Lee R. *Elements of Film.* New York: Harcourt Brace Jovanovich, 1969. A work covering both theory and fundamental techniques.

Kingson, Walter K., and Rome Cowgill. *Television Acting and Directing.* New York: Holt, Rinehart & Winston, 1965. A very basic work which should prove very useful for those who have no experience with television equipment.

Mercer, John. *An Introduction to Cinematography.* Champaign, Ill.: Stipes, 1967. An excellent book for beginning filmmakers.

Millerson, Gerald. *The Technique of Television Production.* New York: Hastings House, 1961. A very sound text on all phases of television.

Roberts, Kenneth H., and Win Sharples, Jr. *A Primer for Filmmaking.* New York: Bobbs-Merrill, 1971. Specializes in 16mm and 35mm film techniques.

Smallman, Kirk. *Creative Film-making.* London: Collier-Macmillan, 1969. Concise outline of the steps in the production of 16mm film.

Books on Directing
and Acting by Directors

Antoine, Andre. *Memoires of the Théâtre-Libre,* translated by Marvin Carlson, edited by H. D. Albright. Coral Gables, Fla.: University of Miami Press, 1964.

Appia, Adolphe. *The Work of Living Art & Man Is the Measure of All Things,* translated by H. D. Albright. Coral Gables, Fla.: University of Miami Press, 1960.

Artaud, Antonin. *The Theatre and Its Double,* translated by Mary Caroline Richard. New York: Grove, 1958.

Barrault, Jean-Louis. *Reflections on the Theatre,* translated by Barbara Wall. London: Rockcliff, 1951.

Belasco, David. *The Theatre Through the Stage Door.* Harper & Row, 1919.

Bentley, Eric, ed. *The Theory of the Modern Stage.* Baltimore: Penguin, 1968.

Burnim, Kalman A. *David Garrick, Director.* Pittsburgh: University of Pittsburgh Press, 1961.

Clurman, Harold. *The Fervent Years.* New York: Knopf, 1950.

Cole, Toby, and Helen Krich Chinoy. *Actors on Acting.* New York: Crown Publishers, 1970.

————. *Directors on Directing.* New York: Bobbs-Merrill, 1963.

Graig, Gordon. *On the Art of the Theatre.* New York: Theatre Arts Books, 1961.

Di Somi, Leone. "Dialogues on Stage Affairs," in Allardyce Nicoll, *The Development of the Theatre.* New York: Harcourt Brace Jovanovich, 1966.

Eisenstein, Sergei. *Film Form and Film Sense.* New York: Harcourt Brace Jovanovich, 1942.

Esslin, Martin. *Brecht: The Man and his Work.* New York: Doubleday, 1960.

Gassner, John. *Producing the Play.* New York: Holt, Rinehart & Winston, 1948.

Gelmis, Joseph. *The Film Director as Superstar.* New York: Doubleday, 1970.

Gielgud, John. *Stage Directions.* New York: Random House, 1963.

Gorchakov, Nikolai. *Stanislavski Directs,* translated by Mirian Goldina. New York: Funk & Wagnalls, 1954.

Gorelik, Mordecai. *New Theatres for Old*. New York: French, 1941.

Gratowski, Jerzy. *Towards a Poor Theatre*. New York: Simon & Schuster, 1969.

Guthrie, Tyrone. *A Life in the Theatre*. New York: McGraw-Hill, 1959.

Hopkins, Arthur. *How's Your Second Act?* New York: French, 1948.

Houghton, Norris. *Moscow Rehearsals*. New York: Grove, 1962.

Jones, Margo. *Theatre-in-the-Round*. New York: Holt, Rinehart & Winston, 1951.

Knapp, Battina Liebowitz. *Louis Jouvet, Man of the Theatre*. New York: Columbia University Press, 1958.

Kommisarjevsky, Theodore. *Myself and the Theatre*. New York: Dutton, 1930.

Laban, Rudolf. *Mastery of Movement on the Stage*. London: MacDonald & Evans, 1950.

Macgowan, Kenneth, and Robert Edmund Jones. *Continental Stagecraft*. New York: Harcourt Brace Jovanovich, 1922.

Meyerhold, Vsevolod. *Meyerhold on the Theatre*, translated and edited by Meyer Braun. New York: Hill & Wang, 1970.

Owen, Alice C. *The Art of Play Directing: A Tentative Bibliography*. Boston: Simmons College, 1943.

Oxenford, John. *Goethe on the Theatre*. New York: Dramatic Museum of Columbia University, 1919.

Shawn, Ted. *Every Little Movement*. Brooklyn, N.Y.: Dance Horizons, 1963.

Simonson, Lee. *The Stage Is Set*. New York: Harcourt Brace Jovanovich, 1932.

Stanislavski, Konstantin S. *An Actor Prepares*, translated by Elizabeth Reynolds Hapgood. New York: Theatre Arts Books, 1936.

———. *Building a Character*, translated by Elizabeth Reynolds Hapgood. New York: Theatre Arts Books, 1949.

———. *My Life in Art*, translated by J. J. Robbins. New York: Theatre Arts Books, 1948.

Tairov, Alexander. *Notes of a Director*, translated by William Kuhlke. Coral Gables, Fla.: University of Miami Press, 1969.

Directors will want to be familiar with the literature in all fields of theatre arts as well as basic resource books in the allied fields of music, art, and dance. It is difficult to select typical works from each field. Thus the following are not offered as the best, the most outstanding, or the most typical. They are merely provided as a suggestion of the kinds of material available.

Theatre, General Works, Histories, Play Collections

Block, Haskell M., and Robert G. Shedd, eds. *Masters of Modern Drama.* New York: Random House, 1962.

Brockett, Oscar G. *History of the Theatre.* Boston: Allyn & Bacon, 1968.

Gassner, John. *A Treasury of the Theatre,* Third College Edition. New York: Simon & Schuster, 1953.

Kernodle, George R. *Invitation to the Theatre.* New York: Harcourt Brace Jovanovich, 1967.

Nicoll, Allardyce. *The Development of the Theatre.* New York: Harcourt Brace Jovanovich, 1966.

Whiting, Frank M. *An Introduction to the Theatre,* Third Edition. New York: Harper & Row, 1969.

Costume and Makeup

Barton, Lucy. *Historic Costume for the Stage.* Boston: Bakers Plays, 1961.

Boublik, Vlastimil. *The Art of Makeup for Stage, Television and Film.* Oxford: Pergamon Press, 1968.

Corson, Richard. *Stage Makeup.* New York: Appleton, 1967.

Music, Voice, and Dance

Blunt, Jerry. *Stage Dialects.* San Francisco: Chandler, 1967.

H'Doubler, Margaret N. *Dance: A Creative Experience.* New York: Appleton, 1940.

Lee, Charlotte. *Oral Interpretation,* Fourth Edition. Boston: Houghton Mifflin, 1971.

Moore, Douglas. *A Guide to Musical Styles.* New York: Norton, 1942.

————. *Listening to Music.* New York: Norton, 1937.

Sachs, Curt. *World History of the Dance.* New York: Norton, 1963.

Shanet, Howard. *Learn to Read Music.* New York: Simon & Schuster, 1956.

Sorell, Walter. *The Dance Through the Ages.* New York: Grosset & Dunlap, 1967.

Thompson, Betty Lynd. *Fundamentals of Rhythm and Dance.* New York: A. S. Barnes, 1933.

Wise, Claude M., and Giles Gray. *Bases of Speech.* New York: Harper & Row, 1946.

Playwriting, Theory of Drama, and Fiction

Clark, Barrett H. *European Theories of the Drama.* New York: Crown, 1947.

Cole, Toby. *Playwrights on Playwriting*. New York: Hill & Wang, 1961.

Lubbock, Percy. *The Craft of Fiction*. New York: Viking, 1957.

Richards, I. A. *Practical Criticism*. New York: Harcourt Brace Jovanovich, 1929.

Rosenthal, Raymond. *McLuhan: Pro and Con*. New York: Funk & Wagnalls, 1968.

Smiley, Sam. *Playwriting: The Structure of Action*. Englewood Cliffs, N.J.: Prentice-Hall, 1970.

Scene Design and Lighting

Bowman, Wayne. *Modern Theatre Lighting*. New York: Harper & Row, 1950.

Burris-Meyer, Harold, and E. C. Cole. *Scenery for the Theatre*. Boston: Little, Brown, 1953.

————. *Theatres and Auditoriums*. New York: Reinhold, 1966.

Larson, Orville K. *Scene Design for Stage and Screen*. East Lansing, Mich.: Michigan State University Press, 1965.

McCandless, Stanley R. *A Method of Lighting the Stage*. New York: Theatre Arts Books, 1950.

Philippi, Herbert. *Stagecraft and Scene Design*. New York: Holt, Rinehart & Winston, 1963.

index